Understanding Girls' Friendships, Fights and Feuds

Understanding Girls' Friendships, Fights and Feuds

A Practical Approach to Girls' Bullying

Valerie E. Besag

Open University Press

Open University Press
McGraw-Hill Education
McGraw-Hill House
Shoppenhangers Road
Maidenhead
Berkshire
England
SL6 2QL

email: enquiries@openup.co.uk
world wide web: www.openup.co.uk

and Two Penn Plaza, New York, NY 10121-2289, USA

First published 2006

© Val Besag 2006

A catalogue record of this book is available from the British Library

ISBN-10 0335 21982 9 (pb) 0335 21983 7 (hb)
ISBN-13 978 0335 21982 7 (pb) 978 0335 21983 4 (hb)

Library of Congress Cataloging-in-Publication Data
CIP data applied for

Typeset by RefineCatch Limited, Bungay, Suffolk
Printed in Poland by OZ Graf. S.A. www.polskabook.pl

Sticks and stones will hurt my bones
Words can break my heart.
(Alteration to traditional saying)

The Hebrew poet Gabriol suggested that there are
three types of friends: those like food, without which
you can't live; those like medicine, which you need
occasionally; and those like an illness which you
never want.

Friendship has no survival value like philosophy or art,
but gives great value to survival.

C.S. Lewis. Quoted in Newcomb
and Bagwell (1996: 290)

I would like to dedicate this book to the girls who took part in the study. They face an uncompromising world with little advantage but with a great deal of humour and courage.

Contents

Preface

It is only in recent years that we have considered seriously the concept of bullying. When I began my work on bullying in the early 1980s, many professionals denied that such a thing existed whereas others thought it a good learning experience. Statistics now inform us of the extent of the problem and we are gaining an understanding of the pervasive, long-term damage that bullying can cause. At last, we are looking at the more subtle social exchanges taking place among our young, such as the covert social interactions between girls that are equally as powerful as the more overt behaviours more usually employed by boys.

The widespread claim, that physical means of controlling peer relations are used more widely by boys than by girls, whereas covert means are preferred by girls, is made from a review of research carried out with extensive cohorts of young people. Clearly, there is a huge overlap in the behaviours used by both boys and girls as many young people draw on a wide repertoire of behaviour using both overt and covert means. However, this book addresses the behaviour of girls and is not, primarily, a study of boys as they are the focus of most existing work on bullying and behaviour in general. The behaviour of boys is more visible, and so more readily understood but the behaviour of girls remains a mystery to many of us.

The core of the book draws on information gained from a study made of young girls in an informal situation, chatting freely among themselves, over a period of 16 months. This is only part of the contents as the book incorporates information gained while working daily in schools of all types, over several decades, as a teacher and later as an educational psychologist. It brings together the content of extensive informal discussions held with individuals and groups of young people and adults throughout Britain, including those from some ethnic minority cultures, and also retrospective accounts given by adults. In addition, I have had the opportunity to work in many other countries and cultures, including parts of Ireland, Australia, New Zealand, America and Canada, so findings from observations and discussions held with students and adults in these countries are also incorporated. The book also includes current research findings from Britain, Ireland and some other European countries, Australia, New Zealand, the USA and Canada. The findings and hypotheses offered, compiled from an amalgam of research, are given with the intent of illuminating an area of behaviour that is causing a great deal of distress but of which we know little. I wrote this book in the spirit of triggering debate. As with my first book on bullying, *Bullies and Victims in Schools* (1989), the aim is to stimulate discussion and research into an area causing great distress to many young people but which has been largely ignored, even dismissed, by adults.

Acknowledgements

It would be impossible to mention the many hundreds of teachers and other professionals working in schools who, over many years, contributed to this book either directly or indirectly. I can only mention those who were central to the research or the writing of the material. Peter Smith has been a valued colleague for many years and had sufficient confidence in the material I had collected to accept me to study for a doctorate. Anne Campbell took over this task when Peter moved to a less accessible city and gave me the support and enthusiasm necessary to do years of arduous transcription work. I should like to thank Helen Cowie for her friendship and her many excellent suggestions in addition to encouragement to continue the work.

I was fortunate to receive a Walter Hines Page Scholarship awarded by the National Union of Teachers and English Speaking Union that allowed me to visit people in the USA, including John Gottman, Don Zimmerman, Carole Webster Stratton and Sibelle Artz. These people gave up their valuable time to speak with me, with infectious enthusiasm, and I learnt a great deal from each.

A Winston Churchill Travel Scholarship awarded to me later contributed to my funds allowing me to meet many people in Canada, the USA, Australia, New Zealand and Japan. At this point I should like to thank Coosje Griffiths in Australia, and John Watson in New Zealand, for helping organize the lecture tours I have carried out in their countries. On all occasions, I have learnt something of value from the teachers and other professionals I met and greatly enjoyed their humour and honesty.

I am also grateful to Gail Stephenson who voluntarily helped me run the activity club.

The support of my friends has been invaluable. Sue Ridgway and Clare Howat, in particular, helped smooth my path by ignoring my absences, of mind and body, and welcoming my presence.

I should like to thank my son, Dave, who has worked with me on the book from the start. His research and technological skills, his intelligence and his patience in proof reading, and his ability to unscramble my scribble has enabled me to write the book while earning a living. We are still speaking.

Above all, I should like to thank the numerous students from many countries and cultures who talked to me or worked with me in various ways. Without exception, all courteously gave unstintingly of their time. In particular, I should like to thank the girls who formed the core of the study. All the names listed in this study have been changed to protect the identities of the girls.

SECTION 1
Exploring the Problem

1 She's my best friend, but I hate her!

Boys fight with their fists, girls with their tongues

In an attempt to identify why girls' friendships appear to be more fractious and disputatious than those of boys, it would seem necessary to begin with a description of the problem.

> *The scenario – The staffroom door in a Leafy Suburb primary school*
>
> There is a knock on the staffroom door. Anne Marie complains that Julie and Melanie were her friends but now they are deliberately excluding her from their games and activities. Anne Marie is upset as they no longer invite her to join them after school. They have made it clear that they do not want her around. Julie and Melanie are hiding around the corner awaiting the outcome of this complaint. The adult in charge settles this dispute with some difficulty only to find, a few weeks later, the situation is the same but the players have changed roles. Now it is one of the girls previously doing the excluding, Julie or Melanie, who complains that she is being ostracized by the other two friends.

Having presented this scenario for discussion with young people and adults, over the past two decades, in Britain and elsewhere, I have found nearly all relate to it immediately. The scenario occurs with surprising frequency seemingly anywhere girls gather. Details may differ, but the core elements appear universal.

The friendship relations between girls appear more unstable and disputatious than are those of boys (Pipher 1994; Harris 1995; Simmons 2002; Wiseman 2002). Those in frequent contact with girls are aware of the fractious nature of their friendships and the process where friends become enemies at the drop of a hat. One minute, two girls are best friends; the next minute they have quarrelled and are at daggers drawn. Each girl appears to come under fire in turn as though on a carousel.

Bitching or bullying?

The names given to girls' quarrels such as 'cat fights', 'silly squabbles' and 'bitching' are denigrating in themselves. In fact, grassing, insult, gossip and rumour are examples of the powerful linguistic processes frequently chosen by girls as tools used to cause distress to others. The potency of these processes has been underestimated. We have advised those girls who complained to 'go away' or 'make it up' without discussing details or considering how damaging the effects have been. Many girls may not understand the harm they cause by their actions. We need to make it clear to all that what seems to be a simple quarrel between friends can be a damaging, destructive process.

We know comparatively little about the dynamics of girls' friendship bonds; the reasons for the instability of their social relationships, the role individuals play in the disputes, and the precipitating factors relating to the conflicts. We appear to have ignored the distress experienced by girls, of all ages, by failing to understand the complex relationships that lie beneath the umbrella label of 'squabbling among friends'. Why is this disputatious behaviour more common among girls than among boys, as the latter do not seem to change the membership of their friendship group with the same rapidity as girls? Is this the way girls control each other? Perhaps boys wield their power by use of physical force and other overt mechanisms (Olweus 1978, 1993; Smith and Boulton 1990), whereas girls distribute power and manipulate each other by changing their friendship allegiances.

Boys appear to use modes of aggression that are visible and easily identifiable to dominate the vulnerable such as hitting, pushing, abusive name-calling and threats of violence (Olweus 1978, 1993; Smith and Boulton 1990). What may have escaped our attention is that there may be a similarly powerful, negative intent embedded in the scenario at the staffroom door given above. This dynamic could be the emotional, psychological or social manipulation of others. Just as boys use their fists or feet, girls may use their friendships as a powerful weapon of attack or defence. In other words, boys fight with their fists, girls with their tongues.

Teachers report the seemingly trivial squabbles and quarrels, constantly breaking out among girls, to be far more time consuming and difficult to address than the occasional physical fight erupting between boys. One of the most disheartening aspects of dealing with girls' quarrels is the revolving nature of the key players in their disputes. A teacher having settled a quarrel between girls cannot relax as the girls will soon return. The group dynamics may have changed, but they will have yet another grievance to air.

There would seem to be another noticeable difference between the friendship behaviour of boys and girls. If quarrels erupt between boys, it would appear that complaints rarely reach adult ears. The disputants often agree to go their separate ways or settle their differences between themselves. It appears that boys rely less on adult arbitration than girls do, whereas it is common for girls to bring their parents or others into school to support their complaint. In some instances, the aggravation even spreads into the community. For whatever reason, most parents of boys in dispute appear less emotionally involved. This could be for many reasons; boys feel they should be able to sort out their own problems or parents feel that the boys should settle their own differences. It may be that boys are more reluctant to talk to others about their emotions or, perhaps owing to the overt nature of their quarrels, they are able to resolve them more easily.

The difficulty in finding a satisfactory resolution to the quarrels among girls highlights the intensity of the emotions aroused and the complexity of the interactions. It may be that we have not identified them accurately as a particularly covert and sophisticated type of bullying requiring further investigation. Adults have misinterpreted the actions of girls, and under-estimated the possible negative effects of their behaviours, making it extremely difficult for victims to turn to them for help. What has confused us is that most troublesome behaviour among girls appears to be integral to their friendships and relationships. It appears unusual for girls to attack strangers. This has provided a smokescreen preventing us from seeing the issues clearly.

The findings culled from the study of the girls' activity club, forming the basis of the research described in the next chapter, support the claim of researchers in America (Maccoby 1999), and Australia (Owens 1999), that their friendships are of the utmost importance to most girls of all ages. Yet, anyone who has had close involvement with girls will be familiar with the paradoxical nature of their friendships. These friendship relations are often characterized by a 'best friend' dyad (Maccoby and Jacklin 1987; Benenson *et al.* 1997), but this close twosome, so familiar to parents, professionals and others, is rarely static over time. Girls commonly refer to having a best friend whose name they will volunteer readily. They often rank these best friends so that a girl may refer to her 'best friend', 'very best friend' or even her 'very best friend in the whole world'. Notes pass from one girl to another seeking reassurance that her friend is still her 'very best friend'. Boys rarely write such notes; most prefer a wider set of 'mates', referring less often to a single 'best friend'. A comprehensive review of the gender differences in friendship relations is given by Daniels-Beirness (1989).

This cosy friendship is not always a stable relationship. The composition of the dyad of best friends appears to change on a whim. The next time the same girl refers to her friends, a different girl may be designated her best friend. Many parents agree that they are heading for trouble should they plan a social event, such as a birthday party, and ask their daughter to invite only one or two friends. They will not be surprised to find the guest list changes several times, depending on how long in advance their daughter has in which to change her mind. A boy may include another at the last minute because they have just met, or the proposed guest has just received a new skateboard or computer game and they have been playing together recently. However, it seems rare that boys change their invitations because they have quarrelled with someone previously invited. The proposition is not that boys are more materialistic than are girls, but that the source of most quarrels among girls primarily lies within their close relationships. One or two of the girls in the activity group studied stated that they would stay away from school should their friend be absent, and this was confirmed by checking the daily register. Another may grieve when her friend changes school, yet these same girls will probably have had the same tempestuous relationship as others in the past.

Covert means are not the only modes used by girls in their attempts to control or dominate others. There is a use of all forms of aggression by both boys and girls. Many consider that a sex difference in preferred modes of aggression is in evidence from the pre-school years (Arnold *et al.* 1999). However, some dispute that there is such a clear gender difference as first appears (Thorne 1993). Confusion may arise as the preferred means of attack may change at different stages of development and in response to different situations. Although there is divided opinion as to whether girls use more verbal aggression than do boys, there appears to be agreement that girls use less physical aggression (Archer 2001). Authors who have worked extensively in the field offer rationales for the aggression of girls and their preference for indirect modes of attack (Archer 2001; Campbell 2004). These are presented throughout this work where relevant.

However, some girls use the overt and physical types of aggression more commonly found among boys (Glazer 1992; Campbell 2004). There are instances of severe physical attack made on both girls and boys carried out solely by girls that are identical to the physical attacks of boys (Glazer 1992; Campbell 2004). The significant difference seems to be that it is more usual for girls to attack those familiar to them, whereas boys are more likely than are girls to attack a stranger. I would suggest that the bar room brawl often stems from a challenge directed to a stranger, whereas women are more inclined to choose their target for gossip or ostracism from those among their acquaintances. As aggressive behaviour among boys is expected, preventative strategies are more likely to be in place. Sadly, what have received less attention are the covert psychological, emotional and social attacks occurring among girls that are often unexpected and commonly carried out under the guise of friendship.

There has been some research into the instability in girls' friendships (Alder and Alder 1995; Harris 1995), and mention made of the cyclical nature of the close bonds made between them (Eder 1985; Alder and Alder 1995). However, there has been little identification of any robust rationale for the frequently changing composition in their friendship relations, or explanation as to why these fluctuations would seem to be more pervasive in girls' groups than in those of boys. The lack of research into the negative aspects of girls' relationships, compared with those of boys, may stem from the more visible manner of boys' interactions as they are louder, more boisterous and more visibly energetic than are girls. It is more difficult to ignore their behaviour as they more usually turn to overt means of physical aggression (Cairns *et al.* 1989; Bjorkvist *et al.* 1992; Whitney and Smith 1993; Crick and Grotpeter 1995). This allows others to understand and address the dynamics of their conflicts more easily (McCabe and Lipscomb 1988). The covert nature of girls' attacks necessitates models of research that are more subtle, time consuming and therefore expensive (Crick and Grotpeter 1995). The use of high-powered equipment is essential in order to pick up the detail of the conversations and nuances of facial expressions of girls in dispute (Maccoby 2002).

Boys' fights tend to draw an audience from other boys. Escalation to a physical tussle, most often accompanied by shouts from bystanders of 'fight, fight', will draw an audience of lads from nowhere. It is common for boys to arrange a fight in advance so that all in school, other than the adults, know exactly when and where it will take place. It appears as if an impresario has arranged tickets for the audience of lads to congregate via the 'bush telegraph'. The dispute will end on the declaration of the winner or appearance of an adult. Conversely, disputes between girls rarely take place in the public arena. They happen in toilets, over the phone, by text messaging and, most relevant to this work, by the changing of friendship loyalties. We may recognize that girls' friendships are more fractious and unstable than those of boys, but we have not had any real understanding of the rationale for this behaviour. We appear to have accepted that this is just the way girls behave, and that squabbling and quarrelling are all part of the process of growing up. We have not understood the power of the underlying mechanisms and dynamics at work in disputes between girls.

In an attempt to understand this covert, complex social behaviour, a study was made of young girls over a period of 16 months, chatting together in an informal activity club. The aim was to analyse their conversations as well as their social behaviour. The following chapter gives a description of the study and a summary of the main findings with other comments and findings interwoven throughout the rest of the book. Amalgamated into the work are insights, opinions and hypotheses relating to the social lives of girls, collated over decades of working with the young in a variety of settings and cultures.

Suggested approaches

1   Adults in close contact with girls as professionals, parents or carers, need to understand fully the dynamics of the girls' friendships. They should have access to relevant literature, materials and workshops.

These adults need opportunities to discuss issues in an informal manner with others. In this way, they should be well informed and know how best to respond before disputes occur.

2   As this may be a new area of expertise to many, it would be useful for those working with girls to network with others in the initial stages of planning strategies and programmes of work.

3   We need to raise the awareness of girls so they understand the dynamics of their disputes. They need to know when they are under attack and the possible reasons for this behaviour. They need to learn to distinguish covert modes of bullying from other behaviours such as understanding how teasing differs from bullying.

4   It would be advantageous for girls to realize that if an action has a negative emotional effect, such as anger, sadness, irritation or isolation, there has probably been an intention to hurt. They need to learn to recognize these feelings stemming from the behaviour of other girls they regard as friends.

5   Girls need to be aware that they may face disappointment; their friends may become enemies overnight. Clearly, such discussions need to be presented in a sensitive manner to avoid suspicion and distrust.

6   We need to help girls to consider what they can do if they are not happy in their friendships. If not, they should know what they could do and feel confident to take appropriate action. Are they prepared to move on? How could they do this? If not, why not?

7   It is advisable for girls to have a group of friends, or to have others in addition to a 'best friend'. They could consider joining a club so they have other girls to call on from time to time.

8   Schools could have in place a peer support system to identify and work with troubled girls.

9   Transition from primary to secondary school is an extremely important time as long-term friendships are often established in the first few days of the transition period. Primary and secondary schools need to work together on transition programmes to help new students establish appropriate friendships.

2 The activity club

From friend to foe

The widespread extent of the multifaceted problem of girls in dispute had been evident in my daily work in schools for many years. Girls, of all ages, appeared in distress over these disputes, and discussions with parents showed that the stress experienced by individual girls could be significant and long term. Those enmeshed in these incidents often appeared depressed to some degree, some girls having had their life in school blighted by the actions of former friends. There appeared little understanding among adults of the processes involved and less about how to bring about a successful resolution.

The study forming the core of this work was designed to identify whether the pattern of instability indicated in the comments of girls, parents and professionals existed in their friendship bonds. The core aim was to uncover the processes underlying these fluctuations in allegiance. In parallel with this, an analysis of the manner in which girls break their friendship bonds seemed to be of relevance. Therefore, included in the aims of the study was an attempt to analyse the mechanisms girls use to entice some into their groups and by which they exclude others. In addition, after listening to the conversations of girls over many years, an analysis of the language they use seemed pertinent to the work.

The questions selected from those addressed by the study are:

- Are girls' friendships more disputatious than those of boys? If so, why is this?
- Why do the quarrels occur most often among those who have previously been friends?
- What are the dynamics involved in this process?

Subsequent analyses covered:

- The identification of rationales for the popularity and unpopularity of girls.
- The roles played by individuals.
- The identification of rationales for bullying.
- Gender differences in leadership.
- The language of conflict.

The ethnographic study – professional gossips

An ethnographic design was chosen for the study. Ethnographers are described as 'professional gossips' telling tales about the lives of others (Schoeman 1994: 72). 'Ethnography is the study of what is ordinarily taken for granted. It is a systematic method of study whereby the depths, patterns and connections, hidden within everyday happenings are identified and analysed' (Eder 1985: 155). Ethnography is a time-consuming model of qualitative methodology rather than quantitative. Instead of collating data for statistical analysis, ethnographic work features watching, waiting and recording. An ethnographer spends a vast amount of time recording, hoping that eventually something of value will emerge from the accrued material. Even more stressful is the crushing doubt regarding one's ability to make any sense of the recordings so painstakingly gathered. However, an ethnographic design seemed best to meet the criteria of this study as the researcher aims to see the world from the point of view of the participants. Based on recordings of direct experience, it appeared to be a more sensitive tool of investigation than some other techniques, and one that would offer the most truthful and valid results. It was essential that the mode chosen would capture the natural behaviour and conversations of the girls first hand, open up their hidden interactions, and go some way to explain their meanings.

A total of 16 hours of videotaped material was recorded during a weekly activity club organized for the girls. Other supplementary modes of investigation included sociometric measures as well as informal, semi-structured interviews held with the girls, their teachers and other adults in regular contact with them. The 16 months spent working with the girls resulted in abundant measures of their interactions and a vast amount of direct observational material. The findings are replicated in material obtained from interviews and discussions held with many hundreds of students, teachers and others in several countries and various settings.

Ethical considerations

Ethnographic models throw up some of the most complex ethical issues owing to the close proximity of the researcher to the subjects studied and the length of time they necessarily spend in each other's company. As ethnography looks closely at the detail of people's lives, there must be a valid rationale to pry, especially into the lives of unsuspecting children. Successful ethnographic studies rely on the participants behaving in a natural manner without contamination from outside influences. Built into the study is the intention that, over time, the participants will become less aware of any observers or equipment. Unfortunately, this opens up opportunities for abuse. The researcher must protect the participants by ensuring that they do not say or do anything that could jeopardize their future welfare. This is especially so with young children as they are more likely to become completely absorbed in their conversations and activities and be unaware of external observation.

As the main aim of the study was to understand hidden social interactions, some of which could be perceived as bullying, it was considered that the work would be justified, as such actions can cause immense suffering to girls even younger than those who took part in the study. Bullying not only affects the targets, as the repercussions can be pervasive, but also other family members, teachers and peer witnesses. Subsequent to the study, practical lines of action have been developed to prevent, or lessen, bullying activities among girls. These are presented in the final section. Hopefully, this validates the ethnographic nature of the study.

One issue that caused concern was the possibility of identifying a child in difficulty prior to the end of the study. To witness bullying and ignore it would be unethical; to intervene would contaminate the results and end the study prematurely. Bullying did occur from time to time but the adults in school identified and addressed the problem whenever possible. The teachers were constantly dealing with disputes and crises occurring among the girls but, unfortunately, many of the more subtle negative behaviours became known only when the video-recordings were analysed. By this time, the girls had been on a residential weekend and the most vulnerable girl had made friends with one of those most powerful. Details of the ethical consideration given to the study are reported elsewhere (Besag, unpublished study).

After completing an observational checklist in a class some years ago, I noticed one young girl had covertly completed her self-made checklist by recording her own observations of my behaviour. She was making a checklist of my behaviour while I was observing hers. Such experiences had taught me to take into account the possibility of an acute awareness of others, a high level of curiosity and immediate awareness of strangers that appears to exist among most girls. Even armed with this knowledge, the first pilot study failed because of the curiosity of the girls observed. The girls in the pilot study were approximately 13 years of age and feeling relatively sophisticated and confident in their secondary school. They became aware of my presence as soon as I entered the playground to observe them informally, thus making it necessary to find a different design for the study. As I was not part of the daily life of the school, my presence would continue to attract unwanted attention from some girls.

The activity club

Setting up the club

An activity club was set up in a local primary school as I considered the disputatious nature of girls' relationships would be the same regardless of age, and that slightly younger children than the girls in the pilot study would perhaps be less sophisticated and conscious of observers. The weekly club was held during the lunch hour, enabling recordings to be made of the girls chatting and interacting informally, in an unsupervised setting, when they would be relaxed and behaving naturally. The school chosen was one where I was well known to the staff.

Agreement was gained from the school, the girls and their parents to run an activity club for all the girls in Year 5 (aged 9 to 10 years) for the summer term of that academic year. This was to run over the three terms of the next academic year should the girls retain their interest. The club ran for a total of 16 months and formed the core of the ethnographic study. By chance, there were 20 girls and only 10 boys in the class but the boys did not wish to take part in the study for reasons given later.

Permission was given by the girls, their parents and teachers, for them to be filmed while engaged in a variety of tabletop activities such as sewing, painting and handicrafts. Groups of six girls were filmed each week in rotation. A talented art and crafts teacher volunteered to join the study, so while filming took place in one room, we worked on the same activity with the other girls in a separate room some distance along the corridor. The composition of the club was not static as absences were inevitable. One girl left the area but returned later in the year; two others entered the school as their families moved into the area. Remarkably, each week at least 18 of the 20 girls in the class attended the club as they loved to sit and chat to each other.

Recording the conversations

The expectation was that the video material would show the language structures used in dispute as well as the instability and fluctuations in the friendship bonds of the girls. To be valid for research purposes, it is necessary to record conversation in context. Material based on recall of previous conversations is not as valid as recordings made directly. Asking the girls to recall what they and others had said would have risked misinterpretation and errors in judgement and recall. In addition, ethical issues would be involved as there would be the possibility of the deliberate altering of information with malicious intent. There would also be the possibility that the process would be construed as gossiping or telling tales about others. It is necessary for conversations to be recorded in full, from beginning to end, to elicit valid and comprehensive understanding of the complex interactions and developments (Boden and Zimmerman 1991). In addition, conflict must be studied by using the actual discourse, recording it and analysing what has taken place (Bavelas *et al.* 1995). This study encapsulated all three factors.

On reflection, the 10 to 11 years age group was an opportune one to have chosen for the study. Importantly, the girls were old enough to be responsible for the video and audio machinery while working unsupervised. In addition, they were still at the cognitive stage where, on uttering a swear word or behaving in an untoward manner, they would first look towards the room, some distance away, where the adults were working with the rest of the girls, forgetting the camera directly in front of them. Fearing possible sanctions, their instinct was to look first in the direction of an adult in charge, even though this adult was out of sight and earshot, ignoring the camera. This indicated that their cognitive awareness that the camera was recording their language and behaviour was secondary to their awareness of adults some distance away. This offered validation that the video material captured their natural, unedited conversations and behaviour.

A long-term, in-depth study was required to amass sufficient detail and observe changes over time. The 16 months allocated for the study allowed changes in the relationships between the girls to be identified, logged and analysed. Any 'snapshot' method of observation and analysis could not offer such a valid record of the subtle, shifting interactions involved. The length of the study, in relation to the age of the girls, meant that there was an unexpected bonus factor. The girls were maturing rapidly over this period, passing through the critical time of development from young girls into early adolescence, so offering the possibility of identifying developmental change.

The neighbourhood

The area had been famous for shipbuilding, coal mining, steel manufacture and other heavy industries, most of which had long since disappeared. At the time of the study, many adults had never been in full employment and hardly any had a job with a career structure. Since the start of the study in 1995, the situation has improved. Employment is now available, for males and females, and signs of an improvement in material standards are clearly evident.

Girls in their final year at the local secondary school had described their expectations of life after school freely and honestly to me some years prior to the study. I found that many held depressed aspirations. Several expected to have a boyfriend and baby soon after leaving school. They did not necessarily anticipate marriage as there was little local stigma about being pregnant while still a teenager or even of school age. Several expected to be physically abused by their male partner should they 'deserve it' (verbatim), and few had any realistic work expectations. Although the girls in the activity club held higher expectations than the older girls interviewed previously, their level of aspiration appeared lower than the average for most girls of their age.

A modus operandi of aggression

Some of the girls in this locality were aggressive in their attitude and behaviour, considering it acceptable to use immediate and overt modes of aggression to settle problems and differences (Miller-Johnson *et al.* 2005). However, girls in other locations may be equally aggressive, albeit not as obviously so. It may be that there is little difference in the quantity of disputatious behaviour among girls across the socio-economic range in western cultures, although there appear to be differences in the modes of expression chosen. There is now more widespread awareness of levels of physical violence among girls of all ages. Sociological reasons may have led to changes in attitudes and behaviour among young females in recent years. Developing sophistication in the design of research methodology, plus the recent emergence of a more questioning and challenging examination of young girls and their behaviour, may have contributed to these findings. In addition, the high levels of alcohol and drugs now imbibed/used by some young females, lowers their inhibition against the use of violence, thus increasing recorded incidents of aggression (Campbell 2004).

It was a joy to work with the girls as they were challenging, lively, humorous, inquisitive and instructive. The study offered insights into the many demands that life placed upon them at such a young age. The conversation, presentation and antics of the girls seemed a million years from a Jane Austen sewing bee or refined Victorian tea party. Several had the elaborate hairstyles in vogue at the time and their language was colourful, spattered with dialect and street argot. Most were energetic, loud in their conversations and dramatic in manner, yet the attitudes and machinations underlying their conversations had clear parallels with the more sophisticated and genteel exchanges that took place in the society houses and fashionable spas of centuries ago.

SECTION 2
Gender Differences in Children's Social Behaviour

3　The power of the peer group: affiliation and differentiation

Nested sets of social contexts

In aiming to identify and analyse the processes involved in the fractious relations of girls, it is necessary to start by considering the rationale, value and effects of peer relationships among the young and to examine the power and influence of the peer group within which they interact. There is now an acknowledgment of the importance of friendships among the young (Harris 1995). The girls in the study valued their friendships highly. Humans are in essence social animals who require social contact to thrive. How many of us have met a true hermit? As humans, we live within more than one set of social relationships, interacting within nested sets of contexts such as a family, extended family, colleagues and acquaintances (Buhrmester 1996). Young people interact with a vast number of students and adults each day in their schools. Many of us will never again need to interact closely with so many others, on a daily basis, as we did during our schooldays.

A high level of skill is required to interact successfully within all these groups, each with their own demands. From birth, we learn to interact socially with an extensive number of people, all with their own distinctive person-alities and agendas. Our social skills are polished and perfected as we meet new people, situations and challenges. If we are to fit in, we need to be adaptable, pliable and responsive. This is a skill learnt over a lifetime, mainly by a process of trial and error, with many embarrassing and hurtful experiences encountered along the way that form the source of much media material and entertainment, whether comedic or tragic. Many young people find it difficult to pass through the fraught time of childhood and adolescence without some degree of scarring.

Socialization is a comprehensive, subtle process encompassing a myriad of sub-skills we must assimilate rapidly into a highly flexible repertoire of behaviour. To survive amicably in human groups, we need emotional, psycho-logical, verbal and social versatility to read differing social situations quickly and adapt accordingly. Moving into a new location, or starting a new job, makes us realize how hard we try to fit in with our neighbours and colleagues, and how uncomfortable it can be if we do not succeed. Most of us remain strongly influenced by 'what the neighbours say'.

The classic study by Philip Zimbardo (Answers.com 2005), of university students playing the parts of prisoners and prison guards in an American penal institution, illustrated how quickly we adapt to the social expectations inherent in a role. Individual personality, and a sense of responsibility for self and others, became subsumed under the identity each student acquired when in the role of guard or prisoner. This happened so quickly and effectively that the experiment had to end prematurely. The humorous and insightful work of Goffman (1963) uncovered the myriad of social rules and regulations we adhere to subconsciously in our daily lives.

The processes of socialization and group acceptance

The ethnographer Bailey (1971) describes an inventive way of coping with the type of social challenge commonly encountered. In the isolated villages of southern France, it was necessary for a housewife shopping to stop and chat at length to anyone met, causing problems for those in a hurry. To stop was fraught with difficulty, as gossip could lead to trouble in such a tight-knit community, but it was considered extremely rude to walk by without stopping to talk. One housewife came up with the solution by hurrying to the shops wearing an apron to signify that she was in the middle of housework and needed to get back home quickly. Subsequently, this was universally adopted. These seemingly trivial social difficulties are often our most problematic as they can have widespread, lasting repercussions on our closest relationships.

It is essential that young people quickly build up a working repertoire of appropriate social skills. Signals indicating that a change in attitude or behaviour is necessary may be subtle, but they need to be read quickly and accurately, and selections and adjustments made immediately in order to avoid peer approbation. Most young people straddle at least four cultures simultaneously each day; the peer group, home, neighbourhood and school, each with its own established set of rules and expectations.

Children have an innate, adaptive mechanism that directs them to learn from any source, but what they learn is highly specific to the context (Rowe 1994; Harris 1995). What they learn in one situation may not be appropriate in another. Good street survival skills may well lead a youngster headlong into trouble with teachers who may interpret effective defence mechanisms as challenging behaviour. Young people can get into serious trouble if they are unable to adapt quickly enough to the different demands met in their home, street and school. Children must learn to function successfully in the wider world.

They need to form alliances that go beyond the nuclear family, moving among a wide variety of challenging and rewarding social situations, in order to hone their embryonic social skills. The skills appropriate to home are not enough (Rowe 1994). Many of the disputes among the girls studied stemmed from their movement between groups, with the resultant processes of acceptance and exclusion. Many were unable to adapt to the differing expectations of the various friendship groups within the class.

The influence of the peer group

The peer group has a particular role to play in the development of these social skills (Tajfel 1982; Hutchins 1991; Maccoby 1999). The most powerful agent a young person experiences is the peer group influence as this is how cultural mores are transmitted most effectively (Eckerman *et al.* 1988; Harris 1995). Humans have a strong identity as individuals but, once categorized as a member of a group, a person takes on the expected rules, standards, beliefs, attitude and conduct of that group (Harris 1995).

Perhaps we have underestimated the importance of the close social relations within peer groups of the young as most children aim to become members of the social peer group and identify with its members. The opinions held by young people of school age about their peers were found to be as good a predictor of psychopathological illness as professional opinion and psychometric measurements carried out in childhood (Cowen *et al.* 1973). Young people were able to identify the vulnerable among them from an early age, presumably because they were in their company for many hours a day for several of their school years. They see each other at their most relaxed, behaving naturally without the restraint of adult eyes.

Peer rules and regulations

Young people take their primary influences from their peers despite the best efforts of caring adults to guide them in a direction they consider more appropriate. Members of the peer group are the primary source of the social mores, dress code, presentation, language, attitudes and behaviour the young person adopts (Harris 1995). Many initiatives against alcohol, sexual promiscuity, cigarettes and drugs have failed to influence the young because they have been adult led. Young people may pay lip service to heroes nominated by adults, while taking their cues assiduously from the most influential group or gang members in the school or neighbourhood. However, they must emulate the peer group with care. To wear outdated clothing labels can be taboo, and the vocabulary in vogue with the young changes rapidly so that using a dated slang word can be a source of ridicule and scorn (Dent 2004).

Academic or social success

In the context of this work, we need to consider the influence of the peer group on young girls. As popularity becomes more important with age, many girls start to become less concerned with achievements, such as academic success, and do not wish to alienate their friends by openly competing against them (Rosenberg and Simmons 1975; Rose and Asher 1999). The negative attitude of the peer group can adversely affect a girl on track for a glittering career so that she falls short of once achievable goals. Commonly, those most influential have been her closest friends. In this way, the low achievement of a girl may be due to her relationships with other girls, not solely with an emerging interest in boys as was once assumed (Eder 1991).

Many of those who most forcibly reject the rules and regulations within the school or home seem to comply meekly with the rigorous social rules of the peer group. Even meeting the requirements of a team game is beyond many, yet what they do, think, wear, drink, say and eat needs to meet the expectations of their peers as every detail is checked out. Young people at risk are not the only ones who challenge adult rules and regulations. A discussion of whether this challenge and confrontation is part of the necessary process involved in preparation for independence, and fleeing the nest, is given in the work of Apter (2001).

Drink, drugs and rock and roll

It often appears that no amount of adult persuasion, or intervention, can change the force of the peer influence as the young themselves decree what is acceptable. We may achieve agreement, amendment, even compliance when talking to a young person alone but, once back in the midst of the peer group, other, more powerful influences often take over. For some, it is too dangerous to fly in the face of peer opinion and support. One of the most influential factors contributing to success in working with the young who offend is whether they return to friends who are continuing in the same pattern of behaviour. Many would be able to kick an alcohol or drug habit were it not for the influence and example of their friends. An effective practice is to separate them from this peer group, but this strategy is fraught with problems as the peer influence is so powerful and valued so highly. Attempts to change behaviour in an individual must take cognisance of the power and influence of the peer group.

Adults may befriend adolescents lacking a strong identity within their peer group in the guise of a religious cult, extreme political party or commercial marketing group. Young people are enticed into such sects by the tacit offer of a ready-made group of peer friends. Many such groups have an agenda relating to financial, sexual or other gain that remains hidden until the young target is enmeshed in the group. It is a sound strategy to attract potential membership by drawing attention to the availability of compatible friends. The current popularity of mobile phones and chatrooms highlights this basic need for social connections among the young.

Assimilation or rejection

Specific influences and mechanisms within groups aid the socialization of individuals (Gottman and Parker 1986; Rowe 1994; Harris 1995; Simmons 2002). As young people look to their contemporaries for guidance and confirmation regarding codes of behaviour, it is necessary to consider the complex, interacting processes involved in belonging to any group. The two opposing influences, assimilation and differentiation, can be daunting, insurmountable hurdles. The process of assimilation, that transmits cultural norms and smoothes the rough edges off individual personality, is balanced by the need for differentiation whereby we display our individuality (Harris 1995). There are cultural differences in how a society views individuality. Fitting into the mores of the group takes on greater significance in some cultures. For example, individuality is prized more highly in western cultures than in some others (White 1987). It is interesting to note how many young Japanese, of both sexes, now dye their hair red or blonde so they stand out from their Japanese peers by having a more western appearance. By doing so, they can impress both sets of peer groups. They aim for an acceptable level of differentiation within the home peer group, in tandem with assimilation within the western style of appearance. In this way, we can see the processes of differentiation and assimilation working simultaneously.

Marking individuality

There is constant flux and change as either assimilation or differentiation can be dominant at any time. As both are necessary, we become engaged in a balancing act. It may be compulsory to wear a certain style of dress, but an attempt to display personal identity may be shown in a radical haircut or the angle at which a hat is worn. Slight nuances of change, and adaptations in style, would appear to be registered more quickly by girls than by boys. Students who are required to wear school uniform show that girls, perhaps more than boys, display their initiative and imagination in a wide range of variations on the uniform theme. It is essential for the young, attempting to stamp a degree of individuality on their presentation, to proceed with caution as only the judgement of their peers is valued. Getting it right allows acceptance into the group and perhaps admiration; getting it wrong may trigger approbation from the more powerful.

This process of jostling between the need to express individuality and the need to remain within the boundaries set down by the group, continues throughout our lives. Even adults appear to make their decisions in the context of the opinion of others. Most of us consider, if only fleetingly, how others will react if we paint our house an adventurous colour, wear an outrageous outfit or voice a radical opinion. Among the impressionable and vulnerable young, adverse peer opinion can have a powerful, hurtful or even dangerous effect.

What's different about girls?

The socialization process whereby individuals establish themselves within the peer group may be especially troublesome for girls. Learning to live in the group context, and acquiring the socialization skills necessary for full social development, throws up many opportunities for conflict. In the case of girls, this often appears to result in changes in friendship bonds. As friendship is a construct with positive connotations, it is easy to miss any negative aspects, yet friendship offers an arena for both conflict and competition (Gottman and Mettatal 1986; Hartup 1992; Menesini 1997, 1998). This is seen in the frequent falling out and ill feeling associated with girls' friendships. Some research shows that conflict occurs more frequently, and the episodes last longer, between friends than between non-friends (Menesini 1997, 1998). This may be because friends feel secure enough in their relationship to voice opinions honestly, or perhaps have more emotional investment in tackling the difficulties rather than moving away to seek relationships elsewhere. Quarrels occurring between the girls in the study were primarily between close friends, or past friends, and less frequently involved girls in different friendship groups.

We are unable to attribute the answer to the cause of the instability of girls' friendship bonds solely to the arena of peer socialization as boys also travel this route. It is necessary to consider if there is a gender difference in the character and quality of the friendship bonds. An examination of the internal organization and functioning of the peer relationships is required in any attempt to uncover an explanation for the fractious friendship relations between girls.

Suggested approaches

1 Discuss with girls what it means to fit into a group and the concepts of affiliation and differentiation. They may like to talk about their experiences of these processes.

2 Talk about the benefits, disadvantages and possible dangers of complying with group demands.

3 Discuss the process involved in joining a group. Most people employ these skills automatically but sometimes it is not easy and we need to analyse the process to find the best way forward. Ask the girls to identify common group entry skills such as staying proximate, making supportive and complimentary comments to existing members, and identifying the expectations of the group.

4 Explain that a new entrant may not be welcomed into the group immediately. It often takes time to establish new friendships.

5 There are programmes to aid young people to form friendships such as Circle of Friends (Newton *et al.* 1996).

6 Discuss the benefits and disadvantages of staying outside the group. What could be the dangers?

7 Discuss peer pressure. See Section 7 for suggestions on how to handle peer pressure.

8 Discuss what friendship means and the costs of friendship. Friendship is a two-way affair. Maintaining a relationship is a different skill from joining a group. Some young people do not realize how much they need to put into any worthwhile relationship. Ask them to consider the iceberg model of benefits and costs. Most of an iceberg is under water: you must be prepared to put more effort into a relationship than you expect to get back.

9 Talk about the necessary skills required to maintain a friendship. Discuss negotiation, sharing, learning how to give time, support and encouragement, and how to give and how to accept friendship. Explain what it means to take a genuine interest in others.

10 Explore why it may be best to approach those with similar interests to their own.

11 Discuss what is meant by 'dangerous friends'. These could include adults.

4 Toys for boys, gossip for girls?

Play preferences

In examining the dynamics within girls' friendship groups, it is necessary to compare their social behaviour with that of boys. A gender difference in the attitude to friendship and play activities was evident in the class studied. Before setting up the activity club, I held informal discussions separately with the boys and the girls in the class to identify whether there were gender differences in the quality of the friendship bonds. Each boy was asked what he would do if he brought a new cricket bat to school and found his friend did not want to play cricket that day. Without hesitation, each said that he would find someone else to play cricket with him. The boys could not see a problem.

Separately, each girl in the class was asked what she would do if she brought her new recorder to school only to find that her friend had not brought hers, or did not want to play her recorder that day. Unlike the boys, the girls considered the scenario posed a problem and immediately tried to find amicable solutions. All stated they would negotiate with their friend to find a way they could play together. The ideas and options they volunteered were extensive and inventive. Suggestions included: persuading the friend to change her mind; go home for it at lunchtime if she had forgotten it; share the one recorder by taking turns; or borrow one from someone else. They offered other ideas, such as dividing the playtime in half and covering two options with each girl choosing one of the activities, or asking the teacher if they could borrow another recorder. Without fail, one option put forward included choosing something both could do instead of playing the recorder. When faced with such a quandary, it appears important to girls that they behave in a fair and equitable manner, so they negotiate, discuss or seek arbitration until a settlement is agreed upon that is satisfactory to all. It seemed necessary to the girls to play together and to retain their friendships at all cost.

Agentic play

It became obvious that *what* the boys did in their free time was of prime importance to them, whereas with *whom* they played with was of more importance to the girls (Lever 1976; Maccoby 1999). The activity appeared of secondary importance to the girls as they said they would choose to play a less preferred activity in order to remain with their friends. The boys did not elect to do this and were happy to canvass for playmates until they found others to play their chosen game. They were happy as long as they had someone to kick a ball to, or engage in a play fight or other physical activity. Boys, more than girls, appear to put more emphasis on the agentic aspect of their play, such as a bat or ball, whereas girls appear far more selective regarding their playmates and companions and use more personal criteria when making their choice. This exercise has been repeated with various groups of young people, giving the same result (Besag, unpublished research).

A game or a gossip?

A similar difference in behaviour was in evidence at break time. When lessons ended, and the class left the room, this gender difference in behaviour became obvious. The boys ambled out of class to the playground or toilets, singly or in clusters, jostling along the paths and corridors where they would casually meet up with friends. Unless they are in the older age range of secondary education, it would appear that most boys start some type of informal game or activity with whoever is interested and competent.

The girls in the class behaved differently. As soon as the bell signalled the end of a lesson, the girls sought their closest friends. Unlike the boys, they would have already decided with whom they would play with that day and would leave the classroom with their best friend of the moment. They stayed close together, chatting, or engaged in a small group activity such as skipping, until the bell signalled the time to return to class. If one wanted to visit the toilet, they would go together and would return to class together, preferring to sit next to each other to chat and exchange ideas. If a girl was in trouble, her friends would gather round to offer solace or advice, whereas a boy in trouble with staff would be left by his mates to sort out his problem as best he could.

Boys practise skills, girls rehearse life

It would appear that boys prefer games with a formula and traditionally accepted rules, pitting their physical strength or skill against those of others.

Their play often centres on the construction and manipulation of toys and equipment (McLloyd 1983; Goodwin 1990; Flannery and Watson 1993; Nicolopoulau 1997; Maccoby 1999). I have found that many toddlers highlight this difference when playing with an unfamiliar object. Girls seem to examine a novel object carefully, perhaps turning it in their hands to catch the light to see if it changes colour, trying it out for sound, smell and taste and delighting in its intrinsic qualities. They will carry it round until bored. In contrast, boys of the same age handed an unfamiliar object seem to squeeze it, bang it, shake it and throw it into the air to discover what it can do and how it can become an agent of their play.

It appears that girls' groups tend to be smaller, their play activities reflecting events in their daily life and relationships (Lever 1976; McLloyd 1983; Buhrmester and Furman 1987; Maccoby 1999). From information collated from informal observations carried out over years while working in schools, I would suggest that girls at play are preparing for adulthood by rehearsing domestic scenes familiar to them, imitating adult behaviour they have witnessed, consolidating what they have seen and rehearsing for the future. Girls frequently take on the role of adults, playing the part of mother or father using dolls to replicate babies, and role-playing future employment by pretending to be hairdressers, nurses and teachers (Goodwin 1990). Although there is now less gender differentiation in choice of employment, it would seem that many girls continue to play games related to their daily life rather than pretend to drive the trains, spaceships and war machines that remain the focus of attention for many boys.

Boys, too, rehearse for future employment, but appear to base their choice less on their daily experiences and more on unrealistic expectation, fantasy, adventure and challenge. Although boys use realistic role models in their play, such as train drivers, they more often seem to emulate the famous racing car driver, football icon or astronaut. Excitement, adventure and competition appear essential ingredients in boys' play. It is rare to see a boy pretending to be an anonymous electrician or plumber in the manner of a girl pretending to serve in a shop.

A glance in any playground seems to show that, from late primary school age until mid adolescence, many girls stand around talking to each other, whereas boys are more likely to be engaged in playing a game, play-fighting, testing the strength of each other or running around. Some aspects of this gender difference appear to last into adulthood as more males can be seen playing games, such as football and cricket, on sunny beaches than females, who more frequently read novels and magazines or chat to friends. A cursory glance at recommended reading lists in both male and female magazines, would suggest that many females choose books and films primarily about interpersonal relationships, whereas most males prefer excitement, action and facts.

Girls' social play

Talk features largely in the activities enjoyed by girls and is interwoven throughout their play (Gottman and Mettatal 1986). The girls studied in the activity group enjoyed activities that involved conversational exchange even when engaged in physical activities similar to those enjoyed by boys such as ball play, skipping or hopscotch. Many of the girls in the group studied were happy to sit chatting with friends without the need of an agent of play such as the bat or ball that featured largely in the activities of the boys. Even an essentially sole occupation, such as crayoning or sewing, was engaged in more happily if carried out with close friends and accompanied by chatter.

Imaginative content weaves through the discussions of girls. Many conversations of the girls in the group started with phrases such as, 'What would you do if . . .?' and 'Suppose . . .', that triggered the imagination. Girls enjoy telling each other stories from books they have read, films and television programmes or stories developed from their imagination (Nicolopoulau 1997). Their oral story telling is often a cooperative affair where all are allowed, even encouraged, to contribute (Nicolopoulau 1997). Boys also use imagination in their play, but the focus appears to be on the activity and not on the conversation, as it is with girls. The imaginative talk of boys more frequently appears to be directly related to their play, as in developing a myth, describing an adventure or in the dramatic enactment of a battle, whereas the conversations of girls would seem more usually to have roots in the events and people in their everyday lives. In summary, the gender difference may lie in the emphasis given to the character and content of their talk rather than a discrepancy in the amount spoken.

All the girls in the class studied agreed eagerly to attend the lunchtime club, saying they would love the opportunity to sit and chat to friends while engaged in an enjoyable activity. The boys were not interested as all wanted to be out in the playground, even during the winter months. Most were happiest emulating the local football heroes, somewhat monopolizing the playground, or standing around watching the other boys playing in informal teams. Sitting around chatting to each other on a weekly basis was not of interest to the boys. Even those not interested in the games and activities the other boys played, were not interested in attending the activity club.

An illuminating experiment carried out by Lever (1976) was replicated on television some years ago. Girls, approximately 6 years old, were shown into a room, a pair at a time, set up with a wide choice of toys. Boys of the same age went through an identical procedure. Both groups were matched for intelligence and family factors and none of the children had met previously. Each pair had approximately 15 minutes to make a choice and play with the selected game.

Soon after the pairs of boys had entered the room, one boy would state what he thought they should play. If the other boy agreed, the game would commence without further ado. If they disagreed on the choice of activity, one boy would emerge as the more forceful, or determined, and make the final choice. If they could not reach agreement, each would play separately with their chosen game, taking little interest in one another. They were not being rude; their behaviour simply showed their preference for play over inter-personal interest. The games and activities chosen were primarily ones of construction, manipulation or skill based. Overall, the boys played with little language necessary to the successful progression of the game. For most pairs, the verbal interaction was primarily a soundtrack accompanying the movement of the toys, the re-enactment of a fight scene or the exchange of comments and instructions directly and indirectly related to their play.

In contrast, the conversations of the girls were rich and extended. Their curiosity about each other appeared unbounded and several pairs began by introducing themselves at length, often with their full name and address. Some exchanged the names of their school, teacher, siblings, parents or friends. Some dyads followed such chatter with a lengthy, verbal exploration to find if they knew anyone in common. Some recalled other girls with the same names, others exchanged names of girls who attended their schools or lived nearby to see if they shared an acquaintance. Important to this study, several of the girls commented positively on the clothes or hairstyle of their partner. It seemed that, even at this early age, they had taken full measure of each other in their first sweeping glance and were trying to make a social connection.

Most of the girls discussed, equably and fully, suggestions for the game they wanted to play, their skills of negotiation and bartering already being evident. Once the game had begun, many continued to chat about incidental matters such as where they shopped with their mother, where they went for a special treat, their favourite books, films and cartoons. The games and activities chosen were those demanding conversational exchange. They were finding commonality and making strong attempts to bond. Most appeared more interested in each other than in the games as, at times, they abandoned their chosen game in favour of detailed conversation. Primarily, they appeared to consider the play activity as a vehicle for social exchange.

A television programme shown in 2003 on Channel 4 in the UK looked at the behaviour of a group of pre-adolescent children living alone in a house for four days with adults next door in case of emergency. The behaviour of the girls was in contrast to that of a matched group of boys. The boys settled their disputes dispassionately or by force of strength or personality. There were frequent disputes, upsets and quarrels between the girls but the group discussed these incidents in full, negotiated endings were attempted, and sophisticated support offered at the sign of any trouble or distress.

Two girls left the house, separately and prematurely, leaving the rest distressed. Without prior discussion, the remaining girls huddled together to talk things through in the place where each absent girl had slept. The girls showed surprising insight into the behaviour and emotional state of each other and seemed to want everyone to get on amicably. However, this did not stop individual jealousy, selfishness and spite coming to the fore from time to time, causing upset and disruption. When this happened, the girls attempted to repair the relationships by discussion, persuasion and negotiation. The experiment succeeded in highlighting a gender difference in the degree of mutual support and emotional enmeshment shown.

Adults: an evening out

I would suggest that it is possible to look to a scenario in the social arena of adults to support this finding. From observations and informal discussions, I would suggest that men, more than women, go a pub or club on the chance of meeting friends. Men are more likely than are women to stay for a drink if their friends are absent. A few minutes spent eavesdropping at a bar will reveal that the talk of most men centres more on impersonal matters such as the weather, sport and politics than does that of women. A close friend is not required in order to open, or develop, such conversations as these matters can be discussed with a casual acquaintance. Depending on the quality of conversation, balanced by the need for a drink and company, a man will leave after a drink or stay to develop a casual acquaintanceship with others at the bar.

I have found that most women say they do not behave in this way. It would seem that a woman wishing to go out socially probably contacts a friend beforehand to make detailed arrangements regarding day, time and venue. What to wear may come into the equation. A woman may stay home if her friend cancels an arrangement, whereas many men are happy to attend a football or cricket match alone. Clearly, many women do not act in this way and pride themselves on their independence. It is not yet clear whether this gender difference in social behaviour stems from social training, genetic predisposition or from specific benefits gained. Future years will tell whether there is a growing movement away from female interdependence on these friendship bonds or, despite a growing ethos of gender equality, women will continue to seek out the company of close friends.

Suggested approaches

1   Some teachers suggest that girls who play in team sports appear less disputatious in these friendships than otherwise. There may be some

    benefit in encouraging girls to look to team activities as well as close friendships.

2   Explore with girls whether they think they enjoy the games they play more than those enjoyed by boys because of social training or genetic predisposition.

3   The girls may enjoy designing and implementing a small experiment to inform their opinion. This could be carried out by observing younger children at play or by interviewing students or adults in their school. They may be able to set up a small experiment with younger children as in the one described in this chapter.

4   The girls may be interested in widening the discussion by researching gender preferences in leisure reading material or choice of employment among adults.

5   Older girls may be interested in the books now available stemming from the work of Deborah Tannen outlined in her book *You Just Don't Understand: Women and Men in Conversation* (1992). There are several popular books on the theme of gender differences in behaviour such as *Men Are from Mars, Women Are from Venus* by John Gray (1998).

5 Girls cooperate, but boys compete?

The young male syndrome

In considering why girls' friendships are so disputatious, it is necessary to look at some of the most influential attitudes underpinning the behaviour of boys and girls. Girls do not appear to have the same competitive spirit as boys. It may be that 'girls cooperate, boys compete', as proposed by Ahlgren (1983). Girls usually play games in a negotiated, turn-taking manner (Crombie and Desjardins 1993), whereas boys more often settle for the strongest or most dominant being first in line (Smith and Boulton 1990; Coie and Dodge 1998). Although girls may celebrate a winner, this is not necessarily the main purpose of the activity. Most boys will be able to name the best footballer among them, but fewer girls regard it as important to know who is the most accomplished at skipping. Primarily, girls appear to play and interact socially and cooperatively rather than competing with their friends (Ahlgren 1983; Hughes 1988).

Males appear to have an inherent competitive spirit – the young male syndrome (Daly and Wilson 1994) – urging them to maintain face in front of their peers at all times. Adult males are thought to be high in competitiveness, autonomy and dominance and low in warmth, sympathy and compassion (Williams and Best 1990; Hoyenga and Hoyenga 1993; Feingold 1994). In an experiment to show this gender difference, young boys, given the same game to play as girls, were the more competitive, as the girls considered displaying a competitive attitude could spoil their relationship with their friends (Ahlgren 1983; Hughes 1988).

The games played by boys tend to include an element of competition, challenge and daring-do (Manning and Sucklin 1984; Whiting and Edwards 1988; Crombie and Desjardins 1993). Informal observation of boys playing on their bicycles appears to encapsulate this gender difference. It would seem that most boys given a bicycle immediately try it out as an instrument of challenge, competing to find who can ride the fastest, furthest, without hands and per- form the most daring stunts. Boys seem to enjoy competing against their past record and that of others, whereas girls appear less interested in such matters and enjoy leisurely cycle rides with their friend, chatting as they ride. Few girls are observed attempting 'wheelies'. Casual observation of most popular sporting events shows more males than females watch or play competitive sports. Competitive arcade and computer games do not seem to attract as many girls as boys; few girls appear to hang around games arcades other than those waiting patiently for the boys.

Male dominance hierarchies

Dominance hierarchies appear more characteristic of boys' friendship groups than those of girls. Young boys gain some idea of where they fit into the physical dominance hierarchy of familiar peers that is established in the early years (Omark *et al.* 1973; Pellegrini 1988; Smith and Myron-Wilson 1988; Smith and Boulton 1990). Boys engage in play fights, rough-and-tumble play and direct physical competition from an early age in order to establish dominance (Pellegrini 1988; Smith and Myron-Wilson 1988). They settle their arguments and challenges with feet and fists (Loeber and Hay 1997). Many primary school teachers recognize that young boys will take every opportunity to roll round on the floor engaged in play fighting. Even waiting to go on stage for the Christmas Nativity play, undeterred by shepherd's garb of dressing gown and striped tea towel, they will most probably snatch every opportunity for a tussle on the floor. Young girls, with flimsy paper wings attached to their backs to depict angels, do not entangle themselves on the floor to test out their strength in mock battles. However, these demure 'angels' may well be weighing each other up, and making harsh and destructive comparisons, albeit in a different manner. Their competitive spirit may present in a different, covert guise. On one occasion, I watched helplessly as a young angel, of 8 years, jealously eyed the spectacular wings of her best friend and silently unhooked them leaving her to go on stage wingless.

Some form of play fighting seems to be an essential part of the interaction between young boys (Pellegrini 1988; Smith and Myron-Wilson 1988; Smith and Boulton 1990). Boys would seem to be constantly testing out their physical strength against that of their companions. Dominant boys gain practice in leadership skills and in establishing, maintaining and increasing their dominance and confidence. Those vulnerable at an early age fail to get practice at establishing a confident presentation, leaving them even more vulnerable.

Cock of the midden

In parts of England, boys from the age of approximately 9 to 13 years voluntarily fight for the coveted title of 'cock of the class'. The winner of the scrap, usually held on the playing field out of sight of staff, gains the accolade that defines him as being able to fight all-comers. This young fellow then struts around school basking in glory while sceptical adults refer to him as 'cock of the midden', rather than 'cock of the class', midden being the Old English word for dung heap. This refers to the cockerel standing on the farm dung heap crowing to announce his dominance, his ownership of the hens and his ability to ward off all challengers.

The boys in the class studied formed a dominance hierarchy based on physical strength and confidence. All were aware of who was the most powerful in the group, but they allowed others to use and display their skills in the cause of winning a game. Any competent player would be welcomed in a group playing a board game, with a computer game or engaged in a physical activity such as football. They ignored those unskilled or not interested. The girls were far more selective, exclusive and personal in their choice of friends.

Caution is required in any examination of gender differences as we may be looking at the issue through what Bem (1993) has described as gendered lenses; our own gender bias may be subconsciously embedded in the design or interpretation of any hypothesis or research model. However, as this gender difference in attitude towards play activities and companions appears so noticeable, it is of interest to consider the possible origin and rationale of these behaviours to explain why girls' friendship relations are so different from those of boys. We need to consider why it is necessary for boys to constantly test out their strength and power against that of others. It may be because boys tend to use the more obvious means of physical and verbal aggression to resolve their conflicts (Loeber and Hay 1997). A confident boy merely needs to use his powerful presence to warn that he can take on all-comers just as older males, such as Hell's Angels, choose apparel that lessens the chance of challenge. Their dress code holds the dual function of giving an active display of power alongside a passive warning to contenders that mirrors the cockerel crowing on top of the midden to ward off challengers. Boys may draw upon as broad a repertoire of social skills as girls but more readily embark on competitive and challenging activities to display their power.

Adult behaviour

The same discrepancy between genders, regarding competition and cooperation, seems to occur in adults. Females seem to take a group-oriented, negotiated leadership style, whereas males tend towards a task and self-enhancing leadership style (Tannen 1992; Buss and Schmidt 1993; Cross and Madson 1997; Rose and Asher 1999). Many adult males admit to remaining wary of other males in potentially aggressive situations, surreptitiously weighing up the physical strength of other males present before taking risks such as challenging inappropriate behaviour (Archer 2001). Perhaps many women constantly compare themselves with other women but on a measure of physical attractiveness rather than physical strength.

Directives or discourse?

Watching boys and girls at play shows why we have assumed that girls are less competitive and aggressive than boys. Not only are boys more likely to be involved in competitive games, with accompanying shouts of encouragement and challenge, but there is also a gender difference in the use of language. By listening to their language, when there is a difference of opinion, we can discern that girls do not use as much directive language as boys. Boys appear to come straight to the point, with little preamble, with those most forceful and confident giving the orders. Perhaps girls are taught to consider the feelings of others and so use a different style of language, preferring negotiation, barter and persuasion (Tannen 1992; Chung and Asher 1996; Rose and Asher 1999). We do not expect girls to show dominance or anger when frustrated or in conflict in their peer relations (Underwood 2003).

Analysis of the language used by the girls participating in the activity club showed that many used a different style of language from that of the boys in the class in their informal conversations. However, directives spattered the conversations of the more aggressive girls, resulting in their language being similar to that used by the boys. These forceful linguistic structures direct the action, telling others what to do. Examples of directives are 'We will . . .' and 'You must . . .'. Most of the girls in the group used few directives, more readily seeking consensus by negotiation. This supports the findings of Collins and Laursen (1992) who found this latter style of conversation characteristic of adult females. If they challenge their friends directly, it seems many girls experience feelings of sadness and guilt (Whitesell and Herter 1996). If there was a dispute over materials or equipment, most of the girls attending the activity group used the language of negotiation and barter as in 'Let's . . .', 'Shall we . . .?', 'What about . . .?' They sought consensus by asking 'Who wants to be first?' Questions, phrases and sentences such as, 'Why don't you have the scissors for half the time, then we'll change over?' were plentiful, the conciliatory question mark being an essential element. However, most of the girls resorted to directives in anger or frustration when their conciliatory language proved to be ineffective.

Observation of the boys in the class showed that they decided quickly on the game they would play and how they would play it. This was reminiscent of the experiment shown on television and described in Chapter 4 (pp. 27–8) as the dominant lad in the group would state what the game was to be. For example, he would declare that they would play 'aliens', so putting the onus on any who demurred to challenge. In this way, the meek were 'wrong footed' as confidence is required to challenge a decision. Dominant adults use the same technique to thwart the timid (Tannen 1992). The dominant boy would, for example, take the role of captain of a spaceship, placing one or two of his friends second in command while allocating the role of aliens to the more submissive boys who would figure minimally in the action. The leader and his friends would have an exciting time chasing after the rest of the group. I have found that it is often possible to identify the hierarchical positions in a group of boys simply from the allocation of roles in their games. In a similar manner, a queue of boys often parallels the 'pecking order' in the group present.

One potato, two potato

If there is no clear outcome to a quandary or dispute among girls, traditional rhymes, songs and games often come to the fore. For example, the traditional rhyme 'One potato, two potato' is common to many areas of Britain. Rhymes are integral to many skipping and ball games and enjoyed as much as the activity itself. They help keep the peace as the climax of the rhyme signals the winner, loser or who is to have the first or next turn. There are few arguments as the rhyme ending indicates the outcome in a decisive and impersonal manner. Similarly, males use drinking songs and rhymes to signal turn taking or the winner, but they appear less central to boys' games than those of girls as the dominant males more frequently take the decisions. It would appear that males, more often than females, use songs in a competitive manner to build up or confirm team spirit. Warring male fans can be heard at professional and amateur games singing from a repertoire of stirring songs, sung long and loud to incite the opposition while promoting their own team's strength and power. However, this obvious gender difference in behaviour may be because fewer females participate or watch competitive team games.

The language of leadership

The gender difference in the use of language appears to continue into adult-hood. Some research shows that males see an argument in terms of a tussle for power and, more often than females, want to see they have led the conversation and had their own point of view accepted by force of argument (Tannen 1992; Cross and Madsen 1997). It would seem more important to males to know that they have won an argument, whereas many women have a different agenda, considering a compromise position equally acceptable (Eagly and Karau 1991: Buss and Schmidt 1993; Cross and Madson 1997). In their eyes, it is not a matter of identifying a winner, and subsequently a loser, as there can be a genuine 'better for both' solution (Fisher and Ury 1983). It would seem more important for a woman to keep her social bonds intact and preserve harmony than to be seen as the winner (Crick and Grotpeter 1995; Cross and Madson 1997; Galen and Underwood 1997). The source of this apparent gender difference may be that many females are trained from a young age not to show an openly aggressive or competitive attitude (Gottman and Mettatal 1986; Underwood 1997; Denham 1998).

The polite phrases used by girls may be misleading as it was evident from transcripts made of the conversations of the girls attending the activity club that, despite conciliatory linguistic exchanges, some more easily achieve what they want than others. If girls' social relationships are the more egalitarian, then in the words of George Orwell (*Animal Farm*), 'some are more equal than others'.

Suggested approaches

1   Ask girls what it means to be assertive, compliant and aggressive, and to identify the differences and possible outcomes of these behaviours.
2   Girls need to consider whether they are too compliant and cooperative in their friendships. Cooperation does not mean giving in to others. Do they feel other girls always get the best deal? Explore how they can recognize when others have not treated them fairly.
3   Perhaps girls need training in assertiveness so that they are better able to make their preferences known. Many fear annoying or upsetting others and so become overly compliant. Others may use language that is aggressive rather than assertive.
4   Compliant girls would benefit from training in finding 'better for both' solutions (Fisher and Ury 1983) rather than failing to state their own needs and preferences. They need to know that this is acceptable and there is no need to please everyone all the time.
5   A submissive attitude can lead to resentment, revenge, hurt feelings and grievances. Girls sometimes think it is not safe to say what they want from a dispute. Discuss what could be the outcome of taking such risks.
6   Adults teach girls not to show negative emotions such as anger. It could be useful to discuss when anger could be an appropriate response and how the girls could express their anger appropriately. There is no need to become angry on most occasions but girls need to

be able to be appropriately assertive, not compliant, angry or aggressive.

7   Mediation and other forms of conflict and dispute resolution are useful life skills. These are discussed in Section 7.

8   Many girls are reluctant to publicly celebrate winning. Discuss what would be appropriate behaviour in winning or losing a game.

9   Perhaps we train girls to negate compliments. Many women habitually respond with comments such as, 'This is just a cheap thing I picked up in the sales' when complimented on a new, expensive dress. Why do many females respond in this way? Are they afraid of making their friends jealous? Accepting compliments and winning gracefully are skills taught to the young in some other cultures.

10 Girls may enjoy researching gender differences in the language used in play among younger children. They could consider differences in the effects of directive language and the responses it provokes as opposed to the language of conciliation and negotiation.

6 When things go sour: bullying

Invisible girls

In stating that boys are competitive but that girls are cooperative (Crombie and Desjardins 1993), we may not have looked closely enough into the complex dynamics hidden within girls' friendship interactions. Analysis of these may offer insights into why girls change their friends more frequently than boys do, and why this process gives rise to such upset. We are beginning to understand that a wielding of power is identifiable among groups of girls as well as boys (Owens 1996; Xie *et al.* 2002; Salmivalli and Kaukiainen 2004). If we reframe many of the changes in friendship relations among girls as manipulating power for their own advantage, we can define the process as bullying:

> Bullying is a behaviour that can be defined as the repeated attack – physical, psychological, social or verbal – by those in a position of power, formally or situationally defined, on those who are powerless to resist, with the intention of causing distress for their own gain or gratification.
>
> (Besag 1989: 4)

Bullying is a relatively new area of research. An extensive literature search carried out prior to writing *Bullies and Victims in Schools* (Besag 1989) showed little had been written on the issue. The seminal book, *Aggression in Schools: Bullies and Whipping Boys* by Olweus (1978), was out of print. This latter title shows that the complex nature of girls' relationships had received scant attention although studies examining the bullying behaviour of girls had begun (Roland 1988; Besag 1989; Munthe 1989). The general assumption was that there was no gender difference in bullying behaviour. Recently, we have come to realize there is far more bullying among girls than was previously thought but that it may take a different form from bullying among boys (Besag 1989; Pipher 1994; Boulton and Hawker 1997; Simmons 2002).

There is some dispute as to whether girls are as aggressive as boys (Salmivalli and Kaukiainen 2004). Confusion arises because girls seem to use less easily identifiable modes of attack (Largerspetz *et al.* 1988; Owens 1996; Xie *et al.* 2002; Salmivalli and Kaukiainen 2004). In addition, the use of varying methodologies, sample size and age of participants makes comparisons difficult (Smith *et al.* 2004; Archer and Coyne 2005). The term 'two cultures', used by Maccoby (1999) to identify gender differences in the social lives of the young, has been challenged (Bem 1993; Thorne 1993; Zarbatany *et al.* 2000; Underwood 2003).

Definition of indirect aggression

There is significant controversy regarding the labelling of the covert, manipulative behaviour seemingly preferred by girls, such as gossip, stealing friends, social exclusion and malicious teasing. Some researchers in Finland label it 'indirect aggression', describing it as behaviour in which the perpetrator attempts to inflict pain in a covert or vicarious manner so hiding the intention to hurt (Bjorkqvist *et al.* 1992b). The American researchers Crick and Grotpeter (1995) prefer the term 'relational aggression' as this stresses the intent to harm by manipulating relationships using a circuitous mode of operation. Others have argued for the term 'social aggression', claiming this describes specific behaviours that cause harm by damaging social relationships (Cairns *et al.* 1989; Underwood 2003). As all bullying involves social relationships in some fashion, the original term 'indirect aggression' is used in this work. Underwood (2003) gives a useful and succinct description of each of these terms but states that there would appear to be such overlap between them that they could be subsumed under one heading. This confusion of terms is best described as 'everyone treating their definitions like toothbrushes – everyone must have his or her own' (Watkins 1990: 328).

Developmental changes

From the age of approximately 3 years, children understand the power of indirect aggression to hurt others (Crick *et al.* 1997). At this age, indirect aggression takes a simplistic form such as refusing to share or hiding a favourite game (Underwood 2003). As they get older, children start to dislike those who are aggressive, preferring those who are sociable and supportive (Gottman and Mettatal 1986), so it becomes advisable to hide aggressive intent. The character of bullying behaviour, used by both boys and girls, appears to change from direct and overt to more indirect and covert as they get older and develop a more sophisticated level of social intelligence (Bjorkqvist *et al.* 1992b; Rivers and Smith 1994; Smith *et al.* 1999).

The older and more socially skilled the attackers, the more subtle will be their bullying behaviour. As children mature, they learn to wait and plan their actions for best effect rather than responding in anger, or reacting without thinking through the consequences of their actions (Ferguson and Rule 1988). Older children have the insight and ability to delay gratification and to store information for later use on the most favourable occasion. They are able to use a more subtle range of indirect aggressions and wait for the reward of seeing the effect of their actions. For example, they hold on to gossip until they can use it to their best advantage with the result that, as they enter adolescence, their bullying becomes more sophisticated. Girls, in particular, become better able at dissembling and hiding their emotions and become more capable of employing premeditated and malicious covert behaviours (Underwood 2003).

Research on bullying puts the peak age of incidence of physical aggression, by both boys and girls, at 9 to 11 years, with a significant decrease in the number of incidents after this age (Olweus 1978, 1991; Whitney and Smith 1993; Smith et al. 1999). A preference in use of modes of indirect aggression by girls is at a peak a little later, coinciding with puberty, when they compete most intensely (Vaillancourt 2005). In the later adolescent years there is less gender differentiation in modes of aggression as, by this time, each boy has found his place in the male dominance hierarchy so physical challenges become increasingly rare (Ahlgren 1983; Pellegrini 1988; Smith and Myron-Wilson 1988). More subtle means of displaying power replace the physical fights between boys so common in their earlier years. As there is more use of indirect aggression by boys, the gender difference lessens.

Statistics show a decrease in bullying incidents among older students and young adults but this may not reflect the severity of the problem accurately. Those bullied at an older age may be the victims of more subtle but damaging attacks that go unnoticed by those who could help. These young adults may have been bullied throughout their childhood and so lack the confidence necessary to cope with these attacks or to seek help. In addition, they may be living away from the supportive networks they relied on in the past, or may fail to seek help, feeling that, being older, they should be able to cope. Many young adult males appear to display power and potency indirectly with fast cars, engagement in competitive sports, an excessive consumption of alcohol or a threatening style of presentation. Indirect strategies become increasingly complex and manipulative in both genders. For example, Bjorkqvist et al. (1994) describe forms of covert aggression used in the workplace such as unfair judgement and criticism of another's work, although even here there are gender differences in the choice of tactics used.

Bullying or benign leaders

Contrary to myth, research suggests that many bullies are socially adept and possess an adequate range of social skills to allow them to manipulate the group to achieve their own goals (Sutton *et al*. 1999). If many bullies are socially skilled, why do they behave in such a negative fashion? It is suggested that male bullies are often confident, assertive, energetic, good communicators and more popular with their peers than are their victims (Olweus 1978, 1993). It is difficult to discern what is wrong with such a profile as it represents that of an effective male leader. Many school prefects, captains of sports teams, managers in industry, and others in a prime leadership role fit this description. Although indirect aggression relates to particular social skills, such as social intelligence, it relates negatively to empathy (Kaukiainen *et al*. 1999). It may be that a benign, empathic leader uses these skills to lead in a democratic manner, whereas a bullying leader, lacking empathy, uses the same skills in a dominant, autocratic manner to the advantage of self and disadvantage of others.

Girls say why they bully

Focus groups held with adolescent girls in Australia found the girls used a range of indirect aggressions to attack others, including gossip, attacks on sexual reputation, stealing friends and social exclusion (Owens 1999; Owens *et al*. 2000). Some of the reasons the girls gave for their behaviour were boredom, jealousy, seeking attention, anger, revenge, self-protection and power. They also mentioned excluding others to show they themselves were included in the select group. These rationales are similar to those given for gang membership in both America (Joe and Chesney-Lind 1995; Chesney-Lind and Sheldon 1998; Chesney-Lind 2001) and Australia (Houghton and Carroll 2002). Investigation into the sexual bullying among adolescent girls in Britain gave similar findings (Lees 1993; Duncan 1999).

Although the girls in the activity group studied were only 10 and 11 years old, they used the same behaviours as the Australian adolescent girls in their attacks on others. Most considered their aggressions in the context of retaliation for real or imagined slights, injustices and the disloyalty of friends. However, some had reached the stage of social development where they were able to recognize the role their own emotions, such as jealousy, played in these interactions. Unlike boys, it seems that most girls, if challenged, readily offer a rationale and justification for their attacks on others although these excuses are rarely based on fact.

Rather than there being a clear gender difference in modes of attack, it may be that the context influences the mode chosen (Campbell 1999; Pearson 1999). For example, there is evidence that females revert to overt forms of aggression, similar to those used by males, when resources are scarce (Cook 1992; Glazer 1992; Campbell 2004; Ness 2004). In addition, the effects of different cultural experiences and expectations play a part in how boys and girls differ in their expression of aggression (Richardson and Green 1999; Tapper and Boulton 2004). It would seem likely that there is a continuum, termed 'borderwork' by Thorne (1993), with considerable overlap of direct and indirect aggression used by both boys and girls.

Other cultures

Most research findings incorporated in this work come from studies carried out with girls coming from countries and cultures having their roots in a Western heritage. With this in mind, the issues were discussed with girls with an Indian, Pakistani, Bangladeshi, African and Afro-Caribbean background. All were of the same age, born in Britain and attending schools in the North East, Midlands and South of England (Besag, unpublished research). The findings given are collated from discussions held with the girls, observations of them carried out while working with them and other girls, and discussions held with their teachers, parents and members of their communities. From this limited personal experience, I would tentatively suggest that there are some bullying issues of particular relevance to girls from ethnic minority groups living in Britain that may not have received the attention they warrant.

Concise and clearly presented information on issues concerning the young from ethnic minority cultures living in Britain can be found on the following web sites; Commission for Racial Equality (http://www.cre.gov.uk/); ESRC Research Centre for Analysis of Social Exclusion (http://sticerd.lse.ac.uk/case/) and Department for Education and Skills (http://www.dfes.gov.uk/). However, there appears to be less information about the issues involved in bullying among girls in these ethnic groups, the emphasis of research being on bullying by white girls against those from ethnic minorities. Although ethnic bullying occurs primarily between differing cultures (Eslea and Mukhtar 2000; Pepler, Connolly and Craig 2004), girls may also be at risk from those in their own ethnic group.

Discussions held with girls from India, Pakistan and Bangladesh, showed they drew upon a range of indirect strategies in their disputes in the same manner as the girls studied in the activity club and elsewhere. Informal discussions held with adults in their schools and communities confirmed these comments. Initially, these girls denied that quarrels and disputes occurred among them, appearing more reluctant than other girls to talk about the negative aspects of their friendships. After some time spent on general conversation, the girls grew less wary. Eventually, all admitted disputes occurred and they discussed them openly.

There appeared to be little difference in the way they behaved in dispute than most other girls. The reasons they gave, such as the jealousy of others, the disloyalty of friends, the dominance of some, and the name-calling and gossip of others, were reasons given for their disputes by girls from other cultures. The girls readily gave the positive facets of their friendships that they valued highly. They behaved in both positive and negative ways within their friendships in the same way as most girls elsewhere.

Any query about quarrels being about boyfriends resulted in shy giggles and denials. Eventually, all agreed that there was talk of boys but few admitted to having a boyfriend. This was partly because some adults in their communities class associating with a boy as 'shaming'. Any suspicion of a girl being in contact with a boy offered leverage for others to hold power over her. The girls said they were reluctant to seek help if bullied. This is the case with girls from other cultures due to fear of reprisals but, particularly in the case of Pakistani, Bangladeshi and some Indian girls, it could be those from their own ethnic group who threatened to tell their parents of behaviours disapproved of by their families and communities. Some girls are afraid of adults hearing of their behaviour, even if they do not have a boyfriend and the threat stems solely from malicious intent. Such a threat is a powerful weapon to use against these girls.

A further reason adding to the power of the threat, and for the reluctance of the girls to seek help, is that some parents could respond by taking their daughter from the school. This results in these girls suffering this abuse from others in silence. An additional factor was that some of the girls who disclosed these concerns appeared to accept these threats passively feeling that they had betrayed their family and so were at fault. None had considered approaching any adult in school for support or advice.

Several teachers had noticed recent changes in the behaviour of girls from these ethnic groups; some now appear more confident, even challenging, when under attack from peers and are starting to return the negative 'looks' from others. A few have even used physical aggression in their own defence. Some now use make-up and adjust their school uniform in ways similar to other girls in their school. There could even be the beginning of a 'ladette' culture (Muncer et al. 2001) among a minority.

Most of the Afro-Caribbean girls interviewed were less reticent about discussing the negative aspects of their friendships. Many claimed to be less tolerant of verbal abuse and threat than many of the girls they knew from Pakistani, Bangladeshi, Indian and African families. School discipline records confirmed they would be more likely to challenge and confront those who annoyed or attacked them. In this way, they appeared to behave more like girls in most Western cultures, appearing to be more ready to resort to physical aggressions such as standing over or crowding around their target, in addition to hitting and pushing (Miller-Johnson et. al. 2005). They seemed to consider it more honest to express their emotions openly and act in ways they thought appropriate at the time. It appeared to them that they would gain little from using what they considered less effective modes of defence. Discussions held with the girls and their teachers, along with observations and records, would suggest that many use a full range of indirect and direct modes of attack as used by the white girls in their schools. Research into aggression among Afro-American girls living in North America, Scandinavia and Canada has found similar results (Bergsmann 1994; Bjorkqvist et al. 1994; Osterman et al. 1994; Xie et. al. 2002). As with all other girls interviewed for the study, the Afro-Caribbean girls in Britain valued their close friendships highly. Several teachers, and other adults, were eager to say that sometimes the energetic and boisterous presentation of many of the Afro-Caribbean girls and boys belies the fact that some lack confidence and self-esteem. When challenged, some appear genuinely surprised that adults in school listen to, and accept, their explanations.

In summary, all the girls interviewed, whatever their cultural background, held similar attitudes to their friends. Their loyalty and appreciation of their friends, and their dependence on them for comfort, solace and entertainment, were identical to the young girls studied in the activity club and the vast majority of girls interviewed elsewhere. However, as stated, there may be specific issues concerning girls in some of the ethnic minority cultures that deserve further investigation.

Almost without exception, the opinion of the teachers, and other adults in the schools, was that girls from nearly all cultural backgrounds were becoming less resistant to using physical aggression in frustration, attack or retaliation. Females from many cultures appear to be turning to physical aggression more readily in recent years as shown by an increase in overt violence among young females in the U.K. (Campbell 2004), and the U.S.A. (Snyder and Childs 1997; Snyder and Sickmund 1999). We may be witnessing a modification of evolutionary factors, and the beginning of less gender differentiation in the use of physical aggression. Few would deny that some girls are physically aggressive. In a recent broadcast (BBC Woman's Hour 10.10.04.), Campbell suggested that women have always been willing to use physical violence in the home and that rates of female domestic violence may equal those of males. It would seem that there has been a marked decrease in recent years in female resistance to using physical aggression as, without doubt, there are gangs of overtly aggressive girls in many schools and communities, some equally as aggressive as boys. These highly aggressive girls are discussed further in the chapter on gangs.

Why use indirect aggression?

Why do girls prefer to use indirect modes of aggression when direct attacks such as pushing and hitting have immediate effect, whereas attacks using an indirect route, such as gossiping, take longer to have the desired result? Do boys in conflict behave differently from girls because of their upbringing or because of factors present before birth? It is most likely that the explanations encompass more than one factor, with gender differences in the expression of aggression lying in an interaction between genetic, physiological and socio-cultural co-determinants (Eron *et al.* 1983; Rowe 1994). Some authors suggest cultural and socialization factors, such as training and early influences, are the primary causal factors (Eron *et al.* 1983; Rowe 1994); others place the emphasis on genetic forces (Campbell 1995).

We cannot look to weaker female physique as the reason that girls use less physical aggression in conflict than males, as females compete more with other females than with males. Girls often use indirect modes to support more direct and forceful attacks or if the attacker is less physically strong than her target. However, even among girls of equal physical strength, indirect aggression is often their preferred mode of attack (Crick *et al.* 1999).

It appears that girls have emotional as well as practical reasons for avoiding the use of physical aggression. Perhaps their small, closely knit, friendships mean that they must jostle for a favoured position (Charlesworth and Dzur 1987; Alder and Alder 1995). They may be reluctant to resort to physical attacks in their struggles as it is likely that they will have been trained to think of others (Rose and Asher 1999). An additional explanation may be that they value anger control as their female peers reject those who display anger (Gottman and Mettatal 1986; Chung and Asher 1996; Underwood 1997).

Although cross-cultural studies show adolescent girls to be more indirectly aggressive than are boys, a study carried out in Italy found less gender distinction (Tomada and Schneider 1997). This was considered to be due to the close social bonding found in Italian families encouraging males, as well as females, to support each other emotionally (Tomada and Schneider 1997). This Italian study may reflect findings from a study of friendships among Mexican-American, African-American and European-American adolescents (Jones *et al.* 1994). This study found that the European-American group was the only one to show gender differences in levels of self-disclosure. This may have been because most males in the European-American culture are not encouraged to maintain the close relationships that elicit self-disclosure to the same extent as in the other cultures studied. Most cross-cultural studies have been carried out in countries with a western European heritage. As the concept of friendship may be culturally specific, findings may not hold true across social class, race, ethnicity or culture (Pearson 1999).

The structure of girls' friendship groups may lead the girls to use modes of indirect aggression more than do boys. As girls interact in small, emotionally enmeshed groups, by adolescence many have become highly skilled in using these behaviours and have little use for physical modes that are more easily detected and sanctioned. As girls are known to play nearer to adult supervisors than are boys, it is advantageous to them to use more subtle forms of attack (Grotpeter and Crick 1996; Hawley 1999). Girls gradually add more subtle forms to their repertoire of aggression, such as gossip and social exclusion, as these modes demand the small, close friendship networks characteristic of adolescent girls (Xie *et al.* 2002). The small groupings characteristic of girls' friendships are required for these behaviours as they demand knowledge of the personal life of the target. In addition, it is necessary for several people to be involved to spread, prolong and compound the negative effects (Xie *et al.* 2002).

Children seem to use the type of aggression most recognized and valued by their peers (Crick and Grotpeter 1995). It may be because boys form hierarchies built on physical power (Pellegrini 1988; Smith and Myron-Wilson 1988; Smith and Boulton 1990), that they use these modes to attack the vulnerable. As the display of physical power is important to boys (whereas the protection and maintenance of friendships appears more important to girls), it is not surprising that boys turn to physical means to wield power whereas girls appear to look to the manipulation of their relationships. Boys bully using modes of direct aggression that are primarily physical and obvious (Olweus 1978, 1993), whereas girls use indirect modes that appear directly related to the importance they place on their close friendship bonds (Bjorkqvist *et al.* 1992b; Warden *et al.* 1994)

Gender difference in the development of cognition skills may enable girls, more readily than boys, to employ indirect means of attacking their target (Baron-Cohen and Hammer 1997; Keenan and Shaw 1997; Baron-Cohen 2003). Some research shows that, from an early age, girls appear to show superior verbal abilities and social intelligence to boys (Baron-Cohen 2003). These are skills positively correlated with forms of indirect aggression such as gossip, social exclusion and sending malicious notes. Evolutionary psychology suggests that the comparatively slow development of the young human allows time for the development of the cognitive skills necessary for such sophisticated behaviour. There is a suggestion that those who use the most indirect aggression have the highest levels of social intelligence as these modes require a more sophisticated form of aggression so that there is less chance of the perpetrator being identified and reprisals taken (Salmivalli and Kaukiainen 2004). Perhaps girls choose modes of indirect aggression because, although taking longer to have effect than direct aggression, the distress caused can be more destructive and last far longer (Underwood *et al.* 2001).

Evolutionary psychology contributes additional hypotheses for female preference for use of indirect modes of aggression (Campbell *et al.* 1993; Campbell 1995). Female reluctance to use direct aggression could be because females in nomad communities, deprived of strong kinship ties, created new and intimate friendships with females in their new community (Ness 2004). These supportive friendships were vitally important as they provided an effective deterrent to abuse from males in patriarchal societies (Campbell 1995; Geary 1998). Campbell (1995) considers that this need to bond led to female groups being very different from those of males, being less hierarchical, having a weak clique structure, a lower focus on leadership and a less competitive ethos. Campbell suggests that, as females are relatively indifferent to status, they value group cohesion and so avoid the use of physical aggression. This may be how the picture appears on the surface, but there may be a very different scenario hidden below. In the class studied, the elements Campbell lists as having less of a presence in female groups than in male – a hierarchy, leaders, and competitive ethos – were alive and well among the girls although somewhat difficult to identify. This finding is supported by other research (Alder and Alder 1995; Eder *et al.* 1996), and by the ethnographic literature that points to intense, covert competition for status among some girls (Alder and Alder 1995; Eder *et al.* 1996; Pearson 1999).

It is thought that, as females are concerned with maintaining relationships and fostering reciprocity (Campbell 1995), they resolve their conflicts more readily than do males through strategies of compromise and mediation rather than physical force (Charlesworth and Dzur 1987; Collins and Laursen 1992; Charlesworth 1996; Cross and Madsen 1997). However, evolutionary psychology suggests that females prefer these modes of conflict resolution because they would have little to gain, and more to lose, compared with males, should they engage in direct physical combat (Bjorkqvist *et al.* 1992a, 1994; Olweus 1993; Daly and Wilson 1994; Charlesworth 1996). In evolutionary terms, men aim to remain strong in order to take their place in the dominance hierarchy, primarily for best access to resources and reproductive partners (Smuts 1987). For this reason, they show less resistance than do females to the use of physical aggression in conflict.

Females may prefer indirect modes of aggression as they have different priorities from males and avoid sustaining serious injury because of their high parental investment. Mothers remain the primary carers in most cultures and are often still more crucial to the survival of an infant than the father (Allan 1996). In the evolutionary context, it is not worth females engaging in dangerous physical contests, with no guarantee of success, in order to establish a dominance hierarchy. The priority for females is to remain healthy and strong to care effectively for their young. The necessary long gestation, and subsequent lactation period, means females must choose low-risk aggressive action to ward off a predator or rival. It is too dangerous for them to embark on high-risk 'fight to the death' attacks. A female must be in reasonable health for between two and three years if she is to see her baby through the months of gestation plus a possible two years of breast-feeding. After this time, others are able to rear her child, thus freeing the mother to take more risks. However, as women do not become equally as physically aggressive as males after the childbearing years, this does not offer a convincing rationale to explain the preference of females for indirect aggression.

A further reason why females avoid physical confrontation may be their physiological make-up, relating to the availability and uptake of serotonin (Nolen-Hoeksema 2001). Female awareness of danger is acute, activating a faster anxiety or fear response than found in males and resulting in females being less confrontational in situations of provocation and danger. Females take longer to be aroused to a level where they risk their own safety, seemingly because their priority is to defend their offspring. Related to this may be the finding that females suffer from a higher rate of disorders such as phobias and panic attacks (Nolen-Hoeksema 2001).

Women do not appear to have an obvious ranking mechanism, as is seen in the dominance hierarchy of males, but perhaps their ranking system takes a different form. Adherents to the evolutionary hypothesis would suggest that it is more important for females to look attractive to males than vice versa. At the earliest stage of the reproductive process, females play a comparatively passive role. They are the recipients of male sperm, whereas males can choose a mate and impregnate an unwilling female. Females normally need to attract males to them in order to reproduce. If so, they need to protect their presentation and avoid physical risk and disfigurement. This offers a rationale not only for their preference for indirect means of attack, but also for the formation of a hierarchy among females relating to their ability to attract males. In other words, they form a hierarchy of physical attractiveness rather than physical strength. Interestingly, indirect aggression becomes most prevalent in early adolescence around the time of puberty (Vaillancourt 2005) when girls become romantically interested in members of the opposite sex.

The hypothesis outlined above would suggest that there is no point in females establishing a dominance hierarchy for reproduction, as dominant physical power serves little purpose in securing a male mate. As physical strength is not of prime importance to females, they tend to spend less time in developing, maintaining and displaying their physical prowess. Unless a member of a sports team, I would suggest that most females who spend time in gyms seem to do so for reasons of health and beauty rather than to increase their physical strength. As attractiveness is a significant feature for females in securing a partner (Campbell 1999; Campbell, Muncer and Bibel 2001), fear of disfigurement is pertinent. Perhaps this explains why females jealously guard their appearance, constantly assess themselves and others, and are wary of competition. How they look seems of the utmost importance to many females. The girls in the study spent a great deal of time comparing their perception of their own physical attractiveness to that of others.

Gender differences in indirect aggression

Working in the neighbourhood over a period of years, I observed gender differences even within the categories of direct and indirect aggression among the older students. The verbal aggression used by the boys in the class studied tended to be direct, openly abusive with sometimes sexualized name-calling and abusive chanting. Although younger, the boys behaved in a similar manner to the adolescent girls in the study of Duncan (1999). These boys did not appear to use covert verbal modes such as gossip.

As well as drawing from the more common modes of indirect aggression, the girls studied wrote abusive, anonymous notes about their targets. Older girls in the neighbourhood wrote in secret on toilet walls. There was no evidence of malicious writing from the boys in the class, but writing by the older boys in the neighbourhood tended to be in the form of graffiti and was more generalized and less focused on other boys than was that of the girls.

Two types of people write graffiti. 'Taggers' vie with each other to make their mark everywhere, including places that are challenging to reach, whereas 'artists' create intricate messages then may take photographs of these and put them on the Internet. The older boys in the neighbourhood were taggers who targeted authority figures, female sex icons, or wrote comments advertising their own physical or sexual prowess while denigrating that of others. Like animals marking their territory, they liked to claim a wall, or train carriage, by writing their name or logo big and bold. Observation showed they liked to advertise their own power, potency and status, so reflecting their competitive spirit. If they targeted females, there appeared to be some element of a power imbalance, such as threat of sexual attack, dominance or denigration of their target. Both the girls in the study and the older girls in the locality usually targeted their immediate acquaintances. They wrote personal, negative or obscene comments, often to a girl who had been a close friend. Rather than their being an obvious claim to dominance and power, as was the case with the boys, these comments appeared to stem from feelings of jealousy and threat. These girls often targeted another considered attractive, or one suspected of enticing a 'boyfriend' from another girl, although many of these romantic liaisons existed solely in their imagination.

In parallel, there was a gender difference in the use of physical aggression. A few girls used physical attack in the manner popular among boys, such as hitting and kicking, but most physical aggression took the form of behaviours that were difficult to challenge, such as 'playfully' tugging hair, or 'accidentally' knocking into someone. The more aggressive girls occasionally crowded around their target in a tacit but threatening manner, although it was difficult to prove any deliberate intent. These girls did not target adults, but older girls in the neighbourhood occasionally behaved in this manner. Male adults can find this experience daunting as a sexual component seems integral to the threat.

These changes may stem from cultural influences with messages from diverse sources giving permission to girls to behave in this way. Of relevance may be the current trend of less gender differentiation in appearance, skills, language, interests, behaviour and employment. The restraint of 'lady-like' behaviour appears no longer of prime importance as gender differences in behaviour become blurred. 'Successful' and 'independent' are terms prized by many young women, and more females appear aggressively ambitious than in previous eras. As multifarious messages now urge females to compete on equal terms with males in all spheres of life, they may have few inhibitions about employing what were predominantly male modes of aggression. Alcohol, advertising and the lowering of social sanctions, all may have contributed to young women being physically aggressive (Campbell 2004). Intake of alcohol lowers the threshold of restraint, placing the more powerful evolutionary defence mechanism of aggression to the fore. Most young men and women now have equal access to money for binge drinking, and alcohol abuse among young females currently figures significantly in female violence.

Suggested approaches

1   Young people need to understand the actions and subsequent emotional effects of bullying behaviour. Once taught to understand what indirect aggression is, and the negative effects that can ensue, they must then take responsibility for their behaviour. They can no longer claim that an aggressive action, or abusive comment, was 'just a joke'.
2   Discuss the dynamics of group bullying with girls. What roles do the individuals play? Consider the role of assistants who join the bully, reinforcers who encourage the actions, and defenders who go to the aid of the victim (Salmivalli *et al.* 1996). These roles may not be as clearly defined among girls, as boys bully others in view of their peers and their behaviours are more visible. Discuss how these roles may translate into the behaviours used within female friendship groups.
3   Ask girls how the 'silent observers' (Besag 1989) could best support a victim. What factors would prevent them from supporting a bullied girl? Girls are more likely than boys to defend others under attack (Sharp and Cowie 1998; Smith *et al.* 2004). What do they think they could do in those circumstances?

4 Start a discussion on semantics. Words can be more powerful than the sword. Discuss words traditionally used to describe *verbal* acts, such as cutting words, harmful, cut to the quick, to wound, to destroy, to stab in the back, a tongue lashing, poisonous words, sticking your claws in. All these are explicit physical descriptions of the pain suffered by those under verbal attack.

5 Discuss words that vividly describe indirect *physical* acts, such as giving someone the cold shoulder, leaving someone out in the cold, to freeze a person out, to turn your back on someone.

6 Discuss who can help targets of bullying. Girls need be able to recognize when they need help and know where to go and whom to approach.

7 Discuss how the girls could make a challenge if they saw someone being bullied. What else could they do? They need to be able to identify others under attack and offer friendship and support as a group if they are fearful of defending the target alone. If they are not confident enough to make a challenge, they should move away and tell someone.

8 Discuss fear of reprisals and how they can be avoided. Refer to Section 7 for suggestions.

9 Discuss how the girls could work as a group to address bullying. There is a role for all to play. We all have responsibility for the welfare and safety of others.

10 In relation to the above, discuss possible whole-school approaches they consider would be effective and, importantly, those they consider would be ineffective, and why.

7 Mirror, mirror on the wall: cruel comparisons

Who is 'in' and who is 'out'

As it is essential for young people to have some degree of acceptance in the peer group, it is necessary to examine how the processes of acceptance and rejection occur within groups of girls to gain any understanding of why their friendships are so disputatious. Assimilation, as stated earlier, incorporating the process of being accepted and feeling accepted, is one of the basic factors that regulate our social behaviour (Omark *et al.* 1973). The processes of assimilation and differentiation, as described by Harris (1995), are particularly pertinent to any investigation focusing on relationships between girls. This need to show some individuality, yet conform to the mores established by the group, is the source of many disputes and much heartache. In any group of girls there appears to be an ongoing evaluation process present, identifying those considered worthy of inclusion and those to be ignored, ostracized and designated outcasts or ridiculed.

It would appear that girls, more than boys, need to feel accepted as part of a group. The fact that, unlike boys, they tend to interact in small, closely bonded friendship clusters supports the hypothesis that their social needs differ from those of boys (Thorne and Luria 1986; Benenson *et al.* 1997; Maccoby 1999). As girls seem more likely to bully by social manipulation than by physical power, the closeness of these bonds, and the need of most girls for acceptance in the group, offer a powerful lever to those with malicious intent. The close bonding between girls within their friendships offers many positive factors to the relationships, but perhaps the closeness of the bonds gives rise to less positive features. We need to consider why these friendship bonds are so important and how, and why, some girls manipulate them so skilfully.

If acceptance within the group is so important to girls, inherent in the assimilation process will be the threat of exclusion. As stated earlier, the friendship groups of girls are small, so it may be necessary for the girls to jostle fiercely, but covertly, for a preferred social position (Charlesworth and Dzur 1987). There appears to be an ongoing process of defining who will be included or excluded by the group, a process termed 'othering' by Lees (1993). Girls who bully may alienate another simply to prove that they, unlike their target, are part of the group (Lees 1993; Roland and Idse 2001). The girls in the activity club used these tactics to confirm friendships within their group and to exclude targeted girls.

For many girls, the most distressing aspect of this process is the manner in which it is executed (Pipher 1994; Simmons 2002; Wiseman 2002). As these evaluations can change overnight, they are the source of much distress. A girl needs to be aware of the precariousness of her position in the group as the mood of the membership could fluctuate at any time. Any girl in the group studied could arrive at school to find her friends of the previous day had decided to exclude her. To make matters worse, they could have alienated her from the rest of the class. This level of intense wariness of others in the group is contributory to the tension so common in girls' friendship relations. Girls know they must keep a watchful eye on their friends to check for a change in mood as this could indicate a possible change in allegiance.

Even young children become distressed when excluded from the peer group. As adults, we may have been unaware of the importance of this concept to younger children and so failed to identify the distressing process going on before our eyes. The teachers in a school near to where the study took place considered one young girl in their care to be happy but shy and nervous of the energetic play of other children. Close observation showed that the other children were excluding her from their games unintentionally. She was desperate to play with her classmates but, being reticent, she could not make the appropriate overtures. The other children did not notice her timid attempts to communicate so did not play with her, or speak to her, throughout the school day. As a result, she withdrew from them even more, so that, at 5 years of age, she was already suffering from feelings of rejection, loneliness and inadequacy. She was getting no opportunity to increase her social skills while those more socially confident continued to develop.

The influence of the peer group

Girls appear very concerned with how others see them (Simmons 2002). Young people find out who they are by making social comparisons of themselves with others (Harris 1995). This is their most pertinent yardstick as it is within their peer group that many of their most influential daily interactions occur (Harris 1995). These social comparisons are complex in that they encompass physical, social and cognitive skills and abilities. All aspects of their presentation and functioning play a part in this complex process (Hartup

1983). The young person is making a judgement regarding his or her identity as others are judging them, while they are judging themselves. Girls, more than boys, appear more active in this mutual, complex evaluation process of self and others. The young develop their own sense of 'the norm' by which to measure, and judge, themselves and their peers. Failure to match this invisible target can be a destructive experience, made so by a sense of inadequacy or the stigmatization of their peers. For girls, the judgement of their peers appears to be particularly pertinent.

From early childhood, girls are not only evaluating themselves against others, they are involved in rating others in comparison with the rest of the group membership. These complex, ongoing social comparisons are multidimensional in character being physical, cognitive and social (Hartup 1983). 'Human females compete with one another in the currency of physical attractiveness because that is primarily what is valued by males' (Symons 1979: 103). Girls are aware of those among them with the prettiest clothes, the latest merchandise and the smartest hairstyle. They identify the most aggressive, the cleverest, the most attractive and the most popular. For many, it is as though they are living their lives by holding up a mirror through which they see themselves in their social world. This social domain appears a more dominant and influential world than that of exams and academic success. This helps shed light on the finding that girls say that it is more important to them to have friends than to achieve academically (Rosenberg and Simmons 1975; Lever 1976; Eder 1991). This 'covert social sub-curriculum is more important to young people than the academic one presented to them by teachers' (Besag 1989: 113).

The constant reciprocal evaluation between girls contributes to a sense of unease and instability in a group (Eder 1985; Alder and Alder 1995). These comparisons made by girls can be harsh and delivered in ways that could be termed bullying. Girls use this strategy to ensure conformity of attitude and appearance, to enforce rules and social mores and to control relationships (Eder 1985; Lees 1993; Alder and Alder 1995; Fillion 1997). For this reason, there is close monitoring of all that is happening, resulting in a need for the constituency of girls' friendship groups to keep in contact by sight, telephone, email or text. Constant contact is part of the armoury used by the powerful to keep covert control of the group and significant others as well as to check on their own standing. In tandem, the less influential members must keep in contact to pick up signs of what the popular girls are doing, wearing and thinking in order to remain in vogue and acceptable. It seems that females, young and old, are constantly, mutually aware and engaged in making positive and negative judgements. Frequent contact, by whatever means, allows the covert registering of any nuance of change within the group in the appearance, manner or attitude of individual members. Most importantly, it allows girls to be aware of any slight shift in the direction and quality of the relationship bonds.

The most dangerous years

Body image is central to the conversations of many adolescent girls and a major source of concern (Ge *et al.* 1996; Basow and Rubin 1999). Many seem obsessed with their physical appearance and their eagle eyes search for evidence of any developmental change in themselves and others (Eder 1991). Early menarche and physical maturity are of particular relevance to girls making these comparisons, as these features are attractive to males so resulting in these physically mature girls dating earlier (Symons 1979; Magnusson *et al.* 1986). They are gaining valuable experience that will stand them in good stead for when the rest of girls catch up to their stage of maturity. The jealousy of other girls, seeing them have first choice of partner, often leads them to become targets of indirect aggression (Eder 1991).

A rounding of the body shape, currently unfashionable, often accompanies desired physical development and maturity so triggering harsh self-criticism. As a result, girls scrutinize each other's bodies for minute changes and informally rank each other's physical development (Eder 1991). They construct imaginary templates of an ideal shape they hope to achieve. The vast melee of fashion industries is more than willing to promote templates of the currently fashionable ideal body image. Adults magnify this process by making both obvious and tacit comparisons. Shops selling attractive clothing exclusively in tiny sizes give silent, powerful and unhelpful messages to developing girls with a healthy body shape. The media prizing a specific body shape, or offering unsolicited advice on weight loss, tell many healthy young females they are not valued. However the message is given, many feel under a harsh, judgemental spotlight.

It is of particular significance that the time of late childhood to early adolescence equates with the peak time for loss of self-esteem and confidence (Schofield 1981; Duncan 1999). Young people are at their most impressionable during these years when hormonal changes are most vigorous and body shape and size seem to change overnight. The speed of body change outstrips any emotional preparation. The hormonal surge in early adolescence results in many experiencing severe and frequent fluctuations in their emotional equilibrium. This is a time when nothing seems in balance. Sadly, girls come under the harshest and most sophisticated peer judgements when they are at this most sensitive and vulnerable stage in their development (Basow and Rubin 1999). It is no coincidence that this is the age of onset of eating disorders relating to body image (*Diagnostic and Statistical Manual of Mental Disorders* 1994). Some young girls think dieting is the one area where they can be effective in meeting the standards set down by others, so perceive this as an area within their control. This can easily get out of hand and lead to the destructive conditions of anorexia and bulimia. Conversely, depression may result in giving up hope and so trigger obesity. This is also the prime age of onset for other self-destructive behaviours that can stem from depression such as drug and alcohol abuse, smoking, reckless behaviour, cutting the skin and even prostitution.

Fashion fads

It is not only in relation to body shape that the young worry about the opinion of their peers. Girls make this very clear by the covert 'uniforms' they wear. These signal where a girl stands in relation to the group. Older girls in the neighbourhood of the school where the study took place, used labels on clothes and trainers, style of hair and make-up, temporary tattoos and choice of accessories to signal that they were acceptable to each other. They arrived at consensus in a casual and informal fashion so that, eventually, the girls in a particular group would choose similar items. The 'insignia' did not signify a closed group membership, as no one prevented those outside the group from wearing similar things. Others in the school would choose similar items if they were in fashion. However, attempts for acceptance by eager 'wannabes' (Wiseman 2002) could be thwarted by ridicule. Once in common use, those considered trendsetters would quickly adopt a new style. A girl targeted for exclusion may be encouraged to believe that buying specific adornments would gain her acceptance, only to find that she has gone to financial and emotional expense in vain. She continues to be the target of scorn if the rest of the girls in the group have changed their appearance overnight to display their disdain.

Such behaviours are contributory to the obsession with appearance so prevalent among girls from quite a young age. The subtle ways in which girls signal the processes of inclusion and exclusion remain a mystery to many adults; their potency leaves many bewildered. As adults may not understand the subtleties hidden within the processes, or fully appreciate the emotional repercussions of such behaviours, they are unable to make effective challenges. Even if they understand the motives, it is difficult to challenge girls over matters such as their personal selection of dress or choice of friends.

I have found that most girls are aware of what others are wearing on most occasions. Conversely, most boys seem unaware of the presentation of other boys unless one among them has chosen something extreme although there are signs that this may soon change. I would suggest that many men have little idea of what other men have worn at a formal function, perhaps because they dress alike, thus dampening any curiosity. Perhaps they choose to dress alike as they have little interest in competing regarding their apparel. Numerous discussions held with women found that within a few minutes of entering a room, most will have scanned the room and know what others are wearing.

They will have assessed which are the most striking outfits, those women looking particularly attractive or unattractive, and whether or not they themselves have chosen wisely (Besag, unpublished research). A woman may consider the occasion ruined if someone else is wearing the same outfit as this negates her individual style. If she considers that she has chosen a garment too dull or outrageous, she could spend the evening feeling invisible or overly conspicuous. The ideal is to wear something that fits in with others while showing individual flare.

This process of comparing while being compared, assimilating into the group while marking individuality, with the attendant anxieties and uncertainties, is rife among young girls. The girls studied, particularly those more physically mature and precocious, were acutely aware of the presentation of other girls. They expected comments and compliments on their own appearance, and failure to offer positive feedback, even on choice of small items such as hair decorations, could cause resentment. It must be stressed that these findings are from research carried out with adolescents and adult males and females in Britain, Ireland, Italy, Australia, New Zealand, the USA and Canada plus participants from the Pakistani, Indian, Afro-Caribbean and African communities living in Britain. They may not be relevant to those from other cultures.

Body image

The comparisons used among girls may be multidimensional, but the girls' major concern is physical attractiveness (Goodwin 1980; Schofield 1981, 1982; Kennedy 1990; Maccoby 1999). As stated earlier, girls rank each other's physical attractiveness, incorporating styles of clothing, as they consider this is how boys rank them (Eder 1991). Early adolescence signals a growing interest in boys that becomes a new area of concern (Larson and Asmussen 1991). Most adolescent girls like to feel that they are attractive to boys, even if they are not actively seeking a relationship. However, those considered to be flaunting their sexuality, by choice of dress and make-up, are particularly stigmatized by others (Eder and Sanford 1986; Walkerdine 1990, 1992; Lees 1993). Many girls must walk a tightrope, wanting to appear both attractive to males but not so attractive that they risk alienating their girlfriends. It may take several hours of anxious indecision before a girl decides what to wear. Her friends could greet her with effusive compliments on her attractive, daring outfit – or they may openly scorn her, saying she looks like a 'tart'. This will probably be couched in falsely positive terms such as, 'I'm only telling you for your own good' if they wish to keep the friendship intact. If this is the case, the girl's friends may exchange their negative opinions behind her back. A couple of centimetres in a neckline, or skirt length, could call up one or other extreme evaluation.

A snap decision may be made by the most powerful girl, with others following suit. The decision of the dominant girl, to make a positive or negative remark, may depend solely on the quality of her relationship with the girl under the spotlight and on how confident she is in influencing the opinions of the others.

Club rules

Related to this need of the membership to check each other for standards of group acceptance, is the finding that girls' groups appear to have stricter boundaries for compliance than those of boys (Alder and Alder 1995; Eder *et al.* 1996). Girls appear less forgiving than are boys to any girl not adhering to their covert rules. No small detail escapes their attention regarding dress code, language, fashion and behaviour. The boys in the class studied had a broader band of acceptance regarding their friends. Boys' groups appear to be looser and less focused on personal qualities and the presentation of individual members than are those of girls. A boy who could hit or kick a ball straight and hard was more than likely included in a game even if he was not in the friendship group.

In summary, girls may use a range of indirect aggressions to manipulate their own social relationships and those of others solely in the context of making and breaking friends. For some, the conscious intent is to alter the dynamics of the friendship group, not to demonstrate or abuse power. However, for some, social exclusion can be aggression and a power strategy and a conscious and effective mode of attack on others.

Suggested approaches

1 Discuss how a girl knows she is accepted or excluded.
2 Explore with girls how the exclusion process happens.
3 Suggest they collect pictures from magazines to make a collage of people who are famous for being attractive. Point out that each one has different physical features. Who do they *really* think is the most attractive? Are they swayed by group opinion?
4 Present a collage to the girls of people that they would not know and who are considered attractive. Confidentially, ask them to vote for their favourite. Encourage them to discuss that it is not what you have but the way you cope with it that is important.
5 Let girls know that research appears to show that many males consider humour, confidence and an equitable temperament as important as physical features. Smiles are powerful.
6 Encourage girls to think of ways to maximize their best features. They could get magazines and books from the library on how to make the

best of themselves, their clothes and accessories. Help them identify relevant websites. Discuss the fact that *no body* is physically perfect. Healthy shiny hair, good skin and skilful dress sense can detract from, or hide, most sins. Older sisters and relatives may be able to help.

7 Ask the girls to make a list of all the harsh comments that females make to each other, then get them to change them round. What are the attackers really saying? Ask the girls to listen and then run an alternative, perhaps more truthful, commentary. Examples might be:
   - That skirt is so rubbish. (I wish I had bought one. It looks really good.)
   - God, you're fat. (You have sexy curves. I wear a padded bra but no one knows.)
   - Stick pin. You'd fall down a crack in the pavement. (I wish I could lose some weight.)

   Stress that if the attackers were confident and happy within themselves they would not care how others looked.

8 Encourage girls to identify and own up to their own emotions – jealousy, anger, disappointment and pride – and their effects. It could help them to understand better the negative behaviours of others.

9 Discuss whether girls should be less dependent on the opinion of others. If so, what does this mean? How could they change their attitude without causing offence?

10 Discuss what girls get from associating with the 'social stars'. Is it company, fashion tips, gossip or protection? Could they get these things elsewhere if they are unhappy in the friendship?

SECTION 3
Groups

8 Cliques, groups and gangs

Social groupings

Young people need to adjust to a wide range of social groupings. For most, there is the additional grouping of a clique, group or gang as well as the class and school population. In searching for an explanation for the puzzling, cyclic formation and reformation of friendships among girls, it would appear necessary to consider the dynamics of their small, closely bonded friendship groups and the larger peer groupings within which these interact. It is of interest to look at the characteristics of these groupings and their impact on the social behaviour of the constituent membership. Groups, cliques and gangs fulfil a primary social need which adults meet by going to pubs, social, political and sport settings for companionship and entertainment. The most popular media entertainment, such as situation comedies and soaps, centres in pubs and clubs.

Groups

Friendship groups have less rigid boundary maintenance, and a more fluid membership, than is found in cliques, so outsiders have a better chance of being accepted (Alder and Alder 1995). Despite exceptions, the membership of girls' friendship groups is more closely matched than that of boys, with more commonly accepted norms, mores and attitudes in evidence. There is a high likelihood that members of groups identify each other as mutually connected, as girls look to those they consider to be like themselves when choosing friends (Alder and Alder 1995). They select their friends on compatibility of personality, preferring them to reflect themselves (Erwin 1985). Their groups are composed of those who tend to be of similar age, with the same interests and outlook, with all members sharing ideas, idols, style, attitudes, likes and dislikes.

The results of the questionnaires given to the girls in the activity club revealed they chose as friends those they considered to hold similar attitudes and values to themselves, as suggested by the research. It would appear that girls, more than boys, gather into friendship groups of those they consider like-minded, perhaps because they spend a great deal of time discussing inter-personal topics concerning themselves and the lives of others (Lever 1976; Thorne and Luria 1986; Goodwin 1990; Alder and Alder 1995; Eder et al. 1996). As boys' friendship interactions tend to focus on activities, they are more likely to gather with others who share those interests and skills, putting less emphasis on mutual attitudes and values. Informal observations of the boys in the same class as the girls studied, plus other boys in the school, revealed that they chose to play with those who were competent and could contribute to their game regardless of their friendship status.

Named groups

There are numerous identifiable friendship groups of young people in schools, clubs and neighbourhoods. Many have a national or international base but fit the criteria of a group by having an open membership with shared aims and interests. Specific groups of young people associate themselves by name and dress code such as the Teddy Boys and Punks of yesteryear, and international groups such as the Scouts and Guides. It would seem that many young people attach themselves to groups with high visibility, their presentation advertising their ethos and attitudes so giving them a clear identity. There appears a need for the young to belong to distinctive groups identifiable to themselves and others. However, these identities change as the rationale for many of the informal adolescent groups appears to be that they are up-to-date and outside the establishment. The frequent change in the behaviour, interests and social mores of the young is brought about partly to keep adults excluded and in ignorance, so that much of the culture is 'underground' and the detail remains a mystery. Over time, the mystique fades and the search begins for new social groupings with a novel presentation. The rapid changes found in adolescents' slang highlight the transitory nature of their codes. Their vocabulary changes rapidly to signal a change in fashion and to keep it separate from the adult domain as well as signalling those in and those out of the social peer groups. By the time adults have learnt a few phrases, those phrases are out of date and their use open to ridicule.

Goths

One of the most prominent and long-standing named groups is that of the Goths. Young people identifying themselves as Goths are of particular interest to this work as their dramatic clothing and make-up may mask vulnerability.

Within this group may be those not included in friendships in the school or community. One way of dealing with such a vulnerable, problematic social position is to do what animals have always done: make the outward appearance as different or startling as possible in order to ward off attack. The music and literature interests of many Goths reflect a depressed affect. Not all Goths are emotionally depressed, but those who are socially isolated often find a loose connection to an undemanding group to be a way of forming a tenuous social bond. High levels of approach made to community call centres such as Samaritans by those stating that they are Goths suggest that many may be in a precarious social or emotional position and signalling a cry for help,

Cliques

There would seem to be some confusion between the categorization of cliques and groups although cliques differ from groups in several ways (Feshbach and Sones 1971). Cliques are more exclusive than groups, having specific criteria for membership, more rigid boundary maintenance, a hierarchical structure and a dominant leader (Alder and Alder 1995). Some friendship groups among the young girls in the activity club showed these characteristics and there was an understanding that not all who desired membership would be accepted. Those who are not members may recognize a clique as such, but the term 'clique' is not one that girls commonly use to describe their own group. Many deny that their group is a clique as they understand the negative connotations of the word and wish to avoid sanctions or adverse comment. The girls in the study who were in a clique were reluctant to admit to being in one, while others readily complained about groups being 'cliqueish', using this as a pejorative term to describe a group from which they felt excluded.

The status of the clique is recognized by its place in the hierarchy of the full group, whether a class, club or neighbourhood. Alder and Alder (1995) state that there will be only one clique dominating the upper rung of a class identified by members and non-members alike as the 'popular clique'. Part of the power of cliques is that they gel quickly. Once the new school year has begun, there is less opportunity for new entrants to infiltrate even a newly established clique (Feshbach and Sones 1971; Alder and Alder 1995). This leaves some young people feeling isolated and excluded from the start.

There is differential power and status within a clique of girls (Alder and Alder 1995). In the class studied, the hierarchy appeared to be internal to the cliques, unlike the sole dominance hierarchy of the boys that covered the whole class. It would seem that, within a class, there could be several cliques of girls, each with its own internal power structure. Males, of any age, rarely appear to speak of cliques, although specific clubs exclusive to males would fit the criteria. It may be because the large majority of male friendship groups are less cliqueish that they use the terminology less often.

Gangs

Both girls and boys form gangs, although we more commonly assume the constituency of a gang to be male. Boys and girls join for the same complex reasons: a mixture of boredom, a sense of belonging, availability of drugs, guns and money, for sex, power and kudos within the peer community, and self-protection (Joe and Chesney-Lind 1995; Chesney-Lind and Sheldon 1998; Chesney-Lind 2001).

A gang can be defined as a group or a clique with deviant intent common to the membership. The agenda could emerge over time, so that a group may change its nature from group to gang over a period of months or years, or it may happen suddenly in an opportunistic manner. For example, several girls standing at a bus stop would be a group if they were just waiting for the bus. If the same girls suddenly ran amok in the street, throwing bricks through shop windows and threatening passers-by, observers would describe them as an unruly gang.

Gangs such as Hell's Angels incorporate the features of a clique, having a recognized leader, closed membership, a dress code, logo and clearly defined terms of mutual interest. Other gangs may be more loosely structured and have less clearly defined boundaries. The definition may change according to the moral judgements of those categorizing the group. The members may not recognize the deviant agenda as such, describing their behaviour as 'having a bit of fun', whereas a source external to the group, such as the police or judicial system, may allocate the label of 'deviant' and describe it as a gang. Whether others describe the group as a gang will depend on how they assess the behaviour of the membership. A member of the Hell's Angels may describe his chapter as a group of mates, whereas a disapproving outsider could describe it as a gang. Members may use the term 'gang' in a bid for peer status.

Girls in gangs

Male gangs tend to have their own idiosyncratic turn of phrase, logo, clothing, territory and common heroes (Joe and Chesney-Lind 1995; Chesney-Lind and Sheldon 1998; Chesney-Lind 2001). Members of some of the recently emerged female gangs also acquire such accoutrements. From observations carried out and discussions held with girls in gangs, it would appear that the girls' behaviour reflects how they perceive themselves. If they regard themselves as a gang, their group dynamics and behaviour will be similar in some ways to that of male gang members. Even so, significant gender differences will be evident.

Most girls in a deviant group do not think of themselves as members of a gang, although, from common parlance and news reports, it would seem that gang membership is now a more acceptable, and perhaps fashionable, activity among a minority of girls.

It is rare for girls' groups to have an identified leader and few have the nicknames, logo and recognized outdoor territory more usually associated with boy gangs. Unlike male gangs, who prefer an outdoor venue, girl gangs usually meet indoors. They often meet in the homes of older girls or young women where they sit and chat, drink or use drugs. They often meet in these houses because the older females are the suppliers. The deviant behaviour of girls, unlike that of boys, will include the theft of items such as make-up, clothing and jewellery for immediate personal use. Mobile phones and credit cards are now on the list.

I have found dyad and triad friendships present within female gangs. As with other female groups, disputes and conflicts focus on arguments over boys and suspicion of the infidelity of group members to their female friends. Discussions about boys often dominate their conversations.

The girls show less tolerance than do boys regarding the flaunting of the social mores held by the membership. Boys in gangs usually have their own deviant behaviour high on their agenda for conversation, including the repetitive recounting of past exploits they claim they or their friends have carried out. Many such dialogues are fantasies. There are efforts to impress, with use of exaggerated and competitive talk.

The research of Houghton and Carroll (2002) in Australia found the social image of delinquent females to be similar to that of males in that they admire delinquent behaviour in others. They have little compunction about breaking the law, they desire freedom and autonomy, and they admire behaviours such as bullying, smoking, truancy and theft. They aim for low adult control and for independence, yet adhere closely to the tacit, informal rules of the gang. In considering self-image, Houghton and Carroll found that gang members were proud to be troublemakers, anti-authoritarian and familiar to the police, judicial system and the community. Unlike other girls, but as with boys, they consider aggression is best carried out in front of an audience as this enhances their reputation among their particular peer groups and older gang members. This means that public sanctions could be counterproductive.

Houghton and Carroll (2002) have shown that by the time these delinquent girls and boys are 11 years old, many are good planners with future goals. This is the time when, moving to the secondary schools, they divide from the more compliant young people by their choice of goals. The transition stage in education has been thought to be influential in this choice of non-compliant goals, yet this division seems to occur even when there is no transition stage at this age. We may have underestimated the skills and achievements of these young girls as they select and accomplish specific and challenging goals. Unfortunately, these are not the goals society would have them choose. There has been an assumption that these young people, boys as well as girls, are not able to achieve because of restricted skills, opportunities or motivation. The research now seems to point to many of them having the ability to meet challenges and achieve; they simply do not want to meet the goals most adults set down for them.

The long-term prognosis for highly aggressive girls is pessimistic with regard to their physical and mental health, their place in the community and future parenting (Farrington 1991; Ensminger and Slusarcick 1992). As they reject the accepted goals of school, these young people often truant or manage to manipulate situations so that they become excluded. Being out of school poses a risk for them and we could say that if they are out of school, they will be into trouble and at risk. They will experience not only a loss of academic opportunities, but also a loss of social opportunities as they will be exposed to restricted social mores and codes of behaviour and, more worryingly, only inappropriate role models. They will have only restricted social bonds as they will be interacting only with those of like mind.

Many of these highly aggressive girls suffer mental health problems such as feelings of alienation, loss, helplessness and depression (Farrington 1991; Ensminger and Slusarcick 1992). If life has little to offer, they may turn to self-destructive, risk-taking behaviour for the rush of adrenaline and excitement this brings, and to alcohol, drugs and promiscuity for immediate relief from pain. Their lifestyle leads them to exposure to adults who may aim to manipulate them for their own gain. Many of these girls are precociously sexually experienced. They may suffer from a range of sexual diseases and are vulnerable to physical and sexual abuse from older males, and many turn to prostitution (Farrington *et al.* 2003).

Groups, cliques and gangs in the study

As stated earlier, more than one clique may be evident in a class depending on the range of interests, maturity and allegiances of the membership. The girls in the class studied divided themselves into groups and cliques primarily according to interests related to their level of maturity. Some of the girls were precociously mature; others remained immature; whereas the majority fell between the two categories. One clique held a more dominant position in the manner described by Alder and Alder (1995). This was the clique containing the more aggressive girls (although not all were aggressive), several of whom were the most physically mature in the class. These girls erroneously considered that they were the most sophisticated and formed a distinct clique with clear boundary maintenance. Entry into this group was difficult for out-siders although the membership was not stable and a girl could find herself excluded at any time by consensus of the other members. At the other end of the spectrum, there was a clique of comparatively immature girls. This group had a more open membership but they, too, were somewhat selective. The rest of the girls were at varying levels of maturity and formed a number of different friendship clusters.

The friendship clique containing the more precocious and physically mature girls displayed the most aggression. From time to time, verbal and physical attacks would occur between them and particular others. These were more likely to occur in the community than in school where there was closer supervision. These attacks gave the group the identity of being deviant and therefore fitting the criteria of a gang. At such times, other girls would refer to them as a gang, usually naming it after the girl most likely to have instigated the attack. This girl, more than the others, fitted the profile of a female gang member although she had not begun to be involved in the quality of anti-social activities that would lead to police action. However, her family and extended family were known to the judiciary.

When there were no aggressive incidents occurring, the other girls did not refer to the group as a gang. For example, during the time of the study, one girl fell foul of Rachel, the most aggressive member, who subsequently led the group to target her for a range of insults, threats and physical attacks. This resulted in the target girl requiring an escort to and from school until the situation was resolved. For some time afterwards, the other girls referred to the group as Rachel's gang. Presumably, these girls did not have the permanent identity of a gang because of their fluctuating membership and the inter-mittent nature of the eruptions of violence. The individual girls who could be involved from time to time were powerful personalities but the fractious nature of their allegiances lessened the cohesion, and consequently the iden-tity, of the group.

Although the more mature girls did not have a uniform as such to indicate their allegiance to the clique, they wore a more mature style of clothing than did the other girls. This set them apart from those less precocious. Most of these girls were extremely conscious of what they and others wore. Some occasionally made abusive remarks to one girl, referring to her clothing as 'babyish' as her mother sometimes bought her inappropriate party dresses from charity shops to wear to school. The other girls in the class did not remark on her clothing but the more 'mature' girls were quick to offer their unsolicited opinion, not about the origins of the clothes, but their inappropri-ate style.

Suggested approaches

1   Explore with girls the differences between a group and a clique, identifying the advantages and disadvantages of being in each.
2   Discuss with girls how being in a group or crowd can be fun. Are they comfortable in the situation? Are they making their own decisions or is someone else doing it for them? If so, are they happy?
3   Ask girls to consider how they would go about leaving a group if they felt uncomfortable. Look at the benefits and costs of the various ways of making an exit move.
4   Talk about peer pressure with the girls. Explore with them why some want others to smoke, drink alcohol or take drugs. Is it to give permission for them to do these things themselves or to have a hold over the target girl in order to get money by threatening to disclose her secrets?
5   Ask the girls to identify the dangers and negative consequences of being in a gang. What benefits could the gang gain from their membership?
6   Suggest to the girls that if they are not in a friendship group, they can get the same emotional and friendship support from other groups. Suggestions for making friends are given in Chapter 20.
7   Approaches for working with girls in gangs are given in Section 7.

9 Dyads, triads and lovers' quarrels

A perfect match

An examination of groups, cliques and gangs alone does not offer a clear explanation of why friendships between girls are characteristically fragmented, querulous and beset by unrest (Savin-Williams 1980; Cairns et al. 1989; Alder and Alder 1995; Harris 1995). To elicit relevant information, it is necessary to examine more closely the smaller friendship formations within these larger groupings and the differences in the emotional features of these relationships.

Perhaps girls' friendships are less stable than those of boys because girls appear to prize different characteristics in their friendships. Unlike boys, girls prefer small, cohesive, closely bonded groups where members are well-known to each other (Savin-Williams 1980; Nicolopoulau 1997). Perhaps it is because boys' groups are not as cliqueish, exclusive, intimate and as emotionally intense as those of girls, that their friendship relations are less disputatious, more static and long-standing (Thorne and Luria 1986; Benenson et al. 1997). 'Girls' relationships are equalitarian but emotionally vindictive, whereas boys', in contrast, inhabit conflict filled but emotionally uninvolved worlds' (Alder and Alder 1995: 159). The friendship groups of boys may be similar in size to those of girls, but girls' groups are more emotionally enmeshed (Urberg et al. 1995). Boys seem to enquire less intently into the lives their friends lead when not in their company. I have found many boys' groups to have a more ad hoc constituency, with several members knowing only the nickname of some in their group. As girls select their friends on compatibility of personality, preferring them to reflect themselves (Erwin 1985), girls tend to choose their friends from a small circle of acquaintances, leading to an emotional enmeshment of social interactions, exacerbating envy, rivalry and competition (Maltz and Borker 1982; Eder 1990; Eder et al. 1996).

Not only is it important for girls to have friends, but the quality of their friendships is also significant. Girls' friendships have been compared to the relationships of lovers, with both the positive and negative aspects comparable to those of the romantically involved (Lever 1976). Unlike many boys, girls actively promote and reward intimacy in their friendships. Emotional connections such as unity, empathy, solidarity, plus mutual support, feature largely in girls' friendships (Gottman and Mettatal 1986; Nilan 1991, 1992). These are characteristics of most lover relationships.

The need of girls for a close emotional commitment would determine the character of the friendship groups. Girls who are close friends not only develop an emotional enmeshment similar to lovers, but also behave in many ways like lovers. They like to display their friendships and make them public. It could be that, in the same way that boys like to display their physical prowess in front of an audience of their peers, so girls enjoy showing that they have access to close friends. The girls in the activity club enjoyed being in close proximity to their friends, linking arms, hugging each other and huddled together in conversation. They liked to sit by their friends in class, sharing tasks and ideas, not necessarily copying each other's work. Girls like to closet themselves away for private and endless chats (Lees 1993), so that a girl without a close friend can feel like a social misfit. I have found that, like lovers, two girls in a friendship dyad often write messages to each other to confirm and consolidate their relationship. It is not only that most boys are less inclined to write about anything than are girls, but boys appear less committed to keeping in such close contact. Many parents of girls are aware that their telephone bills have rocketed in recent years due to the advent of chatrooms, mobile phones, emails and text messaging.

There is often a sense of wariness and unease underlying the relationships of girls owing to the fragile nature of these friendships. Like lovers, girls frequently check on where they stand with each other, each liking to know of every move the other makes. Within their informal chatter, they may be covertly checking on what each other is doing when they are apart, seeking frequent reassurance that their emotional bond remains intact in the manner of lovers. They may not seek reassurance openly, but most girls are adept at reading interpersonal signals. It would seem that, perhaps subconsciously, they are acutely alert to minute changes in the style and content of conversations and the nuances of body language. This would seem to be at least part of the rationale for the frequent passing of notes and text messages between friends, the covert seeking of confirmation of affiliation and loyalty, all features of a lover relationship.

Lovers' quarrels

The gender difference in the character of these friendship bonds appears to be reflected in the source of disputes displaying a gender difference in the use of power. Girls' groups may appear to have a less openly competitive and status-driven ethos than those of boys as they actively discourage open competition and attempts to display power differences (Buhrmester and Furman 1987; Hyde 1990; Maccoby 1990; Tannen 1992). Consequently, they appear less aggressive and dysfunctional although closer examination might show that this is not the case.

Boys in conflict, more than girls, appear to focus on impersonal matters such as skill prowess and the physical strength and dominance of their opponent, so their disputes, although visible and aggressive, can be settled quickly and unequivocally. There is likely to be a clear winner and loser in a dispute between boys, whether they settle the argument with feet or fists or by use of aggressive or dominant language. Girls seem to attack much more personal and intangible areas, such as individual style and presentation, where the markers for success are less easy to defend. These negative, subjective and unsolicited opinions are an important factor in the subsequent distress often present in disputes among girls.

There is a dichotomy of interests inherent in girls' friendships. The positive quality of their relationships, involving characteristic intense emotional investment, appears to contribute to the negative and destructive interactions so frequently present. As girls prize these close emotional bonds, the threat of loss is enough to instil an ethos of uncertainty and tension into the relationship. It would seem that these jealously guarded bonds are at the root of the quarrels and conflicts so frequently occurring between them. Just as in a lover relationship, the close friendships enjoyed by girls can give rise to quarrels as jealousy, suspicion and possessiveness may underlie both relationships. Their emotional commitment to their friends is a double-edged sword whereby the intensity of the enmeshed relations lies at the root of the querulous nature of their friendships.

Loyalty was a quality highly prized by the girls in the study. The root of many quarrels between these girls was the element of jealousy that erupted when a girl suspected her friend of being unfaithful. Having made considerably more emotional investment in their relationships than boys, girls expect more loyalty, commitment and attention from their close friends (Gottman and Parker 1986). This appears reflected in the seemingly uneven emotional commitment often made by young women and men to their romantic entanglements, leading to differing expectations and demands, not always made explicit at the outset. If ignored or misunderstood, these differences cause upset, confusion, disappointment and dispute (Gottman and Parker 1986).

Just as a young female may keep a watchful eye on her boyfriend if he is in the presence of other girls, so girls appear to monitor the behaviour of their friends as others may be waiting to replace one or other of a quarrelling duo. Even before a quarrel erupts, these girls on the sidelines could make bids to infiltrate a dyad or triad friendship. The possibility of this occurring exacerbates the atmosphere of unease, suspicion and unrest in many of these friendships. The dynamics of this process are discussed in Chapter 10. These changes in loyalties, involving fluctuation in the distribution of favour, appear to be at the root of much of the trouble between girls and contribute to the constant complaints, low-key bickering and calls upon adults for arbitration.

Boys may ignore another without friends, unless he is the unfortunate target of bullying, but many girls who have excluded another from their group appear to go out of their way to highlight her distress and draw attention to her isolation. The close emotional bonding between girls can leave poisonous tendrils intertwined long after a separation. A girl found lacking in her commitment to her friend could find herself the target of a complex revenge strategy. Feelings of disappointment and rejection seem more keenly experienced by girls than by boys in dispute. The break-up of a friendship may be devastating to a girl, and to adult witnesses, as they often seem comparable in emotional intensity to lovers' quarrels.

On resolving a quarrel, the girls in the study needed confirmation from each other that they were still friends. They wanted reassurance that they could resume the closeness and mutual trust of the prior relationship. The boys in the class appeared to behave in a different manner and rarely asked for such reassurances. Boys angry with a friend would fight it out and then forget the dispute, or find another mate without fuss. Boys do not seem to experience the repercussions of such strong emotional entanglement as is shown by girls and generally appear to be more relaxed about their friendship relations. Boys may shake hands to signal a quarrel is over, but this appears more to indicate that the fighting will stop than that they have resumed their relationship. There appears far less need for boys to secure reassurance that a broken friendship has been repaired.

'Sneaking friends'

The girls in the study valued their friendships enormously. They gave clear and rapid responses when asked for the names of their friends, though these could change over a short space of time. Any breaking of the friendship bonds could be fraught, even violent. The fact that these partnership changes most often occurred within the friendship group contributed to an atmosphere of suspicion and acrimony as each girl was wary of others encroaching on her 'best friend' relationship. Several of these girls experienced family problems, some seemingly insurmountable at the time, yet the fear of another 'sneaking' their friend was of paramount concern to them all. As sneaking (stealing) of a friend was quite likely to happen – as can be seen from Figures 9.1 to 9.4 on pp. 77 and 78 charting the instability of the friendship bonds – these girls were rarely absent from school. Above all, they wanted to protect their friendships even though they could quarrel irrevocably at their next meeting.

Wagging off

This close bonding supports findings gleaned from a truancy project carried out in a secondary school in the mid 1980s (Besag, unpublished research). Contrary to urban myth at the time, the girls who were regular truants were happy enough with most aspects of school life. Most enjoyed a supportive relationship with many of their teachers who realized that several of these girls had more to cope with in life than appeared on the surface. Most of the girls attended school as a matter of course unless they met up with a friend, when the conversation could turn to truanting. On meeting a friend of like mind, they would readily truant together and go round the shops or sit at home and chat. A girl would rarely truant alone unless there was collusion from her family, some of whom considered their daughters would serve a better purpose by helping in the home than attending school.

Triads of tension

If girls value their friendships so highly, why are their relationships so fractious and disputatious? In addition to the suggestion offered above, regarding their emotional commitment and subsequent jealousy and wariness, part of the answer may lie in the construction of their friendship groups. Friendship groupings and relationships among girls are often more intricate than a simple 'best friend' dyad. As stated earlier, the composition of these twosomes fluctuates and, in many cases, the role of a third party is highly influential (Toth 1978; Goodwin 1990).

Most pre-adolescent girls prefer to interact in a dyad, triad or small group than in a crowd (Maccoby and Jacklin 1987). Observations of the groups in the class studied showed that, even though the dyads interacted in a full circle of friends, these pairs would have a particular relationship not shared by others. Unfortunately, the dyad membership can change over time. Even within a triad, it is likely that there will be one member of the group positioned more as a peripheral than a constant, or there could be changes to the dyad composition with the girl on the periphery moving in to replace one in the dyad. 'Triads of tension' is an apt name given to these groupings by Toth (1978). Boys appear to accept a threesome more readily and amicably than girls (Feshbach and Sones 1971), perhaps because they have less emotional enmeshment with their companions. This unstable, mercurial friendship pattern among girls is not exclusive to the dyad and triad formation. It seems that in a group of any size this alignment and realignment pattern is evident. Characteristically, a larger group contains more than one dyad or triad. However, there would be a likelihood of frequent realignment and changes in the composition of the closest dyads as other girls could be waiting in the wings to displace partners as in the smaller groupings.

The size of the groupings may change over age. In one study of young girls, only one-third said they had more than three friends but, by the age of 12 to 13 years, they had groups of friends rather than one best friend (Lees 1993). Younger girls appear to have fewer friends as they prefer to interact within the dyad or triad, as did the girls in the study. Several girls drew friendships from across the class but retained a small cluster of close friends. Although older girls tend to interact within a larger group of friends, I would suggest that these dyad and triad relationships persist within these larger groups with the attendant pattern of fluctuation present as in earlier years.

Although studies have found girls to have smaller and more emotionally intense social networks than boys (Lever 1976; Belle 1989; Benenson 1993), the latter also enjoy twosome relationships but these are usually less emotionally intense. Research findings are somewhat generalized and relate to cohorts of children, so may not apply to the individual boy or girl. As stated earlier, Maccoby (1990, 1999) urges that we consider gender on a spectrum of masculinity and femininity rather than concentrate solely on gender differences. For the purposes of this work, it is useful to point out the differences in the way girls view their friendship relations compared with boys in order to uncover the subtle dynamics hidden beneath the surface. This is not to dispute that many boys may feel and act in a similar manner.

The group dynamics of the girls in the study

Figures 9.1 to 9.8 illustrate the dyad formation of the friendships among the girls in the class studied and show the presence of a third party forming a triad relationship. Importantly, they illustrate how these groupings changed over the course of the four terms of the study. Later studies replicate the pattern of these findings (Besag, unpublished research). Most research on girls' friendships concerns the interactions between individuals but these figures show how the interactions can range over the whole class group. These small friendship clusters are embedded in a network of peer relationships.

Figures 9.1 to 9.8 draw from information gained from sociogram material for the first three terms of the study, and from the semi-structured interviews for the fourth term. The dyad and triad relationships show reciprocal friendships when nominations for best friend, plus one other choice, were allowed. Arrows and circles mark reciprocal relationships. The figures show the degree of fluctuation of the reciprocal 'best friend' dyads among the girls in the class.

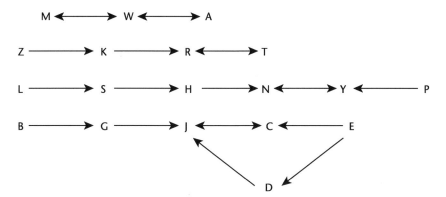

Figure 9.1 Friendship clusters based on best friend plus one other nomination: term 1.

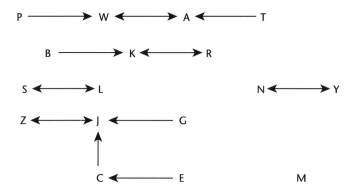

Figure 9.2 Friendship clusters based on best friend plus one other nomination: term 2.

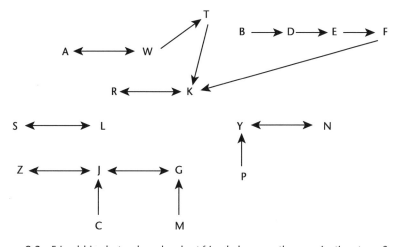

Figure 9.3 Friendship clusters based on best friend plus one other nomination: term 3.

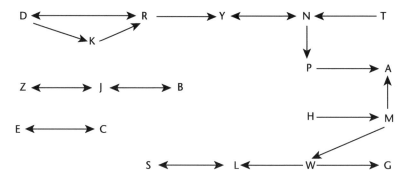

Figure 9.4 Friendship clusters based on best friend plus one other nomination: term 4.

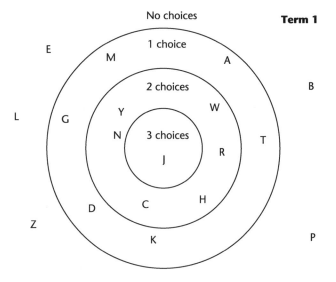

Figure 9.5 Sociometric circles based on best friend plus one other nomination: term 1.

When asked about their friendships, I have found girls of any age often quote several close friends but this may not be based on fact. This may be due to a misunderstanding of the question, although the more likely reason is that girls seem to perceive the number of friends they have as reflecting their popularity and power. In studying the friendship relationships of girls, it is important to use some form of direct observational work along with questionnaires or interviews. This is to control and cancel out the responses of those girls who give replies showing them to be popular rather than offering an accurate response. An attempt was made to lessen any exaggerated responses the girls would make about the number of friends they had by allowing them to give the names of all their friends then asking them to nominate their 'best friends'

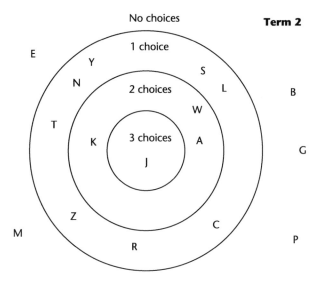

Figure 9.6 Sociometric circles based on best friend plus one other nomination: term 2.

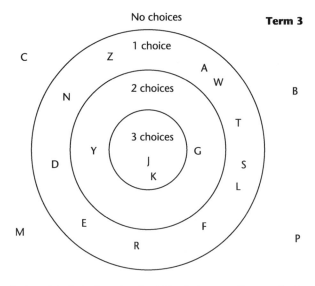

Figure 9.7 Sociometric circles based on best friend plus one other nomination: term 3.

from those chosen. Observational work, plus interviews with teachers, confirmed the findings. It must be stressed that these findings were taken on one day in each of the four terms. They do not represent the friendship relations of the girls throughout each term.

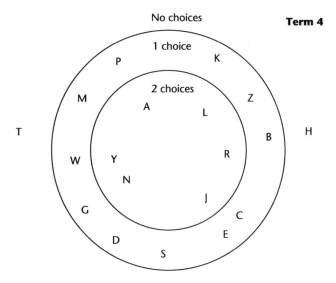

Figure 9.8   Sociometric circles based on best friend plus one other nomination: term 4.

The fluctuations shown within this group of girls would give reason enough for the anxiety most of the girls expressed about another girl 'sneaking' her friends away. The figures show how others on the periphery of a dyad could be influential in causing, or exacerbating, any instability. The influence of the wider peer network seemingly contributed to the disputatious nature of the dyad relationships.

The triad of tension in the study

Without doubt, the most disruptive influence in the relationships was the presence of a third girl alongside a dyad, forming a 'triad of tension' (Toth 1978). There were four clusters of triads among the girls in the class, resulting in frequent redistribution of power brought about acrimoniously. Only the reciprocal choice of Nikki and Yvonne as best friends was stable over the four terms of the study. Although not shown on the figures, Yvonne chose Rachel as second choice but Nikki, who was Yvonne's dyad partner, did not choose Rachel. This meant that Rachel was on the periphery of the dyad of Yvonne and Nikki resulting in ongoing antagonism between Rachel and Nikki throughout the time of the study. As Rachel was the most aggressive girl in the class, most considered her the most powerful. She used a variety of techniques to cause trouble between Yvonne and Nikki. Rachel often attacked Nikki verbally, who would retaliate in kind. Rachel frequently threatened her with physical violence when tempers flared, but this rarely materialized. As Yvonne became a mediator between these two girls, the skills she honed in this role contributed to her becoming one of the most influential, and therefore powerful, girls in the class.

Rachel was what Crick (Crick and Grotpeter 1995; Crick *et al.* 1999) terms a 'controversial' girl. Although she was a central member of the class group, she was strongly liked by some girls yet strongly disliked by others. The girls who liked Rachel counted her as a friend, enjoying her humour, sense of fun and knowing they could rely on her loyalty. However, she was disliked and feared by those wary of her aggressive attitude. Many socially aggressive girls habitually filter out ambiguous cues, with the result that they react aggressively to what they interpret as social rejection (Crick and Grotpeter 1995; Arnold *et al.* 1999). Rachel was quick to rise to what she interpreted as provocation. These children see rejection and aggression where none is intended and the prognosis is that they will continue their behaviour with increasingly negative consequences. In addition, Rachel modelled the attitudes prevalent within her close and extended families.

The provocateur

Like Rachel, Kate too wanted to be a close friend of Yvonne and Nikki. In her bids to secure a close friend, Kate used covert means of infiltrating the friendship dyads such as lying, grassing, initiating gossip and parroting adverse comments to prolong disputes. Although Kate was a member of the larger friendship circle, the other girls appeared to sense her mischievous behaviours.

Joanne and Zara also had a stable dyad relationship over three of the four terms of the study. As can be seen from the figures, Joanne was a popular girl with plenty of friends, whereas Zara was not as popular and her reliance on Joanne for companionship increased throughout the time of the study. This was an unsettling factor in the relationship. Unlike Rachel, Zara was not an overtly violent girl, but she was extremely jealous and possessive of her friendship with Joanne and did all in her power to keep other girls at bay.

New entrants

Two unrelated girls, Elaine and Mandy, entered the class just prior to the study as their parents had moved into the area. Mandy formed a friendship immediately with Wendy, causing upset to the dyad of Angela and Wendy who had been friends since starting school as their families were long-standing friends. The friendship between Mandy and Wendy eventually faded and Mandy remained outside a dyad relationship for the rest of the time of the study. Elaine eventually formed a close dyad relationship with Charlotte in the last term of the study. They had become close friends when the class went on a residential study week. Elaine had always wanted this friendship as she was appreciative of the help and support Charlotte gave her when she was new to the class. Although Charlotte played with Joanne at home, the unpleasant behaviour of Zara in protecting her friendship with Joanne caused Charlotte to seek other friendships in school. Until the final term when she formed a dyad relationship with Elaine, Charlotte nominated Joanne as her closest friend.

Floaters

Two girls were extremely disruptive in the class due to their repeated squabbles and conflicts. These girls fit the description of 'floaters' (Ladd and Kochenderfer 1996). They went from group to group seeking friendships, but instead caused dispute along the way. Each girl was a forceful factor in the disputatious nature of the friendship groups in the class as their conflicts mainly concerned their relationships with other girls. Both were often on the periphery of one group or another attempting to infiltrate the friendships or entice an established member away. From time to time, one or other was allowed into a group but this would soon result in intra-group conflict as both girls were argumentative, insensitive and domineering. Disliked and rejected children often develop extensive, but fleeting, play contacts as they are 'bounced' from group to group because of their lack of social awareness and skills (Ladd and Kochenderfer 1996). Consequently, they never get the chance to learn how to socialize appropriately. Neither of these girls was prepared to wait to assimilate gradually into a group as each wanted to be the 'best friend' of the most powerful girl in the group. Immediately on entry, each made bids for a dominant role, neither being content with a secondary position. As their tactics were obvious, and as their aggressive and challenging behaviours did not endear them to the leader or the other girls, they did not win friends. Others quickly ejected them from the groups. Occasionally, one or other of the two girls would cause inter-group conflict and serious disruption to the whole class. This was rare as the maturity and interest levels of the girls varied significantly so that most of the aggression occurred within the groups. Occasionally, one or two troublesome members from other groups contributed from the sidelines.

Becky had no friends until the last term of the study. The more aggressive girls scorned her inappropriate clothing and her reluctance to join in their boisterous games. This rejection led her to exaggerate, which the girls perceived as lying. On one occasion, she lied about the class teacher and this led to further rejection as all the girls regarded their teacher highly, even though one or two could be challenging on occasions. As Becky was vulnerable, her contributions to discussions were shouted down. The attacks came mainly from the two floaters rather than from the more aggressive girls. In the last term of the study, during a week-long residential field trip, Becky shared a room with Joanne, who was the most popular girl. This relationship continued when they transferred to the secondary school.

The more precocious and physically mature girls rarely became involved with those at the other end of the spectrum as they had few interests in common. This resulted in there being few inter-group incidents. Although the majority of girls would not interfere with those in other groups, should a girl fall out with those in her group, or suddenly be rejected by them, she would drift to the periphery of another group and would either be accepted or cause conflict there. This could give the impression of inter-group conflict although this was not the case. In summary, there was little evidence of inter-group rivalry or trouble but, on occasion, individual girls could cause friction both across, and within, groups.

Friendship maintenance skills

In recent years there has been increasing awareness of the value of peer friendships, and a range of techniques and strategies that have been successful in helping children to make friends are referred to in Section 7. However, there has been comparatively little emphasis on the equally important skills of friendship maintenance. The skills needed to initiate a friendship may differ from those required to sustain the relationship after the initial period. Sociability, a non-volatile attitude and a willingness to accept the point of view of others are important in the maintenance of friendship bonds (Gottman and Parker 1986; Asher *et al.* 1996). The skills of negotiation, bartering and mediation come into play (Gottman and Parker 1986). The girls in the study said that a willingness to make up after a quarrel, along with a need to renew the friendship as soon as possible, was a factor that they valued highly in a friend.

Surprisingly, the more aggressive girls in the class held the more stable relationships. However, these girls displayed many of the conflict resolution skills, as outlined earlier, in their social interactions within their own group. For example, one girl was a skilled mediator. However, the few volatile girls gave their group its reputation. Although they often appeared united, suspicion and jealousy underpinned these relationships, sourced primarily in girls on the periphery of the group, or in the close dyad relationships, trying to gain entry.

Most of the more aggressive girls had a surprising number of positive social skills. In addition to the conflict resolution skills of bartering, negotiation and willingness to make up after a quarrel, they were sociable, gregarious, amusing and could be tolerant, kind and empathic. Most had a good sense of fun and they often had the most ideas for games and activities. They prized loyalty highly, showing loyalty to those they considered their friends at the time, and they defended a friend in trouble. They had effective, if not sophisticated, linguistic skills and most would relate events in a dramatic and humorous manner. These factors may relate to the finding of Sutton *et al.* (1999) that those who bully often have a range of effective social skills.

Suggested approaches

1 We need to consider if we are to blame in any way for a dispute. Discuss this with girls. Are they able to apologize? How could they do this most effectively without losing face?

2 Explore the issue of forgiveness. If they cannot forgive, who is the loser? How can they show forgiveness?

3 Remind girls that they can ask for a mediator if in dispute. Many schools have students who are trained mediators. If the dispute is seriously affecting others, the process of Restorative Justice may be considered. See Section 7 for further information.

4 Girls should recognize the hurt they are feeling. Often they blame themselves for the rejection.

5 How would they know if they had hurt the feelings of a friend?

6 Discuss what they could do if they were unable to resolve a dispute amicably. Encourage girls to consider if they need the friendship. Is it worth renewing?

7 Sensitively alert girls to triads of tension and encourage them to think about having more than three in their group.

8 Train girls to speak honestly, but with dignity, if they believe another girl is breaking an existing friendship. They could say that they believe someone is trying to spoil the friendship and they are unhappy about this. This approach may not work but, in such cases, they must walk away and be prepared to lose this friend.

9 Discuss the concept of resentment. What does this mean? Who is affected by resentment?

10 Discuss the concept of bribery in the context of friendships.

10 Little Miss Popular

The power of popularity

A group of girls may appear amicable and egalitarian in character, but there can be turmoil within any friendship group, clique or gang of girls. Within a large group, such as a class, there is a high probability of significant unrest with constant movement within and between groupings as they meld, erupt, overlap, disperse and reform. Much of the disputatious nature of girls' friendships relates to the role of influential girls causing friction and unrest. This unease and instability could stem from the behaviour and attitude of just one powerful girl or from those less powerful aiming to enhance their status.

Gender hierarchies

There would appear to be different rationales for peer status in relation to gender. The social needs of girls are different from those of boys, as seen in the urge that boys have to confirm their physical prowess (Wachtel 1973). As boys use their physical strength to wield power in the group, their rank in the hierarchy relates to their ability to dominate subordinates, a quality prized among boys (Pellegrini 1988; Smith and Myron-Wilson 1988; Maccoby 1999). Their hierarchies are reasonably stable as boys are able to settle challenges to their status visibly and rapidly, by force if necessary and regardless of whether the challenges come from those within, or outside the group. In consequence, this stable hierarchy of power is identifiable to all within the group plus those in the wider peer network. From quite an early age, some boys learn that they can walk around school with a quietly confident air, an assertive presentation, or even an exaggerated swagger. Others realize they are more comfortable keeping a lower profile, avoiding or deflecting physical confrontation.

Males inclined to do so, tend to attack others within sight of their peers (Wachtel 1973). The drunken brawl usually takes place in front of an audience when the aggressors confirm their power and status, establish and advertise their position in the hierarchy and ward off challengers. This is reminiscent of the 'cock of the class' described earlier. Boys appear to display and confirm their physical power by using mock fights, wrestling, arm locks and various other means of rough-and-tumble play in front of their peers (Pellegrini 1988; Pellegrini and Smith 1998). Such behaviours appear to continue into early adulthood.

We are beginning to understand that girls also rank themselves, and each other, but this is through social success rather than physical prowess as in the case with boys (Eder 1991). It may be that boys use physical prowess to establish, confirm, display and redistribute power, whereas girls manipulate their social relationships. Just as boys use rough-and-tumble play and physical attacks to test out their ranking in the male hierarchy, girls appear to test out their positions of power by using or abusing their popularity. This seems to be the currency employed by girls to mobilize support against challenges and to attack those considered threatening. Covertly aggressive girls may seek power by means of affiliation and the manipulation of friendships then, once established within the group, use their position to alter the dynamics to their advantage. There would appear to be a gender difference in the modus operandi chosen by those who seek power, but the common aim is to gain and display control while, in parallel, avoiding domination by others.

The fluid movement within girls' friendship clusters is often a function of the ranking process carried out by particular girls who hold power over others in relation to their popularity. Competition regarding popularity among girls appears to reach a peak between late childhood and early adolescence. At this age, the process of ranking each other on a scale of popularity, possibly in a subconscious manner, is already established. The position of girls in their power hierarchy is less stable than that of boys. A powerful girl today may be powerless tomorrow, finding herself shunned by the group. There would seem to be a 'chicken and egg' dynamic, in that the more popular a girl is, the more power she holds; the more power she holds, the more popular she is thought to be. This leads others to defer to her, thus increasing her power.

While particular girls are popular, they are powerful; loss of popularity results in a rapid fall from grace. Subtle and complex dynamics underpin the distribution and wielding of power among girls and there is often one girl holding a more powerful position than the rest no matter how democratic the group appears. These girls accrue their popularity, retain it and use it to their advantage by drawing on a repertoire of social behaviours surprising in their level of sophistication. As these positions of power are frequently in a state of flux, it seems reasonable to propose that they contribute to the disputatious and conflict-ridden nature of girls' friendship groups.

Defining popularity

There appears to be confusion among young people in distinguishing among the concepts of power, popularity and those who have close friends. Being popular and having close friends are different concepts. A child can be popular among peers, winning votes in any relevant poll, yet lack a close friend. Conversely, a child having the benefit of a close dyad relationship may fail to win many votes in a survey of popularity. The characteristics defining the popularity of boys would seem to differ from those of girls. There appear to be two categories of popular boys, one containing those who are pro-social and considered studious, good leaders, well behaved and non-aggressive. Another category comprises those who are anti-social, powerful, tough and athletic (Rodkin *et al.* 2000). This finding mirrors the profiles of Australian boys who, around the age of 11 years, divide into two similarly contrasting groups regarding attitudes to school (Houghton and Carroll 2002). Boys consider those who are aggressive, and who can 'handle' themselves, socially competent (Hawley 1999), whereas girls do not consider physical aggression a positive female attribute.

Girls perceived as popular are said to be those possessing glamour, prestige and influence (Parkhurst and Hopmeyer 1998), plus money and family background (Eder 1985). Eder focuses her concept of popularity on the peer election of cheerleaders in American schools, chosen for their physical attractiveness, money and family background. Their high visibility allows these girls popularity. The girls in the activity group listed personal qualities such as being friendly, kind, amenable, peaceable, helpful and trustworthy as attributes contributing to popularity. They listed play skills as important: the ability to suggest, invent and join in games, plus the ability to make others laugh. They liked and respected those who would listen when a friend wanted to talk about her problems. The ability to defend oneself and others was also listed as important. Interestingly, several said it was important to them to have friends who would not get them into trouble with their teachers.

The characteristics the girls noted as unpopular echoed the findings of Borja-Alvarez *et al.* (1991). These authors found unpopular girls to be bossy, attention seeking, self-centred and those who disrupted play activities. The girls in the study listed those who were bossy, conceited, aggressive and quarrelsome. They did not wish to associate with girls who were in a gang as they would find that frightening. They disliked those who called others names, told tales, gave away secrets and lied. They mentioned friendship disloyalty such as 'sneaking' friends, gossiping about a friend or calling her names behind her back.

Joanne was nominated the most popular girl because of her sense of humour, her willingness to play games and sing to entertain others. She often attempted to settle arguments arising between the less aggressive girls and this contributed to her popularity, as is suggested by Gottman and Parker (1986). Although small in stature, she would challenge others when she thought it appropriate, knowing that those more powerfully built would come to her defence if necessary. Angela and Yvonne were ranked highly as they possessed effective peacemaking and arbitration skills. Unfortunately, Angela went through a difficult time due to family issues and began to steal for a brief period which led to a loss of popularity.

Girls tend to aim for friendship with the most popular girls as they associate status with social success (Alder and Alder 1995; Eder *et al.* 1996; Merten 1997). As males consider physical attractiveness, and physical maturity, highly desirable qualities in females, girls appear to seek the company of those displaying these qualities. Perhaps this is to confirm their own attractiveness (Merten 1997), or because, in this way, they are sure to be in the company of high-status boys. As a result, highest-status cliques contain the most physically mature and attractive girls with others on the periphery hoping to be included. This results in intense competition for close friendships with the popular girls (Eder 1985).

The most physically mature girls in the class studied clustered in what others regarded as a high-status clique. These were the most dominant girls, some of whom could be aggressive. High-status girls appear to draw power from their popularity and are able to manipulate those of lower status or less powerful (Sumrall *et al.* 2000). The high-status girls in the class studied could take a dominant, and occasionally aggressive, attitude with the other girls, but more often they interacted independently of the other friendship groups.

Tracey most closely fitted the profile of a popular girl given by Eder (1985), as she was physically mature, attractive and came from a more financially advantaged family than others in the class. However, the other girls eventually rejected her and she became the target for attack. This was due to her spiteful remarks and pompous attitude, plus the jealousy of the others regarding the combination of her attractive appearance and provocative manner with the boys. Her popularity with the boys was the final straw for the other girls. Tracey's frequent sulks and disputatious nature led to her ostracism from the other groups in the class so that she eventually became isolated. Having an advantage of any kind does not necessarily result in triggering negative behaviour from other girls. A girl can become a target for attack as a result of various factors. In some cases, but not all, the attitude and personality of the target girl play an influential role in the social dynamic leading to rejection. The complex emotional dynamics that lie beneath such rejection, on the grounds of jealousy, are explored in Chapter 17.

Not all who appear popular are so. Some may even fear a so-called popular girl but consider it unwise to make any overt challenge. Rachel appeared to have a close group of powerful friends. Many girls considered her popular because even those afraid of her gave every appearance of supporting her powerful position. Rachel was always the centre of attention, dominating the group, and this led to one of the most intelligent girls in the class naming her as the most popular girl. On reflection, she added a perceptive comment saying that the number of friends Rachel claimed to have related to the hold she had over the group. She added that it was wise to compliment Rachel at every opportunity, as failure to comment favourably on any new acquisition could lead to trouble. As Rachel was a volatile, physically aggressive girl, it was not wise to rebuff her offers of friendship. It was better to be her friend than to be her enemy.

Although Rachel was high on the list of girls nominated as popular, several girls she counted as close friends talked about her behind her back and found ways of avoiding following her lead. She had less effective power and influence in the group than her boisterous and dominant manner suggested. However, she was loyal and supportive to those she considered her friends and her sense of fun, and somewhat basic ideas concerning fair play, made her an acceptable member of the group. Girls once popular may become unpopular if others recognize their modes of indirect aggression (Crick and Grotpeter 1995), as was the case of the two girls who were described earlier as floaters.

The tall poppy

Clearly, popularity can be transitory and popular girls quickly become unpopular if they arouse jealousy in others. They can be intensely disliked if others are jealous of their social success. The Tall Poppy syndrome (Merten 1997), refers to the unfortunate tendency for those who succeed beyond the norm to become the target of jealousy, just as the tall poppy in the field is cut down. Many cultures have the equivalent of this Australian expression; Japan has 'knocking down the raised nail' and Britain has 'cutting down to size'. Popular girls may have a coterie around them but these followers may not be loyal. Any build-up of jealousy can put a popular girl in a precarious position by setting up a dynamic that eventually leads to her downfall. Tracey's downfall was dramatic; she was genuinely popular at the start of the study but she eventually became ostracized by the other girls.

Some research shows that processes of inclusion and exclusion centre on high-status cliques, with other girls trying to break into the groups while those within jostle for position. Some girls use intense forms of indirect aggression in their determination to manoeuvre themselves into favourable positions (Richardson and Green 1999). LaFontana and Cillessen (2002) showed a surprising positive association between indirect aggression and popularity over a four-year period, with high-status girls using more indirect aggression than those of lower status. Presumably, the girls chose covert modes of aggression in an attempt to maintain their popularity yet avoid the risk of identification and retaliation.

Even the most powerful high-status girls are under threat of losing their favoured position in the sun owing to the carousel nature of popularity among girls (Eder 1985, 1991). Eder uses the term 'cycle of popularity' to describe the process whereby status in popularity changes within the group. The social stars, and established members of the high-status coterie, must be wary of associating with those less popular as this could put them in jeopardy of losing their exalted positions (Eder 1985, 1991). The glue of exclusivity holds their position intact so that association with less popular girls could diminish the star status they enjoy. The leader, in particular, must be careful in choosing her associates, especially if she is not secure in her position. As popular girls may not have time to cope with all the demands for their friendship, many hoping for their attention are disappointed. The attention given to those girls with aspirations may fall short of their desires and expectations (Eder 1985, 1991). Girls disenchanted or ignored may destroy the popularity of the leader by gossiping and making disparaging comments about her. They behave like sharks circling their target. This can leave her isolated as, sensing a decline in her power, her former friends may reject her.

Entry bids

There would appear to be two main lines of approach used by girls with aspirations to higher status. In addition to the machinations of the leader to maintain her position, challenges may come from both within and outside the group from girls wishing to improve their status. Alder and Alder (1995) describe the dynamics of unrest arising within the group when less powerful members on the periphery of the clique make bids to move closer to the leader to enhance their position and power. They may even be plotting moves to depose and replace her. Bids from those within the group come directly, in linear fashion, from those on the edge to those holding a central position (Alder and Alder 1995).

In parallel with the overtures made by girls in less powerful positions within the clique to get nearer the vortex, others outside the clique may be making approaches to gain entry into the group. The social avenues used by these girls are usually in the form of low-risk moves that add to the unrest within the group (Eder 1985, 1991). Girls of lower status do not aim for the central positions at the start of their campaign for acceptance as this could expose them to rejection and ridicule. They prefer to approach those on the periphery, considering that they will have a better chance of acceptance by association with girls of lower status than with girls from the central coterie.

One path towards entry is to know a popular girl who would promote nomination to the group; another is by rekindling association with a popular girl to gain kudos in a vicarious manner. Wise girls progress slowly nearer to the vortex and leader. A carefully acquired position near the leader offers kudos and protection whereas a move too close, too fast, could arouse the suspicion of the leader and result in a speedy ejection.

Those less popular embark on a hazardous path when they aim to move to a more influential position in the group. A new entrant, or one whose star is in the ascendant, will probably enjoy a flutter of popularity within the group for a while, the other members of the group taking their lead from the most powerful girl in welcoming her. This popularity may be short-lived; should she become too popular, the leader will initiate moves to get her deposed. Established members may also reject a girl. The effusive welcome given to a new entrant, and her closeness to the leader, could set up jealousy within the ranks with the result that other members of the clique reject her.

On entry to the elitist clique, the new member will almost certainly be encouraged to drop old friends and ignore overtures from girls external to the group. Once the new member is exclusively friendly with those in the clique, she is in a vulnerable position as a downward spiral in popularity may set in. She may find herself transferred from popular to unpopular in a matter of days, especially if she has been enticed into leaving her original friends. As shown in the results of this study, most girls prize loyalty in their friends, so those previously close to her may refuse to have her back, having felt rejected when she left their group. As a result, she will be isolated from the 'friends' who have turned on her and, perhaps more importantly, her original friends. Physical, emotional, social and psychological abuse can follow a fall from favour. If the girl retains the affection of the leader, any threat to her position from lesser members must be of a covert nature.

A process of entry, and subsequent exclusion, is common to the models of Alder and Alder and of Eder. Both illustrate the sense of unease and unrest so evident in girls' friendship groups. Whether the attacks made towards the leader, or others, come from within or from outside the group, they appear based on a need for the status and power given by popularity. The role of the leader and her coterie is the same in both models, that is, to use a wide range of imaginative strategies in order to retain powerful, privileged positions. Even though these social relationships may cause significant distress to girls targeted for exclusion, it may be difficult for adults to intervene in any meaningful way. We continue behaviours we find rewarding, so those enjoying power and popularity may see no reason to forfeit their position.

Striving for acceptance

Those striving for inclusion, or a prestigious position in the group, try to behave in ways that are conducive to acceptance by the leader and her coterie. A proven entry skill is for a hopeful entrant to imitate the behaviour and style of the leader and established members (Gottman and Mettatal 1986). As stated earlier, girls tend to favour those who are similar to them, so those with aspirations must copy the behaviour, attitudes and style of the most powerful members in the hope this will result in a successful entry bid. It is not difficult to identify girls in friendship groups as often they have a similar appearance, an idiosyncratic vocabulary and a manner of presentation in common. They also have a mutual core of interests, hobbies and idols. Intending members need to tune in and adjust to the group mores and behaviour if they wish to succeed. Being in the group allows them to monitor closely any changes that occur, thus allowing them to adjust their own behaviour at speed. As it is essential to be able to identify the nuances of change and keep up with the latest trends, a girl outside the group will not have the benefit of this shared knowledge so others are less likely to welcome her into the fold.

The class studied

Challenges and unrest in the groups and cliques in the class studied stemmed from those within groups jostling for a more central position along with those from outside groups bidding for entry. It was not apparent to the girls that they were bidding for dominance or power. The arguments, quarrels and fights erupted primarily over relationships and friendship status between the girls. Who was the best friend of whom? Who had invited whom to stay overnight? Who had said something abusive about whom? Who had looked at whose boyfriend? Who had copied whose work? Who had said what about whom? Who had insulted whom? Who had called someone's mother an abusive name? These disputes occurred equally between girls who were in the groups jostling for position, and those who were on the outside making bids for inclusion. Social invitations gave clear messages regarding where each girl stood in the group hierarchy. It was as though an invisible league table existed with a weekly bulletin announcing the position of each girl on the current social ladder. In addition, the girls appeared to distribute these invitations with the intention of announcing, publicly, the formation or break-up of their friendship alliances. On occasions, they delivered and received them as implicit invitations to a verbal or physical confrontation.

Whatever the source of the unrest, it is primarily the most powerful girls who control and direct the actions of others. The manipulation of popularity, in the form of inclusion and exclusion techniques, is the mechanism used to keep down potential threat and to stigmatize anyone currently out of favour. The work of Duncan (1999), on girls' sexual bullying, outlines the use of similar strategies in a specific context.

The social stars

Life can be very different for those within the powerful group of social stars from that of those excluded. The girls enjoying the favour of the most powerful girls will be in their confidence; they hear the latest news, current gossip and take some part in the decision making. They form a tight coterie around the powerful girls, enjoying the privilege, excitement and kudos this allows. Others in the group remain on the outside, in the cold, and do not enjoy the close bonding experienced by the favoured few. The social life of a class, or even year group, will appear to swirl around the powerful leader and her closest friends. A girl targeted for exclusion from the group can find herself without friends and without a social life. In small towns and villages, where there is little choice of schools, clubs and meeting places, such a girl may face a lonely existence.

Many girls do not wish to be in the group of social stars and will be happiest among their own friends with their shared interests and attitudes. They may not wish to join the more dominant group of girls, many of whom may have precocious social attitudes, and/or are more physically mature than their peers. If included, they may feel uncomfortable or threatened. However, a few girls may be eager to join the social stars. Some may once have been in the group; others may feel rejected and deeply upset by their failure to be invited into the clique, and some may cause a great deal of upset in their strenuous efforts to gain entry. There may be little aggravation between the friendship groups in a class, but there will most likely be one or two girls causing trouble by trying to find entry into a particular group, or causing mischief when excluded from one they wish to join.

Those who are unable to join the group formed by the most popular girls learn to make the best of things, perhaps forming a group with others who will accept them. This means that there are often several groups of girls in a class. It may be possible to rank these groups, as well as individual girls, on a scale of popularity. It is a hard but essential lesson to learn that acceptance into the group of choice is not always possible. Many adult clubs, organizations and societies practise modes of exclusion in either an overt or a covert manner. Blackballing is a well-known mode whereby an established adult group decides whether to offer membership to an outsider. We can only join those who allow us to do so but, sadly, many young people fail to understand this and become upset when rejected. The young can reject others in an unthinking or cruel fashion, leaving the target with emotional scarring that may take some time to heal.

Suggested approaches

1 Describe the behaviour of Little Miss Popular. Discuss the fact that she may appear popular but she may not be liked. Other girls may be keeping quiet if they are afraid of her tongue. Explore ways forward: for example, they could stick together and make it clear that they do not appreciate her behaviour.

2 Little Miss Popular is popular only because others allow it. Explore with girls why she would be allowed to behave in this way. What could others be getting from her friendship?

3 We can only be friends with those who accept our friendship. If girls feel rejected, it may be best to forget those who reject or ignore them and move on.

4 Girls who feel rejected or excluded could try to analyse what the attraction is of being in the group that is rejecting or excluding them. We continue only those behaviours that are rewarding. What is rewarding about being a member? Do these girls go to interesting places or do exciting things? Do they give praise and compliments to their close friends? Are they a laugh or good fun, or is it that they present themselves as the 'most important and popular girls'? Excluded girls may be able to get these things elsewhere.

5 Suggest that if they make their own friendship group and do exciting things, others may want to join their group.

6 It is advisable to warn girls not to drop reliable friends. Loyalty is very important to girls. The new friends may drop them and then their old friends may not want them back.

11　Madam Machiavelli

Popularity and leadership

A girl with many friends is in a powerful position as she is giving tacit messages that she can choose her friends from a circle of attendants. In addition, she enjoys the protection of her coterie. Backed by her supporters, she is able to use a range of both direct and indirect forms of aggression in bullying campaigns against targeted girls. Others may not recognize her behaviour as a deviant use of power, but simply regard her as the most popular member of the group. Her popularity proves that she has the admiration and permission of the group, so making it difficult for any individual to make a challenge. These girls may refuse to accept that their negative behaviour is a form of bullying. Many seem to have the skills to quickly justify their behaviour and so seldom receive punishment (Crick and Grotpeter 1995). Those excluding others often ward off challenges by stating that they have the right to choose their own friends and reject any suggestion of including a girl they have sidelined or bullied. They may even suggest that the fault lies with the targeted girl, claiming that the latter has rejected their overtures of friendship.

Often a group of girls will have a leader who is unrecognized as such and her influence underestimated. Both boys and girls can have difficulty in identifying a leader and often appear unfamiliar with the concept in this context. To tease out if there is a leader in the group, it is useful to ask for the name of the person most likely to make the decisions that others follow. The girls in the study found the concept of leader difficult to understand but could give the name of the girl who most frequently instigated schemes and carried them out with the consensus of the majority, and whose opinion they valued.

The role of leader is not always an easy one. The girls studied often reached consensus regarding any decision only after protracted, disputatious discussion. The leader needed to fend off challenges by reasoned argument, negotiation and mediation. An important facet of the skills displayed by these leaders was their ability to think through suggestions made by themselves and others and to plan how to translate these ideas into feasible actions. This reflects the findings of Gottman and Parker (1986). The leaders among the girls studied managed this difficult role with the most challenging constituent membership – without the benefit of expensive professional management training.

The arbitrator

One skill highly prized in a leader is that of being calm and fair-minded in disputes (Gottman and Parker 1986). A girl who can arbitrate between warring parties, and bring things to an acceptable close, is more likely than others to be accepted as leader, or at least to have influence within the group. Yvonne was the leader of the aggressive clique of girls. She rarely initiated any aggression and only became involved in incidents when, in her view, she was rightly defending a friend or principle under attack. Yvonne did not seek the role of leader, and neither she nor the other girls thought of her as such. As the ideas she presented were intelligent and practicable, the others adopted her suggestions, so tacitly electing her leader. Yvonne displayed the qualities that Gottman and Parker (1986) suggest are necessary in making and maintaining friendships. Her most valued qualities were that she was fair-minded, trust-worthy and drew upon the skills of negotiation, bartering and mediation in disputes. She displayed tolerance and a non-aggressive response to frustration. She had the ability to accept the point of view of others, a willingness to make up with a friend after a quarrel and a need to renew a fractured friendship (Gottman and Parker 1986). In addition, she had a quiet, non-confrontational demeanour and manner of speaking, and a democratic style of leadership. These qualities made her one of the most popular girls and therefore one of the most powerful.

Bids for leadership

Trouble in the group came from others, with less developed leadership skills, vying for her leadership position or inappropriately challenging her decisions. If one of the more aggressive girls tried to become leader by intimidation, the group would stand together in defiance, or wait until the girl had gone away and then dismiss her claim. This dismissal was often in the guise of humour as the girls gained a lot of entertainment by mocking those they considered 'uppity'. It would be up to the leader to meet challenges directly, if necessary. The others would then support the girl they preferred in an overt or covert manner, depending on the relative strength of support they had, and the level of aggression the pretender to the throne would be likely to use.

Angela and Charlotte had effective leadership skills. Both girls were academically able and so others looked to them for advice about their schoolwork. In discussions, both girls gave good eye contact to each speaker, they listened to the opinions of others and sought consensus by looking at each member of the group in turn asking, in a sincere manner, for their opinion. Both had effective mediation skills that they used to settle disputes between the other girls.

Rachel appeared to make unsuccessful bids to become the leader in her group but her aggressive and dominant personality echoed that of a male bully. She had some of the characteristics of a leader, but tended to use them in a bullying manner to the disadvantage of those more vulnerable. As her style of interaction was autocratic, the other girls did not want her as leader and usually managed to reject her attempts to control them. Whenever there was a discussion, and a decision required, Rachel would shout her suggestions over the voices of the other girls. If they ignored her, or told her to go away, she could become abusive. As she was a powerfully built girl, her close physical presence could be intimidating. Eventually, it became clear that Rachel did not have the tenacity to be a leader. She soon lost interest in any discussion and, after making her opinion known, would wander off or become distracted.

Tracey had some leadership skills. She had good ideas and she was confident and gregarious but she alienated other girls, not having the prerequisite skill of an effective leader which is that of understanding, or perhaps caring, how others think (Sutton *et al.* 1999). Tracey did not identify and assimilate knowledge of the desires and needs of others. Whenever she made a bid for leadership, by making a suggestion, or trying to override one already made, she did so forcibly, without taking cognizance of the opinions or feelings of others. She was unable, or unwilling, to register the nuances of the dynamics within the group. In frustration, she dealt with opposition by dismissing challenges or negating them with scornful, abusive or sarcastic comments. If all else failed, she would threaten violence towards those less powerful.

The techniques used by autocratic leaders allow them to dictate what others can do. Some girls achieve such a powerful position in their friendship groups that they are able to manipulate others to smoke, drink or begin sexual experimentation to give permission for their own behaviour. In addition, they realize that knowledge of the illicit behaviour of others offers them opportunity for further control and so they accrue even more power. This is bullying as it is adverse to the welfare of others. If others consider the popularity of the leader demonstrates that she must be right, a secondary dynamic may be triggered. If she remains unchallenged, others may consider the seemingly willing subordination of the group membership validates her attitude. This may lead them to disregard their own moral code, respond to her influence and act to her command.

The queen bee dethroned

The role of the leader is not a relaxed one. Her powerful position may be constantly under threat as she reigns only with the permission of the group. Once a girl has achieved popularity, power or leadership, she will need to be alert to those plotting her downfall. Leaders maintain their tenuous position through the attractive qualities and important contributions they can offer the group. More importantly, their power also lies in their inherent grasp of the subtleties of group dynamics and their ability to wield power within the group (Alder and Alder 1995; Sutton *et al.* 1999).

Those wishing to manipulate others in order to achieve, display or retain a powerful position may draw upon a repertoire of sophisticated psychological techniques (Eder 1991; Keise 1992; Lees 1993; Alder and Alder 1995; Duncan 1999; Sutton *et al.* 1999). A leader needs to have the energy and ability to monitor closely the attitudes, behaviour and alignments of other members and to show a personal interest in individuals (Lemert 1972; Reicher and Potter 1985). A girl who is leader must be sensitive and responsive to changes in the group, constantly monitoring alterations in popularity and making adjustments to retain power in order to avoid a coup or mutiny. She will be aware that some may be making deliberate bids to topple her from her throne, or they may become more favoured by the rest without needing to solicit support. The leader must read the social dynamics at speed, and act with appropriate haste, if she is to avoid or quell any possible threat. She needs to be mistress of a range of well-honed social skills she employs like a punter at the fairground, trying to hammer down a raised peg, only to find that another springs up immediately elsewhere.

The conductor of the orchestra

In the clique structure described by Alder and Alder (1995), the leader has the power to define choice and criteria for membership, maintain clear boundaries and establish exclusivity. These girls rank others according to their own criteria and agenda and define the stratification of popularity, thus delicately balancing the power structure within the group. The leader will decide who are to have the favoured positions closest to her and who are to be relegated to the outer edges of the group. She may encourage those she feels she can control to venture into the group to enhance her power, while cutting out the more powerful who may threaten her reign. In the manner of the conductor of an orchestra, she brings some individuals into focus while leaving others waiting in the wings for their cue to enter into the spotlight.

Should the most powerful girl identify another in the group as a threat to her dominant position, she may make moves to dispel the popularity of this contender by using a range of sophisticated skills to instigate and rally adverse opinion towards her. The leader may use a tangential approach, issuing invitations to non-threatening girls to join the inner sanctum at the expense of any threatening her power (Alder and Alder 1995). Another girl, from inside or outside the group, may be courted and feted simply to take attention away from the girl considered a threat. The spotlight turns onto the less popular, less threatening girl who then moves up the hierarchy to be second-in-command to displace the one previously a favourite.

By drawing upon a range of strategies, the leader diminishes the power of any she considers threatening. Scorn, ridicule and gossip are effective techniques employed to deflate the popularity of any contestant (Parker and Gottman 1989). The most powerful girl may elicit support from the group by encouraging them to laugh at any withstanding her direction. She may be scornful towards group members who desist, while wielding the carrot of approval for those who comply. Coercion and sanctions will result in the group following the leader in stigmatizing or ostracizing a targeted girl. If the leader is aggressive, her followers may be afraid not only of her disapproval but also of physical attack. Perhaps the most powerful tool in the repertoire of a leader is that anyone who rejects her lead may become her next victim. In this way, the power of individual members is adjusted constantly, described as repeated travels through a cycle of inclusion and exclusion (Alder and Alder 1995). These processes serve to manipulate other members into submission and dependence. Clearly, these strategies make for uncertain loyalties and an unstable group membership.

If not challenged in the early stages, the powerful may come to consider their negative behaviours the norm, and the targets to view themselves as unworthy of the attention of the social stars. There may be a rapid acceptance of these behaviours, and their consequences, by the principal actors and witnesses. Powerful girls gain practice in leadership skills and grow in confidence, while others find it increasingly difficult to challenge their role. As the power and confidence of the dominant members increases over time, so do the feelings of inadequacy and vulnerability of those targeted or ignored, leaving them feeling disenfranchised. All may seem calm to observers outside the friendship groups of girls, but there is likely to be a melee of emotions, ambitions and disappointments ebbing and flowing within.

The transitory positions of those within groups, the bids of those trying to get in and the exit of those ousted, must be considered when exploring the different explanations for the fractious friendship bonds and disruptive relationships between girls. The catalyst for these changes is often a powerful leader. Her complex strategies are not necessarily premeditated but, whether her actions are planned or spontaneous, an accomplished leader often resembles a juggler coping with many plates in the air at any one time. One-third of the conflicts in one study of Grade 7 girls (aged 11 years), were found to be due to social manipulation (Cairns *et al.* 1989). These are not necessarily maladaptive behaviours as, in some circumstances, they are adaptive social mechanisms used effectively in the contest for the friendship of the popular girls.

Suggested approaches

1 Explore the concept of leadership with girls. Discuss the difference between an autocratic, bullying leader and one who is democratic and benign.

2 Ask girls if there is a leader in the groups they belong to at home and at school. Who takes most of the decisions?

3 Leaders are only leaders because others allow them to lead. If others are not happy with their leadership, they may use bullying tactics to depose the leader. Explore with the girls whether they feel happy with the decisions made by the leaders of these groups or if they feel they are being manipulated.

4 Perhaps others in the group think the same. How could they identify whether this were so? If it were so, what could they do?

5 Girls need to be able to recognize, in the initial stages, the power bids and destructive behaviours used by some girls. How can they remain independent? Could they challenge these behaviours? How could they do this in an amicable manner?

6 Identify if the girls are able to recognize dominant behaviours and powerful friends who make the decisions without adequate consultation in their close dyad and triad relationships. This needs to be done in a sensitive manner without names being disclosed.

7 Help the girls to identify all the behaviours of dominant leaders they find hurtful.

SECTION 4
The Language of Conflict

12 The language of conflict

The language of conflict

Many studies indicate that girls tend to avoid conflict by using the skills of discussion, compromise and negotiation (Miller *et al.* 1986; Collins and Laursen 1992). However, not all girls have these skills, and those that do are not always prepared to use them, with the result that intense arguments erupt between girls. Although it would appear that fewer result in physical combat than is the case with boys in dispute, such confrontations do occur. There was a wide discrepancy shown between the stages of moral development in the girls studied. Some had well-developed skills of empathy and reciprocity, whereas others saw their own needs as most pressing. These latter girls flaunted the rules, both those set by school and the code of conduct tacitly agreed to by the girls. Joanne was told by her mother to 'fight your own battles', and translated this as a physical response to conflict being acceptable, whereas Charlotte said she had been taught that 'violence never settles anything'. As most girls appear to rely primarily on their language skills in conflict, it may be that they draw upon a wider and richer range of linguistic structures than do boys. The forms of conflict language found most prevalent and powerful in the study – grassing, insult, gossip, rumour – are considered solely in the context of their influence on the fractious and disputatious nature of girls' friendships.

Surprisingly little is known about these forms of verbal abuse as they usually take place out of sight and hearing of adults. It is notoriously difficult to examine gossip owing to its behind-the-back nature. The analogy of the elusive butterfly is apposite: the more you chase it, the more it will fly away from you, whereas if you sit still, it will land on your shoulder (Almirol 1981). In addition, there are subtle differences in interpretation of these forms of abuse not easily discernible to those external to the verbal exchange. We know that a valid understanding depends on accurate interpretation of the tone of voice, gestures, body language and facial expression of the participants (Gilmore

1978). Furthermore, the context must be taken into consideration when seeking to identify the intent hidden within the spoken words. It is possible to interpret identical wording as either benign comment or verbal abuse, and there are regional variations in the meaning and potency of individual words. The ethnographic style of the study, using a combination of video and audio recordings, offered the opportunity to gain insights into the rationales, nuances and impact of these language structures. In addition, as the study lasted 16 months, it allowed the collation of a bank of information about each girl that gave insight into the development of her social mores, behaviour and intentions that helped place her language into a wider context.

Language is an active process as it shapes beliefs and challenges existing attitudes. It shapes our own belief in who we are and influences the view others form of us. Our self-image and confidence slowly accrue from an early age as we learn to match our own perceptions with those voiced by others. Herein lies the pervasive and destructive power of abusive language. A young person develops a sense of identity from the evaluation given by the peer group, more than any allocated by adults or by academic success (Harris 1995). Typically, girls come to understand themselves through an exchange of values and ideologies with their friends (Harris 1995; Hey 1997). If we encourage young people to listen attentively to what we say to them in instructional and benign settings, we cannot be surprised at the power of negative language to influence their self-perception in an adverse manner.

In recent years, the negative, long-term emotional effects of verbal abuse have been identified (Hawker and Boulton 1996). Rumour mongering and gossiping were found to be more distressing than most other types of bullying (Sharp 1995). In a study carried out with Australian adolescent girls, those wishing to cause distress to others spread rumours, betrayed secrets and criticized their clothing, appearance or personality (Owens *et al.* 2000). The emotional damage caused by these attacks was so severe that several students sought a new school and teachers reported some to have contemplated suicide. As the target succumbs to the repeated onslaught, the attacks escalate and become more ferocious. Even would-be aides step back from these concerted attacks (Pepler 1996; Salmivalli and Kaukiainen 2004). The insulting, singsong, rhythmic chants encourage wider negative audience participation.

Abusive language is a tool with which to wield power and influence others. Challenges and criticisms form a regular part of the play of boys, giving a presentation of open hostility, although these grievances usually last only a few minutes (Goodwin 1990). The play interactions of girls are quieter and less volatile but the gossip, ridicule, accusations and insults allocated to non-present girls lead to some being ostracized for weeks or even months (Eder 1990; Goodwin 1990; Duncan 1999). The damage may be pervasive, destructive and lasting. One study of adolescent girls found that many of the more influential girls used the sophisticated carrot-and-stick strategy of raw coercion, alongside friendliness, to keep others subservient and under their sovereignty (Duncan 1999). These girls could turn on those under their liege with vicious intent, their verbal skills honed by frequent practice.

Conflicts serve a variety of purposes. Girls turn to adults for arbitration in their conflicts more than boys do, but resolution may not be their primary goal. They may have the sole aim of gaining a decision in their own favour rather than valid resolution of the dispute (Maynard 1985; Eder 1990). Other goals may be present in conflict, such as displaying verbal skill as in the ritual insults and verbal contests of some boys. Girls monitor each other rigorously, and vicious insult may be the most effective way of maintaining what they consider an egalitarian state. Some girls use these linguistic forms in an attempt to promote themselves in the status hierarchy, whereas some use them to keep other girls in their place (Eder 1985; Duncan 1999; Owens et al. 2000).

The overall impression given by the language of several girls in the class studied was one of aggression, although an analysis of the individual linguistic forms of grassing, insult, gossip and rumour revealed a surprisingly low frequency in each category. The overall aggressive presentation stemmed from the accumulation of all their antagonistic linguistic exchanges, not only those studied. There was an ongoing language of conflict underpinning the social interactions between many of these girls throughout the school day. Some of these were jocular in intent but even these appeared aggressive in presentation. Low-key aggression and minor disagreements seem to characterize the conversations of many girls (Maynard 1985).

I would suggest that a process of repetition and escalation is characteristic of the disputatious conversations of girls, with a situation of polarity set up and an oppositional model quickly established. It is often difficult for an outsider to spot the start of such rows, but the warring parties will have registered the signals and be ready to act upon them. Unlike an audience observing a physical fight between a couple of young boys, girls overhearing or eavesdropping on a verbal dispute are likely to join in with gusto, confusing the issue even further. In addition to the language structures studied, the conversations and verbal interactions within the group of girls attending the activity club were characterized by disputes, arguments, contradictory turns, quarrels and challenges. There was discussion of conflicts both past and pending; outcomes and effects were dissected in detail; blame and reprisals apportioned. Conversations would flit from topic to topic, with disputing dyads changing focus but remaining in oppositional, argumentative roles. All these interactions were interspersed with good-humoured exchanges, jokes, bursts of singing, laughter and fun.

Most negative linguistic conflict structures are given from those with power to those without, so highlighting a status differential (Eder and Kinney 1995). This allows them to be effective modes in the use and abuse of power. In the group studied, several girls bickered most days but the most confrontational language came primarily from the more aggressive girls. This would spread throughout the class by means of supportive comments, delivered *sotto voce*, and challenges and denials made by recipients and witnesses. The girls used the language of conflict in differing forms to establish or display power, to maintain the status quo, or to create or confirm a power imbalance. The structure of this group of girls was not egalitarian, as described by Eder (1985), Goodwin (1990) and Alder and Alder (1995), who suggest girls strive to keep the 'egalitarian rule'; these girls formed group structures more diverse and intricate. However, there was a similar system of intense mutual monitoring and evaluation used in an attempt to hold each other within a grid of informal rules. The girls would only refer to these rules if they were broken, when they would remind each other of them in a vociferous manner and threaten to grass on the miscreants. As the literature suggests, these girls drew upon the skills of discussion, negotiation and compromise in dispute (Miller *et al.* 1986; Collins and Laursen 1992), but they were also well versed in the harsher forms of conflict language.

The talk of girls mainly centres on 'long detailed personal discussions about people, norms and beliefs' (Eckert 1990: 91). Girls of the age of those in the study monitor and comment on each other's quality and style of clothing, body shape and behaviour (Alder and Alder 1984; Eder 1985; Goodwin 1990). In the studies carried out in Australia by Owens *et al.* (2000), the young adolescent girls scrutinized each other daily for minute changes in appearance, clothing and behaviour. They openly ranked each other's body development and physical attractiveness and commented freely. Adolescence is a time of rapid physical and emotional change so that comparisons and criticisms made by others are particularly hurtful. Sexual jealousy appears to be at the root of many fights between adolescent girls (Davies 1984; Lees 1993; Duncan 1999). Girls rapidly become aware of the socio-cultural values placed on sexual reputation, resulting in exalted status for some boys but abusive labelling for some girls (Artz 2005). Although only 10 to 11 years old, the girls in the study found such issues provided a rich source for their frequent verbal disputes even though they were not based in reality. They used comments that were outrageous and meant to shock, and they would mimic the terms of abuse commonly used by older children and adults in the neighbourhood without fully understanding their sexual connotations.

As has been found in other studies, the girls used dialect in their conflict language as they did in all their informal conversations (Cummins 1984). They were able to transfer smoothly from the orthodox language (cognitive academic language proficiency, CALP) used for formal tasks, to the heavy local dialect (basic interpersonal social competence, BISC) used for informal chatter (Cummins 1984). The girls enjoyed music and most were accomplished dancers although untrained. They sang spontaneously, solo or in chorus, displaying tuneful voices and an excellent sense of rhythm. The transcripts of their conversations show their sense of rhythm and balance. Their language was colourful and expressive although the grammatical structures were simplistic.

Despite the aggressive, abusive and challenging language used among the girls, few episodes erupted into violence. Rather, there would be a series of disputes and challenges, with both parties holding an oppositional stance until their interest waned, or until another event or argument commencing elsewhere deflected their attention. The study based on the activity club looked at the behaviour of girls in an unsupervised situation so the results may not reflect the language used in other contexts. In addition, these girls may not be representative of the majority of others. However, from numerous informal interviews held with girls and adults in a variety of settings, it would appear that, although a few of the girls were more overtly aggressive than those elsewhere, most interacted in ways similar to the majority of girls of their age. The findings may enhance our understanding of how some young girls behave out of sight and earshot of adults.

13 Grassing

Definition of grassing

Greer (1995) suggests that grassing can be defined as the relaying of information to those empowered to bring about change by an individual or group, informally or formally constituted, with or against the consent of those concerned. Grassing may be a covert activity but this is not always the case. Nearly all episodes of grassing carried out by the girls in the study were delivered in front of the target, whether it was telling tales or issuing a threat to do so. The teachers reported that grassing was an ongoing part of the school day and one of the most stressful elements of their contact time with these girls. Grassing events can be divided into threats to grass, as in, 'I'm going to grass on you', and the actual telling tales about another as in, 'Miss, I'm sad to say that . . .'. These two categories do not appear to have been identified in previous work. As the proportion of threats to telling tales was almost 50 per cent, the threat to grass was a realistic mode of social control.

Grassing, commonly understood as informing, seems to derive from Cockney slang: grass–grasshopper–copper–policeman (Greer 1995). Perhaps the most famous informer was the apostle Judas Iscariot. Grassing differs from gossip, rumour and insult in that there is access to those in power who can sanction the offender and change the situation or event. Having access to someone in a position to impose sanctions puts the person grassing in a powerful position, leaving grassing, or the threat to grass, open to abuse.

The function of grassing

Girls grass on others for a number of reasons, described below.

To maintain the status quo

The main aim of the grassing among the girls studied appeared to be to even up a power imbalance or to make a bid to keep the status quo. Girls appear to have a commitment to equality, and grassing was one way in which this could be achieved. As stated earlier, girls give the appearance of wanting everyone to be on an equal footing although this may be only a superficial impression. Any girl considered 'uppity' and pompous will be treated like the tall poppy and 'cut down to size' (see Chapter 10). One way of doing this is to challenge any real or supposed misdemeanour of the target by grassing to those in authority. Tracey was targeted in this way because she became proud and domineering. The other girls quickly spotted any misdemeanours and grassed on her to the teachers. Any change, such as a new girl entering the class, brought about an upsurge in grassing behaviour, presumably in an attempt to restore stability. New female entrants to established situations frequently cause jealousy and suspicion among the other girls, leading to unrest (Maynard 1985).

Frequently, the girls appeared to use grassing in a bid for arbitration whereas, in reality, they were using it as a mechanism to their own advantage hoping that any decision would be in their favour (Maynard 1985).

> Wendy: Miss, Angela has taken all the stuff. I was using it. She won't give it back.
>
> Angela: No, Miss. It was mine. I was having that piece. I brought it from home, Miss.

For personal gain as in financial reward

Few girls receive financial incentives to grass, unlike in the adult world where those in influential positions reward others for giving information. However, girls do threaten to grass and may be dissuaded from doing so by their targets with offers of financial and other incentives.

For preferment

Some girls may hope to gain status and recognition for their efforts in monitoring the behaviour of others and so succeed in becoming selected for preferential positions such as prefects or monitors.

For attention and praise

Girls may use grassing in order to gain attention and praise from those in positions of authority. The psychoanalytical explanation for this behaviour would be that it is a process of transferring those unacceptable aspects of our own personality normally repressed onto those more vulnerable and who display the same or similar characteristics (Klein 1946). A simpler explanation would be that these girls want to highlight their appropriate and conforming behaviour while showing others to be lacking in these qualities.

To get another into trouble
Sadly, the Schadenfreude syndrome (guilty pleasure), still exists whereby some girls deliberately seek to get others into trouble. This is usually due to jealousy, revenge or, in some cases, for their personal satisfaction.

To control deviant behaviour or to protect the vulnerable
The example most relevant to this work is that of those who grass on others who bully. Unfortunately, it remains within our culture that to alert adults to bullying is seen as grassing by many of the young. This is particularly so in the case of boys. Fear of reprisal is not confined to the targets of bullying as witnesses can also be threatened if they alert an adult. Most of the girls in the group studied had a sense of fair play and used grassing to alert a girl to something done by another contrary to her best interest.

Fun and entertainment
Other than the intent to get someone into trouble by grassing to those in authority, seen in the framework of joke, it is the threat to grass that most usually forms the basis of a round or other form of entertainment.

To avoid blame and criticism
Several of the girls studied found various ways of diverting the course of justice and employed grassing to avoid blame or criticism. Several were quick to blame others for their spoilt, substandard or unfinished work.

To destroy reputations
Grassing may be carried out by those intending to ingratiate themselves with those in power to enhance their status to the disadvantage of others. It is also used to destroy reputations. These two aims may be observed in the following:

> Kate: Miss, Angela's been naughty. She's been doing handstands in front of the camera. When you went out. We were all quiet.

In fact, it was Kate who had been doing handstands in front of the camera (forgetting she was being filmed), whereas Angela had said she would 'tell on her' if she did not stop. Angela used the threat to grass when girls broke the covert but accepted school, class or social rules in an attempt to keep order and protect the vulnerable.

To add power to a request
The threat to grass was often used as a forceful shorthand form of requesting a girl to stop behaving in a particular way. This gave emphasis to the request.

> Angela: You keep knocking me. You're spoiling my work. I'll grass on you.

To defeat the opposition
In conflicts between factions, friends would align themselves on opposing sides. It would then be the covert duty of members of each faction to spot any opportunity to get a member of the opposing side into trouble. The easiest way to do this was by grassing.

As a reprisal strategy
The girls used grassing as a reprisal strategy. It was common for them to tell tales about Rachel while she attempted her schoolwork. Drawing attention to her mistakes was the only way they could safely bring about retribution for her aggression. As most of the girls did this, and all blamed each other, Rachel was defenceless. Rachel took no interest in her schoolwork and the girls had identified her Achilles' heel.

Culprits and targets of grassing

Those who featured highest in the ranking for both culprits and targets of grassing were the most aggressive girls who were protective of their own status and power and wary of that of others. They kept a close watching brief on each other, noticing every deviation from the formal and informal rules, and making the threat to grass a realistic and effective controlling mechanism. These were also the most prolific gossips and those who jealously monitored the interactions in the group most carefully. Not a detail went unobserved and they would comment on the flaunting of any rule immediately. These girls were suspicious of any perceived slight or insult and guarded their friendships closely.

Kate and Nikki were involved in the grassing sequences, as culprit, target or chorus whenever they were present. Nikki was considered a troublemaker, in both the passive and active sense, in that she issued threats to grass and she was the main recipient. She frequently ignored or challenged the rules although she was the first to spot anyone else doing so. This behaviour contributed to the high number of times the others grassed about her. As she had the security of being in the only friendship dyad that lasted the 16 months of the study, it may be that her personality was at the source of this behaviour rather than any justifiable suspicion or threat of losing her friend.

Denise had a high rating as a recipient of grassing. She was on the periphery of the aggressive group, often causing conflict and unrest in her attempts to break into established friendships. Grassing on her was how others dealt with her provocative behaviour. The teachers and other girls stated that Denise caused the most trouble in the class. Her behaviour was more problematical than the aggression of Rachel as the actions and reactions of Rachel were more visible and predictable. Denise's pattern of behaviour indicated her inability to establish and maintain friendships.

Topics of grassing

Various behaviours triggered threats to grass. The most highly represented category was swearing. Interestingly, those who swore most were those who grassed on others if they swore. These were the girls in the more aggressive group who constantly monitored each other's appearance, behaviour, achievements and friendships. Other behaviours triggering a threat to grass were those considered to be flaunting some form of school-based rule or the accepted social mores. The girls censored behaviours that adults sanctioned, such as running around the classroom, doing handstands or letting others into the room. A less well-represented category contained misdemeanours related to work issues such as sharing materials and space, copying or spoiling the work of another. Angela had a more mature attitude than some of the girls and often took it upon herself to try to keep the others in order. Her high score of threats to grass reflects this. As she told the teachers of misdemeanours only when it was reasonable to do so, the other girls rarely objected to her self-appointed role of monitor. However, most of the disputes over space and materials involved Angela and Wendy, her dyad friend. As they worked closely together, they squabbled constantly over materials and space using insults and grassing to add force to their requests and demands. As stated earlier, close friends appear to quarrel more frequently than non-friends (Menesini 1997).

A framework for grassing

An analysis of the transcripts of the conversations of the girls showed that a structure was evident in their episodes of grassing.

Accusation
A girl intending to grass usually made her intention clear so giving her target the chance to alter the offending behaviour or make an apology. In other situations, targets commonly do not know that someone will, or has, grassed on them.

Threat to grass
Comments such as 'I'm telling if you do that' were interspersed throughout the conversations of the girls.

Telling tales
If the accuser considered her threat had been ignored, she would feel justified in carrying it out in one of several ways. The accuser could tell an adult directly

or indirectly via the camera. The girls often addressed their comments to their teacher directly to the camera. No preamble was necessary for the grassing, so that an adult could be addressed immediately on entering a room.

>Joanne: They've all been singing, Miss.

Denial

The accusation and denial, followed by repeats of the accusation and denial, could last several minutes.

Counter-attack

The girls did not always take an accusation lightly, and frequently responded with a counter-accusation. There could be extensions and elaborations as the episode continued.

>Patricia (to camera): Miss, Rachel just swore.

Rachel's response was to remain silent but, several minutes later, she addressed a different teacher entering the room.

>Rachel: Sir, Patricia's just swore.

Closure

An episode may end in several ways. The threat to grass may lead the target to stop the offending behaviour. Peer pressure could precipitate this move or, if the accuser failed to elicit support from others, the threat could be dropped. Alternatively, the accuser could lose interest, the denial or counter-challenge could be successful, or deflection or a joke could lead to closure.

Language

The sentences used in the grassing sequences were usually short, factual and to the point, leaving no opportunity for ambiguities or confusions. The language was not as elaborate as that used in the insult, gossip and rumour episodes, lacking the colourful vocabulary of the insult sequences and the storyline characteristic of the gossip. There was some evidence of rhythm and balance with alliteration and repetition giving emphasis. Often, there was a mirror effect, as found in the insult structures, with the vocabulary used by the first speaker repeated by the respondent.

>Kate: Miss, Nikki's just writing them down.
>Nikki: I'm not just writing them down.
>Kate: Miss, Nikki's just writing everything down.
>Chorus: Miss, she's just writing everything down.

This may be a covert form of ridicule as it encourages others to chant in the responses.

Summary

The girls used grassing as a strategy in their continuous struggle for power and influence, but no one girl routinely targeted another. The statements were often genuine bids made by some to keep order or defend a vulnerable girl against the inappropriate action of another. Grassing was also a mechanism for fun and entertainment and no episode resulted in violence. The girls often used the threat to grass in a jocular fashion between friends forming a repartee lasting several rounds and reminiscent of the insult sequences. The cry of 'I'm going to grass on you' would most often get the prompt reply, 'Well, I'm going to grass on you'. Grassing was used primarily as part of the flow of taunting, provocative behaviour and petty quarrels that formed part of the interactions between these girls during a normal school day.

Suggested approaches

Those working with girls need to determine, if possible, the rationale for the grassing so that they can respond appropriately.

1 To maintain the status quo or for a decision to be made in their favour.
   Response: Those working with girls need to be aware that claims for arbitration to restore equality and the status quo may only be bids for a judgment to be given in favour of the complainant.

2 Jealousy.
   Response: Unfortunately, girls who achieve in any way, or who are perceived as being more attractive, intelligent or financially advantaged than others, could become targets of attack. Even those given awards for voluntary work or bravery have been the recipients of the unpleasant behaviour of other girls. These attacks are not always focused on the factor causing the jealousy, as girls often give a different excuse for their negative behaviour. Grassing about any slight misdemeanour is a favourite way of making life difficult for a targeted girl. New girls in particular need to be monitored closely, preferably by a peer supporter who can watch for any covert bullying.

3 For personal gain as in financial reward.
   Response: This should be considered in the framework of blackmail and discussed with the culprit in this context.

4   For preferment.

Response: Girls using grassing for such purposes need be told that this behaviour is not appropriate and that selection for office will be done using other criteria. These criteria should then be made explicit to them.

5   For attention and praise.

Response: This behaviour could be compared to lying. Some adults, as well as young people, lie or exaggerate about their achievements, experiences and accomplishments in order to gain approval from others. Any adult in charge needs to judge how sensitive a response is required. Slow, tactful and factual correction of any exaggerations, and patience with bids for attention, may eventually bring about a change in behaviour. In extreme cases, consultation with the local educational psychology service or with the Community and Mental Health Service (CAMHS) may be useful.

6   To get another into trouble.

Response: Once these girls realize that their behaviour, and the rationale behind it, has been identified, they often cease these attacks. Triggers may be rivalry, jealousy, reprisals or simply mischief.

7   To control deviant behaviour by alerting those in charge or to protect the interests of the vulnerable.

Response: It is beholden on all adults in school to be alert to all forms of bullying so that they identify those involved without the need of information from students. They need to work closely with parents, carers and others in the community to form network links and pre-ventative and protective strategies. There are systems that schools can use to lessen the chance of reprisals. These strategies are noted in Section 7. Other worrying behaviours, such as alcohol and drug abuse, depression and suicide intent, come to adult attention com-paratively rarely. Currently, peers who witness such behaviours feel that they have no right to inform adults as some of these behaviours are illegal and this would clearly be a case of grassing.

8   Fun and entertainment.

Response: Grassing to get someone into trouble could be regarded as amusing. More often, entertainment gained from the threat to grass usually takes the form of a round or joke.

9   To avoid blame and criticism.

Response: Adults working with girls need to be alert to the fact that others may be being blamed for their mistakes.

10   To destroy reputations.

Response: If there is any suspicion of a girl's reputation being harmed, it could be useful to inform those responsible that such things are considered slanderous and can carry a conviction in the adult world. Once lost, it is difficult for a girl to regain her reputation.

11 To add power to a request.

Response: As this is usually a threat to grass given by one girl to another, adults rarely hear of these incidents.

12 To defeat the opposition.

Response: If the opposing sides are equally powerful, and no one is at risk, it is best ignored. Once it has been recognized for what it is, this behaviour usually stops within a short space of time.

13 As a reprisal strategy.

Response: If there is a suspicion that this is the rationale behind the grassing, it could be useful to know why this more deviant manner of challenging the target has been employed. In this way, bullying or other unwanted behaviours may be identified.

14 Insult

Definition of insult

An insult was defined for the purposes of the study as an abusive comment or gesture addressed to another present, with the intention of causing emotional distress. It might be: an individual remark, provoked or unprovoked, deliberately made to give offence; a directive given in a manner intended to demean; or a name used with the intention of denigrating another. Influential to the definition of insult is the interpretation of intonation, facial expression, gestures and body language, as any utterance holds a multiplicity of meanings (Malone 1997). A casual observer may misinterpret a tap to the side of the head as the intention to signify stupidity instead of the simple adjustment of a hairstyle. Context and history of the actors are also influential to an accurate reading, as emotion, rather than knowledge, fires insults. Insults can be delivered in a spontaneous, reactive manner or after a period of consideration, with reference to past grievances. An insult is a two-way dynamic process as the power of an insult depends on the intention of the giver and the manner in which the target receives the comments. Only the actors can fully appreciate the message embedded in the words.

The topics and function of insults

The main function of insulting language is to demean or challenge another. As a degree of confidence is required if reprisals are not to be feared, it is usually those in power, or those considering themselves of high status, who deliver insults among themselves or to those they consider of lower status (Eder and Kinney 1995). This finding was evident in the group studied. The content of the insults distributed among the girls was similar to other forms of conflict language. The topics of the insults passed between the girls in the study can be grouped as follows in order of frequency: comments relating to behaviour;

comments relating to work, skill and abilities in the context of school; insults used in a joking manner; insults relating to the appearance of another. A final category encapsulates miscellaneous topics. Several of the girls did not have the verbal skills necessary to talk down their opponent and would resort to swear words or abusive invective simply to end a contest in a decisive manner.

The largest category of insults contained those used to signal disapproval of the behaviour of another girl, especially if she was discovered to have broken an established school or social rule. These insults also focused on the accepted social mores of the group. The girls had an agreed standard of behaviour and would criticize infringement of these rules, although they themselves could be guilty of behaving in the same way. The function of challenging these unacceptable behaviours may have been to demonstrate their power to do so, rather than with any expectation of bringing about change. The function may have been similar to one of the functions of grassing. By pointing out the mistakes of others, it is less likely that one's own will be noted or will be considered as deviant as would otherwise be the case. Insults were triggered when any girl behaved in what others considered an autocratic or conceited manner, or in a fashion that disturbed the seemingly egalitarian state of the group. Challenges were made to girls found to be, or suspected of, lying or cheating.

Much of the abusive language used by the girls was in the form of swearing. Abusive directives, used in a casual or joking manner, peppered their conversations. Some girls would say 'piss off' to a friend in a neutral tone meaning 'go away'. Swearing triggered return insults from targets and non-targets even though these girls often used the same behaviours. Even when not malicious in intent, such comments, along with command directives, aggregated to consolidate the impression of a high incidence of abusive speech among the girls and an undertone of aggressive behaviour.

Other insults arose when the skills and abilities of a girl were considered to be below an acceptable standard, although there were few critical comments relating to intellectual ability. Those finding the academic tasks difficult could always persuade or demand others to come to their aid. There was common use of derogatory names such as 'dafty', 'stupid', 'thick', along with others common among the young in many areas of Britain, such as 'divvy' and 'spakka', but these were not allocated to specific girls. These were spoken in a moment of frustration, affection or as a joke, or would be called into play when any girl executed a task badly, made a foolish remark or an unwise decision.

Insults were used in a joking manner when all would share the joke. In this work, an insult has been considered a joke only if all found it amusing; any causing distress to the target or to another present has not been classified as a joke. There were occasions when some of the girls accused each other of untoward behaviour in the form of a playful 'round'. Rachel was usually the instigator of this game, resurrecting a fading joke by accusing each girl in turn of behaviour considered shocking. On many occasions the purpose was solely for everyone to enjoy the joke, but it may be that the more dominant girls were taking note of the reactions of each girl to the verbal teasing. Young boys tease out the vulnerable during bouts of play fighting (Pellegrini 1988; Smith and Boulton 1990), and it may be that the dominant girls were doing the same with their use of language. Boys are said to tease each other about sporting prowess and school achievement whereas girls may tease others about their appearance, social relations and behavioural norms (Rauste-von Wright 1989). Regardless of focus, both modes are used to sort out dominance, resilience and vulnerability (Rauste-von Wright 1989; Eder 1990).

The girls made surprisingly few comments, directly or indirectly, about the appearance of others. This is contrary to the work of Eder (1990), who found this to be the largest category of insult. This may have been because the girls in her study were older. The girls targeted Tracey as she was proud of her precocious physical development but, as she was powerful and strong, they called her names behind her back. They mocked her conceit and described her as 'all titty and tramp'. Sexual vocabulary did not have any realistic significance to these 10- and 11-year-old girls but they used words with sexual connotations such as 'slapper', 'slag', 'tart' and 'tramp', and became highly offended should they be the recipients. Girls in competition over boyfriends would use these to describe an opponent, but they had no base in fact. A study of Australian adolescent girls found many such names prevalent (Owens 1996), and Eder *et al.* (1996) found the same in a study of American girls. Duncan's (1999) work on sexual bullying among girls gives a good insight into this form of abuse prevalent among older girls. Most authors agree that the sexual names often bear no relation to practice.

Culprits and targets of insult

As expected, those girls who were confident and considered themselves of high status delivered insults to those they considered of lower status (Eder 1990). The highest number of insults were delivered by Rachel, one of the more aggressive girls to the most vulnerable girl in the class. Insults flew between the more aggressive girls although the most aggressive girl did not issue the most insults. This may have been because she preferred to carry out her disputes outside school, out of sight of the teachers, where there would be less chance of credible witnesses. Several girls kept a check on the behaviour of the more aggressive girls and prevented many disputes from developing into conflict. When any girl insulted one more vulnerable, one or other of these more powerful girls often stepped in and prevented things from getting out of hand. Yvonne, Angela and Charlotte were quiet but powerful members of the class whose equitable personalities seemed to calm the more volatile girls.

Tracey appeared jealous of Charlotte and often insulted or threatened her, but Charlotte was a confident girl, with supportive friends, and usually returned the insult. This gave her an uncharacteristically high count of insults, all given in retaliation. Some insult sequences are more complex than would first appear. Tracey frequently set up a discussion with the aim of eliciting a compliment. On one occasion, she chanted, 'Charlotte's got big boobs' in the manner of an insult in the hope that Charlotte would respond by using an inversion strategy saying her 'boobs' were not as big as Tracey's. In this way, Tracey would achieve her aim, to gain a compliment about the large size of her breasts. Charlotte failed to rise to this ploy and remained silent. Tracey later reversed what she said and called out, 'Charlotte has little boobs'. Charlotte, caught off guard, retorted, 'I'd rather have little ones than big ones like yours, Tracey'. At last, Tracey had gained her hard-earned compliment, via an insult sequence.

The framework and language of insults

An analysis of the language used by the girls in their insults is embedded in the sections below.

The adjacency principal

Seemingly, from an early age, young people learn to identify the structure of an insult sequence and the key elements in the routines. They accomplish the sequence of utterances by using a process of intricate, coordinated moves. The structure is based on the cooperative, adjacency principle (Grice 1975), with expectations built into pairs of statements that determine the meaning. The sequence is based on repeated, reversed turns; the most expected response to an insult being a return insult (Labov 1972; Goodwin 1980; Kochman 1983; Eder and Enke 1991).

Tied comments

The majority of insults appear to be tied comments, insults made with direct reference to a preceding remark (Brenneis and Lein 1977). Tit-for-tat comments, in the form of abusive turns (Maltz and Borker 1982), were plentiful in the exchanges of the girls in the activity club, so that a girl calling another a 'cow' would be likely to receive the response, 'Well, you're a cow, too'.

Younger children make an immediate riposte, whereas older children have the cognitive ability to refer to a remark made earlier.

Topping

A verbal duel could follow the exchange given earlier, where the girl called 'a cow' tops the comment with a superlative.

> Denise: You're a fat cow.
> Joanne: Well, you're a fatter one.

Exaggerations can be used such as, 'Well, you're the fattest cow in all the world'. It is critical to have the last word as this usually signifies the winner in the sequence (Opie and Opie 1959).

A verbal stand-off can escalate quickly with each party aiming to top the other. In the heat of battle, taunts and jeers may accompany claims and counter-claims.

> Nikki: I can make a better one than that.
> Joanne: Well, I can make a better one than yours. Yours is rubbish.
> Nikki: Well then, yours is rubbish. Yours is the most rubbish.
> Joanne: Mine's not as rubbish as yours. *Yours* is the rubbishest. Most rubbish, I mean.

Exaggeration and emotion may lead the discourse to degenerate into nonsense. There are various ways of topping an insult when, for whatever reason, comprehensible words are unavailable. The use of nonsense phrases, based on the vernacular in vogue at the time, is a common response, as in the commonly used phrase, 'with bells on'. A sound pattern can top any insult as it is difficult to respond to a sound pattern as there is no content in the prior comment to which to tie a response. When Charlotte challenges Rachel about a remark she has made, Rachel responds with, 'I didn't'. Charlotte decides not to get into a sequence of repeated turns by replying 'yes you did', as there would be an equal chance of either girl winning. Instead, she resorts to the ubiquitous sound pattern response of 'bla bla di bla bla' to end the contest.

However, this type of response could incite the target to violence in frustration. An aggressive reaction is one of the few responses available to counter a sound pattern other than repeating the sounds louder or delivering a different sound pattern. The girls resorted to chanting rhymes and phrases, swear words and sound patterns when they had no access to more sophisticated responses. These passed back and forth becoming more dramatic and exaggerated in length, tone and gesture to out-talk or shout down an opponent. Nearly all the girls were able to make some form of appropriate response within the expected time limits.

An oppositional stance

A structured and coordinated competition may develop where both parties take up a symmetrical, oppositional stance with insults bouncing back and forth. Positions are fluid and can be aggravated, maintained or diminished throughout the exchange. Several of the girls in the study did not have the verbal skills necessary to talk down their opponent and would resort to swear words or abusive invective to end the contest in a decisive manner. In the heat of a dispute, combatants often mirrored each other's words unintentionally. This gave a sense of rhythm, order and predictability to the scenario.

> Rachel: I didn't say that.
> Denise: Yes you did say that.
> Rachel: No I didn't say that. Stupid.
> Denise: Yes you did. I heard you say that.
> Rachel: No, I didn't say that. You weren't there 'cos I didn't see you.
> Denise: Yes you did say that. I was there, see. You didn't see me.

Ritual insults

The difference between a personal and ritual insult is that a ritual insult must be so outlandish as to be clearly untrue (Bavelas *et al.* 1995). For example, calling a boy 'lazy' could cause irrevocable offence but saying he is 'a snail on crutches' is clearly untrue and intended as a joke. However, the delineation between ritual and personal insult, joking and denigrating insult, is tenuous so that playful and hurtful exchanges often cross over mid-stream. Humorous insult exchanges are a form of fun in some cultures, as in the game of 'dozens' played by some Afro-Caribbean boys in parts of North America where insults fly back and forth until everyone runs out of steam (Labov 1972; Goodwin 1990). Although considered a game, fierce competition forms the base of many such interactions and ritual insults can be attempts to gain status (Labov 1972; Goodwin 1990).

Directives

Directives may be defined as instructions or requests couched in terms of commands. Directive commands start, stop, prevent or prohibit an action and often reflect an asymmetrical power structure (Goodwin 1990). Boys are more likely to use directives and 'grandstanding' where they rely on domineering exchanges without reference to the listener (Goodwin 1990; Maccoby 1999). This is discussed in Chapter 5. Directives can be unsolicited advice delivered with abusive intent as in, 'You don't do it that way, stupid'. The girls studied were quick to give unsolicited advice such as this although their intent was often benign.

Directives are frequently issued in conjunction with a name. Tracey's command directives were often dominant and insulting, as in 'Let's have a look at your work'. If she used a girl's name, it would be to emphasize the command as in 'Angela, let's have a look at your work, then'. Most directives were used by Tracey to Angela in the form of demands to see or copy her work. Angela was intelligent and diligent whereas Tracey was intelligent but lazy. Angela was able to withstand her directives but Tracey's attitude towards Angela caused the others to reject Tracey's overtures for friendship. Tracey seemed to interfere in what everyone else was doing and always had an opinion to offer on how to approach a task. She issued a number of forceful, insulting directives that usually triggered a counter-attack.

Surprisingly, one of the most aggressive girls in the class gave a low count of commands and directives. Rachel was socially dominant but, finding the work challenging, kept a low profile when the class was engaged on academic tasks. She would take a relaxed attitude, laughing and joking, recounting stories of happenings and planning future events. The girls also used directives implying moral persuasion widely in disputes over the sharing of space and materials. The inclusion of the possessive 'my' or 'mine' emphasized a moral obligation to return a possession to the complainant. A girl would ask for 'my scissors', implying that another had appropriated hers.

As stated earlier, Menesini (1997) found that friends enter into disputes more frequently than non-friends. Wendy and Angela were close friends who always shared space and materials. There were many disputes when a continuous stream of directives and counter-directives would flow.

Angela: You've taken too much of that stuff, Wendy. Give it to me
Wendy: No I haven't, Angela. It's mine. You're not getting it. Get off it.
Angela: Yes you have. That's not fair. Give me some more.
Wendy: You snatched that. That's not fair. Give it back. It's mine. I'll tell.

Angela was intelligent and took on the role of instructress when the girls needed help. She was capable of giving positive, accurate directions to the other girls and was rarely abusive although she entered into bickering insult turns with her close friend as illustrated above. Yvonne used directives in a variety of modes. The other girls listened to her when she gave advice as the directives she gave were usually in arbitration and rarely insulting. In contrast, Nikki issued a high count of abusive directives in an insolent and bombastic manner. She was in a secure dyad friendship with Yvonne, yet she was jealous when Yvonne engaged with other girls and tried to dominate whenever she felt unable to compete in an equable manner. Denise erroneously considered that she was intellectually, academically and socially superior to the other girls. Her insistence on directing the others caused upset and triggered many disputes especially as she gave insulting directives, demeaning comments, insults and sarcasm when voicing her opinion. The most vulnerable girl in the class gave no directives although she was the recipient of those from one or two of the more aggressive girls.

Name calling

The most common category of insult would seem to be name calling. This is the most common form of bullying reported by both sexes (Katz *et al.* 2001). Names are undoubtedly powerful. We can underestimate their potency until our own name is abused. Our names are described as labels of primary potency (Allport 1954). Several famous dramas have explored the issue of people not owning or remembering their name. Goffman (1968) suggests that a man without a name has no existence. Those who want to command others, as in the armed forces, lower the importance of personal identity by allocating a number to be used in preference to the person's name. Perhaps the power of name calling stems from nicknames being associated with Old Nick, the devil. The power of this form of abuse to cause distress has long been identified (Frazer 1923; Goffman 1963). As with other terms of abuse, the potency of name calling lies in the manner in which the name is spoken and received.

We need names and labels, as without them we would be swamped by a myriad of anomalous characteristics to remember. We are named to define our inclusion in our family, locality, nationality and race, among other things. In parallel, our name excludes us from other contexts, so that having a name can have both positive and negative ramifications. As stated in the section on insult, the psychoanalytical explanation of why humans use abusive names would be that it is a mode of transferring the repressed, unacceptable aspects of our personality onto vulnerable others who display the same or similar characteristics (Klein 1946). The word 'stigma' originates from markings given by the ancient Greeks to those in their society who were either devoted followers of the gods or, conversely, slaves and known criminals. Once a young person is stigmatized by abusive name calling the verbal label seems no less durable.

We have inherited our library of stereotypes over generations (Goffman 1968), along with prejudices from our ancestors as in a wariness of strangers or those with different or unusual features or characteristics. The young person is targeted because of factors outside the norm, and a negative, possibly destructive, process is quickly in place (Lemert 1972):

1   The characteristic is commented on unfavourably by the group.
2   The subject is now more aware of the characteristic triggering the adverse comments.

3 Tension and anxiety cause the victim to believe that the characteristic has become more prominent.
4 The attacks escalate.
5 The victim believes the attacks are justified.
6 The isolated and fearful victim is unable to seek help.

Most abusive names such as 'pig' or 'Frankenstein' (although Franken-stein's monster would be the accurate use) are dehumanizing. More recent inventions are 'goons' and 'wimp'. The potency of these non-human names is that it places the target outside the human context thus assuaging any guilt and giving permission for the name calling to continue (Besag 1989). Once the subject is seen as being outside the human context, the bullying could escalate to a dangerous level. It is critical that adults and peers identify the process immediately and that it is stopped effectively. Name calling and stigmatization among girls appear not to follow any predictable pattern and to stem primarily from jealousy. Only later is a search made for a rationale.

Hargreaves (1967) offers four conditions which he suggests will determine whether the target accepts the label:

1 The frequency of the attacks.
2 Whether those doing the labelling are perceived as significant to the target.
3 The support those allocating the label have in the group.
4 Whether the labelling is done publicly.

The girls in the study rarely used pre-allocated nicknames, preferring to use names thought up spontaneously. As expected, a large category of dehumanizing names was in evidence, such as 'cow' and 'bitch'. Word play and rhythmic chants, such as 'bitch-witch', were common (Besag 1989). Occasionally, there would be some word play on a girl's name but this was not necessarily abusive. The friendship dyad of Wendy and Angela sometimes used a rhyming game based on their names. Tracey annoyed the other girls but, as she was powerful and strong, other girls called her names behind her back.

Suggested approaches

1 As most insults are delivered in the form of name calling, those working with young people should pay particular attention to this form of abuse.
2 The targets and culprits should know that verbal abuse, such as slan-der, is considered in legislation as potent as physical attack. For

example, mental cruelty is considered alongside physical cruelty as grounds for divorce.

3 It is important for girls to realize that it is not necessarily what is said in the verbal attack that is at the root of the problem. If the culprits want to be unpleasant, they will find something to say. It is better to deal with the name calling as a form of abuse than to try to change such things as body shape.

4 However, it may be appropriate for girls to consider whether it would be to their advantage to change whatever is the focus of the abusive remarks, such as their weight or their tendency to gossip or make spiteful remarks. Clearly, this approach requires the utmost sensitivity as no one warrants abusive name calling. However, it may be to their advantage to alter their presentation, attitude or other characteristics if they would feel healthier or if they are causing annoyance to others. Girls themselves must come to realize that this would be beneficial and must make their own decision. To give the impression that they deserve the abuse is doubling the attack. This approach must only be taken in conjunction with the culprits of the abuse being challenged.

5 A targeted girl may become desensitized to an abusive name if used, with her consent, by a supportive adult in a sensitive manner. An older relative or student could be appropriate for this role. It is advisable for the victim to get used to unkind remarks made by others by practising in a benign situation. The aim is to get the victim to shrug off the verbal insults. Other suggestions for appearing to ignore abusive remarks are given in Section 7.

6 All students should be made aware that name calling, along with other forms of insult, is bullying and will be dealt with as such. They should not support or listen to such attacks. Compliment students making positive comments to others in a sensitive manner. The expected standard of verbal communication should be clear to all.

7 The curriculum offers a number of opportunities for an exploration of names. Names change over history and over nations. For example, students could trace the history of their own name, looking at how it has changed over time. They may be interested in discovering from which language it derives. Diminutives of names can be interesting and many names have a meaning.

8 Girls could consider what the reasons are for name calling. Names given by others can be inclusive as well as exclusive. Many men with the surname White happily accept the traditional substitute Chalky for their first name. The same applies to Dusty Miller and Dickie Bird. These names are given in an affectionate, inclusive context rather than being abusive and excluding.

9 Discuss the difference between nicknames and name calling.

10 Perhaps the most difficult name calling to deal with is when a girl's mother is called abusive names in her (the mother's) absence. Such names are usually local words for a prostitute and are variations on calling the girl a bastard. As the mother is absent, she is unable to defend herself. In addition, no factual evidence can be given to prove she is not a prostitute. The victim needs to know that it is not her mother who is under attack. The culprits know that this is one of the most potent and hurtful attacks and rarely has any direct connection to the mother.

11 All students must know that calling someone by what they consider a funny name is rarely amusing to the recipient.

12 Adults must take care that they do not use a nickname, abbreviation or diminutive without permission from the person concerned. Peers can turn a name given in a joking or affectionate manner into abuse.

13 Peer supporters have a powerful role to play in this work. They can offer support, strategies and friendship to a student under stress and model appropriate social behaviour.

15 Gossip and rumour

If being human is all about talking, it's the tittle tattle of life that makes the world go round, not the pearls of wisdom that fall from the lips of the Arisotles and Einsteins.

(Dunbar 1996: 6)

Definition of gossip

The definition of gossip used for the study was the presentation of an evaluative comment about one or more persons absent, of common acquaintance, followed by comments from one or more of those listening. There were many negative opinions passed between the girls about others, giving the conversations the feel of gossip, but unless there was a development in the form of contributions from those listening, these have not been included. In addition, the remarks had to contain some information that could be new or the revisiting of that given previously. Even within this group of girls, several of whom commonly made negative comments about each other, analysis of their conversations found surprisingly few structured gossip episodes, although there were many comments that could be described as being gossip in character. The episodes occurring did so mainly in the conversations of the 'troublesome' group of girls. The surprising paucity of gossip among the girls appears to confirm the hypothesis that gossip, if defined as above, is a more sophisticated language structure than insult and grassing.

Women have long been associated with gossip. In every known culture, men have accused women of being garrulous, chattering gossips (Geertz 1983). Both gossip and witchcraft are considered predominantly female behaviours. Hines and Fry (1994) found that Argentinean women, more than men, judged others, gossiped and lied about others, excluded persons from social events and interrupted conversations. A different perspective on this is the case of the US politician who, in all seriousness, stated that he never gossiped as his wife did and she told him all he needed to know (Meyer Spack 1985). Gossip is a skill and sometimes an art. More has been written about it from the historical and anthropological viewpoints than considering it a part of everyday chit-chat. The phrase 'to peddle gossip' stems from the peddler carrying his news, no doubt with a penchant for gossip. Gossips are often referred to as washerwomen, as the communal washing area is where the village tittle-tattle would have been exchanged in the past.

In common parlance, it is said people turn to gossip to create excitement if they have no access to action. Elizabeth Gaskell, the Victorian author of *Cranford* describes her character, Miss Pole as spending the morning 'rambling from shop to shop, not to purchase anything, except an occasional reel of cotton, or a piece of tape, but to see the new articles and report upon them, and to collect all the stray pieces of intelligence in the town' (Gaskell 1985). The role played by the lighthearted gossip spread by Miss Pole is in contrast to the role that gossip played in the tragedy of Othello as depicted by Shakespeare. A mediaeval saying encapsulates the potency of gossip: 'People who attack the good name of others are more cruel than hell. Backbiters do kill more men with a word, than souldiers in field destroyes with their sword' (Meyer Spack 1985).

Function of gossip

Gossip has a positive function when used as a testing out process to define boundaries of acceptable behaviour and to refine moral stances (Gottman and Mettatal 1986). Gossiping is a means whereby we establish our identity by comparing ourselves to others, and a mode of instruction whereby we learn from others' mistakes. Through gossip, and the discussion of the behaviour and attitudes of others, we develop an understanding of acceptable social norms and mores. We identify moral defects and the sanctions imposed for deviancy (Rosnow and Fine 1976, 1996). We identify those unworthy of our trust, whether in the role of friends or professionals, so we are better able to avoid or deflect trouble (Gottman and Mettatal 1986). Gossip allows us to rehearse possible courses of action mentally and linguistically. In addition, positive gossip enhances status, allocates praise and respect. Gossip can secure or destroy reputations.

Developmental stages in gossiping

Unlike grassing and insult, there appeared to be definable developmental stages in the language used by the girls studied in their gossip. This would appear to be because the framework of gossip is more sophisticated. As the activity group lasted over the 16 months of the girls' ageing from 10 to 11 years old, there was evidence of a developmental change reflected in their language. When younger, as expected, the girls were still discovering features of their own personality and used gossip as an aid to self-exploration by revealing their discoveries and ideas to friends (Gottman and Parker 1986). As they developed, they were able to use gossip to relate their own feelings and opinions to those of others and amalgamate all into one schema (Gottman and Parker 1986). Some girls remained immature; others became increasingly precocious. Over time, positive evaluations occur more frequently (Gottman and Mettatal 1986). By the end of the study, most girls had reached the developmental stage where they could hold both positive and negative evaluations of the same person simultaneously. On one occasion, Charlotte says of Rachel, 'She can be aggressive, but she can be kind'.

The girls used gossip to explore their emotions and to compare them with those of others. Charlotte claimed her mother had promised her a birthday party in the family tradition. Her younger sister had had a party a few months earlier but her mother said that Charlotte could not have one; she was surprised, disappointed and angry. Charlotte needed to discuss her complex feelings with her friends, feeling guilty at having explosive, negative feelings about her mother. She gained a great deal of support from the group, although the comment of one girl, 'I'd kill her, me!', shocked these loquacious girls, never short of an opinion to offer, into silence even though they knew this to be simply a spontaneous, supportive remark.

The language of gossip

The girls in the study showed a surprisingly highly developed range of skills used in what many consider a carefree, leisure activity. A reasonable assumption is that the girls absorbed their skills from overhearing and listening to gossip from an early age. For example, we may have underestimated the role of the listeners as it is an interactive process. The pause at the start of the process fulfils many functions and these young girls used it to the full. They were skilled in working for, and holding, dramatic tension. They were adept at allowing themselves to be encouraged to give out the gossip slowly, to the best advantage, in order to increase audience participation and give an optimum dramatic presentation. In addition, the person gossiping holds important information so the pause allows the gossip to test out whether the response will be a worthy trade-in. Once the information has been disclosed, their power will be transferred. The strategy of withholding the information may be done to solicit and entice listeners to participate actively, so spreading responsibility and blame for the gossiping. A further process is embedded in the initial pause as it ensures the consensus view will be in support of the gossip rather than the target. The gossip needs to judge that the comments will be acceptable to the listeners, that there will be no loss of face, and that there will be an opportunity for repair work if others dispute the comments. The interaction of these processes results in collusion between the speaker and audience and an underscoring of harmony. The girls studied engaged in a basic contrapuntal style of narration where the gossip story and development wove between listener and speaker.

Gossip as a story

Gossip provides good entertainment (Besnier 1989). Not only were most of the girls in the study skilled in making use of a range of linguistic skills in order to deliver the gossip with the most powerful impact, all enjoyed the dramatic presentations and responses. Gossip is delivered best in story form, and these girls told their stories in whispered secrecy and indignant, scandalized tones punctuated with joking comments resulting in much hilarity. Most could judge accurately when and where each mode was appropriate. Their informal conversations were ungrammatical in structure, and often interspersed with a variety of vulgar and swear words, but their language was functional. The arguments were structured and sequential and there was full use of dramatic tension, suspense, climax and humour.

The proficiency displayed by the girls in their use of gossip, to influence the group dynamics, may link to the identification of the range of social skills at the disposal of the more successful bullies previously mentioned (Sutton *et al.* 1999). It would appear that the potency of gossip, learnt through use over generations, for both positive and negative reasons, has infused the process with a sound structure and a polished and effective mode of presentation. These girls had begun to master these skills at a young age.

The framework of a gossip episode

The framework of a gossip episode is more complex than that of an insult or grassing sequence, being highly organized and presented in a systematic fash-ion to minimize the occurrence of a breakdown in communication (Sacks *et al.* 1974). The conversations of the girls studied showed an identifiable, sequen-tial framework to the gossip episodes. On occasions, the sequence looped back, repeating part of the format, resulting in several mini-episodes appearing within one sequence.

Context

The gossip may be set within a conversation, or it may occur without preamble or reference to prior subject matter. An example of the latter occurs when

Tracey makes an announcement, without context, in the form of a question: 'You know what? Angela says to Elaine that I'm seeing Tony and I'm not'. She then elaborates on this and entices others to join in her condemnation of Angela.

Attention grabbers

There appears to have been no identification of the attention-grabber stage in previous studies of the gossip process. Attention-grabbing phrases and sentences are used for dramatic effect, initially to catch the attention of a possible audience, and to be repeated should the gossip flag. 'You know what?' was the comment most frequently used by the girls to catch the attention of all within earshot. This was effective as it is difficult to resist a direct question. The girls were at an age when most sexual matters were still somewhat mysterious, confusing and taboo (Gottman and Parker 1986), so any remark with a sexual connotation would hook their attention. Nikki is joking when she says, 'Rachel was in bed with Tony last night', but she gets the full attention of those nearby. Specific names were guaranteed to demand attention, such as those of high-profile popular and unpopular girls, the names of teachers and anyone famous – or infamous. A command or demand would attract attention, and single trigger words such as 'party' or 'boyfriend' would command the interest of anyone within earshot.

Permission

Tacit permission is required from the listeners if the gossip is to continue successfully. This can be silence indicating encouragement to continue, or a single utterance such as 'Did she?', or agreement as in, 'I know'.

Core statement

The core statement may be a snippet, given as a taster, to allow listeners to entice more information or a more complex comment from the speaker.

> Denise: Do you know what? Guess what Rachel's done. She's only been and – well, you know what . . .? Well, she's cheeky, she is.
> Chorus: What's she done? Cheeky? Who's she been cheeky to?

Expansion

Expansion, also, does not appear to have been identified and named as a separate stage in other work, but these girls were quick to expand on any gossip they heard. Expansions are not necessarily grounded in fact, and a great deal of enjoyment was gained from escalating, hypothetical expansions. Often this was for fun but could lead to trouble when taken seriously.

Nikki: I'm sure Tracey's had a transplant.
Denise: What . . . transplant?
Nikki: Had them blown up. Boobs.
Denise: That's not a transplant.
Nikki: I know it isn't. But she's had them blown up.
Denise: Where do you think she's had them done?
Nikki: I think she wanted plastic surgery . . . like . . . Michael Jackson. I think she's Michael Jackson's sister the way she looks. Her nose is horrible.

The consensus of opinion is given eagerly, that Tracey's nose is 'horrible – like Michael Jackson's'.

Clarification

Clarifications are given in response to requests for fuller information.

Joanne: Her mam's helping with the dinners.
Denise: Whose mam?
Joanne: Her mam. She's going to help with the dinners. She'll get the best dinner.
Denise: Whose mam?
Joanne: Mandy's mam. That's not fair. She'll get the chips. She'll not get that green stuff we don't like.

Parrot comment

The parrot comment stage is another that has previously gone unrecognized. A parrot comment is one given by a listener who repeats a statement imme-diately, or later, in the conversation. It gives support, confirmation and encouragement to one who has already spoken. The parrot statement is a powerful strategy as it is influential in empowering the one whose original statement is repeated but, as those delivering parrot statements are not initiat-ing the insult or gossip, they are not accountable for any slanderous remarks and so avoid sanction.

Joanne was entertaining and nominated the most popular girl but, at times, she could be a troublemaker. She monitored closely all that went on and was quick to draw attention to the shortcomings of others. Her language structures were immature, and she had a restricted bank of vocabulary, but she was eager to contribute to any gossip she heard. She used parrot comments drawing on her skills of mimicry to full effect. Although a mischief-maker, her sense of play and fun, and her habit of singing tunefully at every opportunity, contributed to her popularity. Joanne had a basic sense of fair play, challenging others she thought to be acting unfairly, that was recognized by the other girls.

Kate also used parrot comments but she was less popular than Joanne. The girls seemed to sense that Joanne contributed to the gossip for fun and dramatic effect, as she would join in the flow of gossip about anyone. The comments made by Kate were directed at specific others with seemingly malicious intent. Unlike Kate, Joanne would parrot remarks made about other girls solely with the intent of providing entertainment for her audience. Kate did not appear to be aggressive, but she was influential in orchestrating attacks on others by adding comments to preceding remarks thus inciting emotional tension. By parroting carefully chosen remarks given by other girls, she was able to trigger verbal and physical attacks on girls she did not like without gaining the reputation of a troublemaker. The other girls seemed to sense this and did not allow her the popularity allocated to Joanne.

> Rachel: Pauline went in when I wanted to play out. She's mean, her.
> Kate: I know. She always goes in. She's mean, that's why.
> Rachel: I said, 'Why are you going in?' She said, 'I'm going in.'
> Kate: She never wants to play out, her. She always says, 'I'm going in.'
> She's always doing that. She's mean, her.

Parroting was also in evidence in the insult sequences. However, the repetition of an insult was simply to add weight to a prior comment, unlike the gossip episodes where Kate used these comments to manipulate opinions about other girls.

The disclaimer

The girls showed an awareness of the moral and social implications of making negative value judgements about others in their gossip. They drew upon the traditional disclaimers, 'I'm sorry to say this, but . . .' and 'I like Marie, but I have to say . . .'.

Challenges

A challenge must be made early in the gossip sequence if it is to be successful (Goodwin 1990). Usually high- or middle-status girls initiate gossip, as they have the confidence to make comments about others in public, so that challenges must come from equal- or higher-status girls. Challenges could come from lower-status girls, and even these challenges may be effective if made early enough, but as most listeners want to hear the gossip, the content becomes increasingly negative as more of the audience participate.

Repair work

Repair work is a strategy used to make a recovery from a successful challenge (Hedstrom 1984). It may be in the form of a correction, an apology (rarely used by these girls), deflection by use of humour or a change of focus.

The following illustrates both a challenge made by Rachel and a repair made by Denise:

Denise: Do you know what? Joanne did a bad thing.
Rachel: What? What bad thing?
Denise: Joanne was in school at night.
Rachel: Well, that's alright.
Denise: No. On Sunday.
Rachel: That's alright. She was in school for the meeting. For the Fair.
Denise: Well, that's alright. For the Fair.

Closure

Various endings are available; the conversation could lose impetus and drift to another topic, an effective punchline or joke could disrupt concentration, or the exit or entry of someone could break the flow.

Nikki: Do you know what? Angela says . . .
(A boy enters the room.)
Nikki: Hey. John. Get out of here. This is for the girls. You're not allowed in here.

The culprits and targets

The most troublesome and aggressive girls were the main gossips. The prime target for their gossip was Tracey who was guilty of several of the behaviours listed in Chapter 10 as reasons why girls are unpopular. The gossips were also guilty of these behaviours but they would monitor closely the behaviour of unpopular girls, taking every opportunity to show that they had broken the code of conduct. As Tracey was physically strong and confident, few girls tackled her face to face, so those less confident found gossip an effective mode of attack and revenge.

The content and function of gossip

Gossip is a mechanism used to avoid challenge, yet it achieves change. A lot of the gossip among the girls was for enjoyment and idle fun but other agendas were in evidence. The girls in the study used gossip as an interactive, entertaining mode of communication to cement, disrupt or initiate their complex interpersonal relationships. Gilmore (1978) proposes that we are most at risk from gossiping friends. The loss of friends was a major concern of the girls in the study and some gossip episodes concerned the behaviour and disloyalty of friends. The deviant behaviour of others, such as stealing and lying, also featured in their gossip.

Negative gossip centres on relationships and the destroying of reputations (Lees 1993; Duncan 1999). The girls in the study used gossip to attack the appearance or reputation of other girls. A common theme of malicious gossip among girls concerns the physical appearance of the target. As men preferred to mate with attractive women in evolutionary history, appearance was critical to female survival and reproductive success (Campbell 1995). Buss and Schmitt (1993) found that a common tactic employed by females, to make others undesirable to the opposite sex, was to attack their attractiveness and stylish clothing. Young people asked about the content of gossip stated that sexual comment was the largest single category (Crozier and Dimmock 1999). The girls in the study used gossip to attack those they considered a threat in an attempt to retain their own influence and confirm their own attractiveness. This is reminiscent of the way boys appear to use physical attacks against other boys to display their physical power. Perhaps the most powerful weapon in a gossip episode is humour and ridicule, as in the sequence related earlier about Tracey having her 'boobs' blown up. Gossip has the positive function of forging group support but, in doing this, the target of the gossip may be excluded.

The gossip episodes tracked the highs and lows of the interpersonal relationships within the class, with the escalation, frequency and severity of the gossip reflecting the quarrels and confrontations. Gossips are often considered popular as they need to have a keen interest in others. In addition, they need to be socially and linguistically skilled (Bergmann 1987; Goodman and Ben-Ze'ev 1994). Bergmann (1987) suggests that gossips are confident and in secure friendships. Nikki and Rachel were frequent gossips yet Nikki was in the only dyad relationship that endured the 16 months of the study. Rachel was not in a secure dyad but she was confident and popular within her group of friends and she had older friends out of school. Both monitored any threat to their friendships, and both were jealous of Tracey's relationship with the boys, her attractive appearance and, at the start of the study, her popularity with other girls. Tracey was the target of almost all the gossip as, along with the rationales given above, she displayed most of the behaviours found to contribute to girls being unpopular. This gave the other girls valid reasons for their attacks, which appeared to be based primarily in jealousy.

Rumour

Definition

I would suggest that the difference between gossip and rumour lies in the proposition that gossip concerns the personal matters of another whereas rumour pertains to the impersonal. As gossip targets the personal, it attracts avid interest, involves a more complex structure, and draws from a more extensive and creative vocabulary than does rumour. The initial pause, used to judge the reaction of the listeners, is common to both gossip and rumour.

Culprits and targets

Below is an example of a typical rumour episode between two of the girls in the study. The underlying factor in these conflict exchanges, presented as rumour, was Zara's jealousy of the friendship between Charlotte and Joanne. Zara had a close relationship with Joanne but, as she aimed to exclude anyone else, many low-key exchanges stemmed from the competition between Zara and Charlotte for the friendship of Joanne. Their rivalry often took the form of argumentative insult turns as described by Maltz and Borker (1982). Zara and Charlotte were to attend different secondary schools after the summer break and had an ongoing contest as to which school was the more desirable. This contest about schools appeared to be the vehicle, or conduit, for their conflict over their relationship with Joanne. The transfer to secondary school was a worrying time for all the girls as there was uncertainty about which schools would accept them. Rumours flourish in times of anxiety and uncertainty (Rosnow and Fine 1976, 1996; Adams and Bristow 1979). These two girls dominated the giving and receiving of rumours, reflecting their mutual suspicion and dislike.

> Charlotte: The toilets in that school are manky. ['Manky' is a dialect word for dirty.]
> Zara: And have you seen the . . . that school? Have you seen the toilets? I bet you haven't. You want to see the state of the toilets.
> Charlotte: Well, my sister . . . That's not what I meant . . . My sister . . . my step sister goes there and she says . . . that . . . she says . . . it's got thingy [graffiti] written all over it.
> Zara: That not it. The toilets shine like gold. I'm telling you.

Topics of rumour

Other rumours circulated at the time of the study about the video equipment, the purpose of the study, whether a particular glue was a hallucinogenic, and confusion about whether harmful rays were emitted by television aerials and mobile phones. There were also rumours about what would be acceptable as uniform in the various schools they would be attending. The ongoing contest between Charlotte and Zara, over which was the better secondary school, was by far the most dominant rumour.

The framework of a rumour episode

The stages of the core statement, clarification, expansion, challenges and subsequent repair work are common to rumour and gossip. As with gossip, rumour may be presented in context or without preamble.

The language of rumour

The language used in the rumour episodes was similar to that used in the gossip sequences but curtailed and presented in a turn-taking style rather than a sequential storyline. However, as the two forms, gossip and rumour, were not employed by the same girls, differences in the language of the girls could account for differences in the language used in the insult and gossip sequences.

In summary, there was little evidence of rumour in the conversations of the girls. The underlying function of the rumour episodes appeared to be the challenging, manipulating or affirming of status. The more aggressive girls used gossip, rather than rumour, as a mode of aggression. The two girls who used rumour most used it primarily to express their antagonistic relationship.

Suggested approaches

1 Gossip can be stopped in the initial stages by anyone but it takes confidence to halt the story later. Discuss how girls can interrupt gossip without giving offence to friends.

2 Suggest they ask the girl gossiping how she found out the factual content of the gossip. Ask how she knows this to be true. Is it an opinion she is offering or fact?

3 Discuss with girls what defines gossip. Explore the difference between good and bad gossip.

4 Discuss the uses of gossip. What can we usefully learn from discussing others in their absence? Suggestions could include professional practice, social mores and acceptable behaviour.

5 Highlight the difference between slander and libel. Stress the danger of gossiping in the context of the judicial system.

6 Discuss the adage 'gossip can come back to bite you'. What does this mean? Emphasize that it is often possible to do a backward chaining exercise. By asking each person in turn 'Who told you?', and working backwards, it is often possible to identify the originator of the gossip.

7 Gossip can be entertaining. Put the girls in small groups of three or four. One of the girls overhears the others gossiping about her. Ask how she feels. Do this with the girls in turn. Even though this is role play, it can help the girls understand that gossip can be unpleasant for the target.

8 Discuss with the girls why anyone would need to gossip about others. It is often a way of sharing and sounding out opinions. Is there a less personal way of doing this?

9 Ask if they accept that malicious gossip is a type of bullying, If so, how could they work as a group to stop such gossiping?

10 Making unpleasant remarks, or gossiping about a person, quickly becomes a habit. There are ways of stopping oneself from joining in gossip or contributing to malicious comments. You could suggest the girls use a traditional way to remind themselves to stop and think. For example, they could pull their thumb or pinch themselves whenever they are about to make an unfavourable comment, or they could match each unfavourable comment with a positive one.

11 Discuss if they think girls gossip more than boys do. If so, ask why this could be. They may be interested in carrying out a survey among other students to see if there is a gender difference and then among adults to see if this behaviour changes with age.

12 Remind girls that people recognize whom they can trust. Could they trust a gossip with a secret? People have greater respect for those who do not pass on information given to them by others.

SECTION 5
Emotional Issues

16 The more deadly of the species?

Hidden problem

As bullying among girls has emerged as a cause for concern only in recent years, there are few reliable long-term studies matched for age, background and culture of participants, size of cohort, situation and methodology. Owing to the covert nature of the indirect bullying preferred by girls, the research methodology needs to be sophisticated. As many of the emotional and psychological effects develop over time, long-term, and consequently expensive, studies are required. Playground observations do not show in sufficient detail many of the types of bullying used by girls. This has resulted in adults having only superficial knowledge of the ways in which girls attack their targets. Many adults have spoken movingly of their adverse experiences during their schooldays and of the emotional and psychological baggage they have carried over the years. For many, these negative experiences have left indelible scars.

Destructive behaviours

A surprisingly high number of young people in our schools are suffering from social-psychological distress, including depression, low self-esteem, loneliness and social anxiety due to bullying (Sharp 1995; Hawker and Boulton 1996). Many are confused, hurt and use irrational self-talk; some absent themselves from school or leave school permanently, and some even resort to suicide (Owens *et al.* 2000). The emotional effects of bullying cause a downward spiral in self-esteem and confidence so that the young person becomes even more vulnerable and at greater risk (Besag 1989). It is not clear whether bullies choose their victims because their vulnerability makes them easy targets, or if victims develop low self-esteem because of the bullying. It would seem reasonable to propose that a combination of both factors may be present.

Although aggression between girls is often less visible, and so more easily missed or misinterpreted than the overt modes more usually employed by boys, we now recognize that it can be equally as destructive (Boulton and Hawker 1997). Verbal, social and psychological forms of bullying can drive a child to suicide, having equal potency to modes of physical aggression (Hawker and Boulton 1996; Owens *et al.* 2000). If we accept the range of indirect aggressions used by girls as forms of bullying, we can begin to unravel the destructive nature of the process. Active rejection, being passively neglected, and being ignored by others are different concepts but all may cause extreme emotional distress in the lonely child. Extremes of low or high status in the group may leave a permanent mark on the personality (Coie 1990). Social exclusion is a good predictor of problems such as depression, loneliness, anxiety and reduction in self-worth (Gilbert 1992; Hawker and Boulton 1996; Boulton and Hawker 1997). Female victims of bullying score low on measures of self-perceived social acceptance compared with those not bullied (Boulton and Smith 1994). In a study carried out by Kupersmidt and Patterson (1991), rejected girls were found to be more than twice as likely, and neglected girls four times as likely, to report high levels of depression in pre-adolescence than other girls.

This book is primarily about girls, but we must remember that boys also become depressed. In several countries, such as the USA, Australia and New Zealand, the extent of this problem has been recognized for some time and considerable preventative work has been carried out owing to the high level of reported suicide and suicide intent among young males. Unfortunately, most boys appear not to seek emotional support from their friends and adults in the way girls do. This means that, although the negative behaviours used among girls appear more harmful than the more direct attacks that take place among boys, the level of distress experienced by boys is probably equal to that of girls.

Although we have gleaned information about the emotional effects of bullying on the victim, we know less about the effect on the bully. The repercussions of bullying affect not only the victims but also the witnesses and bullies. Many aggressors experience negative effects if allowed to continue their bullying behaviour. The bully learns it is possible to gain emotional, social or monetary benefit from the bullying, so their *modus operandi* may become habitual. They learn they can use dominance for their own purposes, an attitude that can lead to a career of crime (Olweus 1993). A significant number of young male bullies make at least two court appearances for anti-social behaviour in early adulthood (Olweus 1978). Social aggression is linked to later peer problems with an expectation of a negative outcome such as delinquency and anti-social behaviour (Coie and Dodge 1998). There are links to depression in girls who bully (Obeidallah and Earls 1999) and a prediction of early pregnancy (Miller-Johnson *et al.* 2005).

Locus of control

There is an established link between being the victim of bullying and posses-sing an external locus of control (Trad 1987). Those with an external locus of control consider others to be in control of their lives, feeling like leaves blown in the wind and at the mercy of whatever life should dictate. An external locus of control results in victims being less able to use effective coping strategies as they consider they will be unable to effect any positive change (Seligman and Peterson 1986).

Those with an internal locus of control feel more in control of their lives. Not all who bully have low self-esteem as many bullies are confident and self-assured (Sutton *et al.* 1999). It is interesting to speculate whether bullies with low self-esteem have an internal locus of control. Perhaps bullies fall into two categories. Those with an external locus of control may bully others as a reaction to events seemingly beyond their control, acting without much faith that the bullying will improve their situation, but using aggression in anger or frustration. A different group of bullies may have an internal locus of control and bully others believing that they are able to have some impact on their victim or the situation. The distinguishing factor between the two groups would be their rationale for bullying and the antici-pated outcome.

Victims are more likely to have an external locus of control if they have been the butt of bullying for some time. Feeling helpless, they are less likely to implement effective coping strategies. These feelings of hopelessness can be instrumental in the emergence of depression. Those who manage to overcome their tormentors will be more likely to develop an internal locus of control. The prediction would be that they would feel more in control of their lives if their coping strategies were successful (Sharp 1995).

Why has the problem been underestimated?

A girlie culture or serious squabbles?

I have noticed that many girls appear to spend a large proportion of their time squabbling over seemingly trivial, low-key matters without adults understand-ing the level of distress such actions can cause. Squabbling, gossiping and telling tales appear to be part of the everyday interactions among many girls. Perhaps it is because 'sneaking' friends is such a common occurrence in girls' friendship relations that the emotional impact is underestimated. Only half the teachers in junior schools, and one-fifth of the teachers in secondary schools, considered deliberate social exclusion to be bullying (Boulton and Hawker 1997), yet this is a particularly common form of bullying among girls (Katz *et al.* 2001). Busy teachers appear to have summarily dismissed these verbal attacks as just 'bitching'. Traditionally, the complaints about gossiping, quarrelling and social exclusion have remained unchallenged, with the result that girls involved in bullying others often consider this an acceptable way to behave. These behaviours have been in the repertoire of common social interactions among girls for so long that many consider them acceptable modes of settling disputes. It seems embedded in our culture to accept this behaviour from girls.

Hidden by a halo

Girls have enjoyed a halo effect in the past as we consider females the more gentle sex. Violence between females attracts more public attention than similar acts of aggression between men. Even professionals are more easily shocked when a murderer is discovered to be female than when a male culprit is identified (Campbell 1995). In white, middle-class western cultures, there remains a trend for aggressive women to be perceived as deficient in personal control, mentally ill or abnormal (Underwood 2003). This results in female aggression being regarded as doubly deviant since it violates the mores of expected sex-appropriate behaviour as well as criminal law (Merten 1997). Perhaps the current increase in overt aggression among females may soon see their halo topple.

Troubled or troublesome?

Many of those most troublesome in our schools and communities are those most vulnerable. Our misunderstanding of the power of such complex emotions as depression and suicide intent in the young may be because even older children and adolescents find it difficult to offer verbal descriptions and explanations of their suffering.

Although not necessarily related to bullying, suicide intent may be evident in children as young as 6 years (BBC News 2001). In addition, research has shown that at least 1 in 5 children has some degree of mental health problem. These findings have been replicated in studies in Australia, Canada, New Zealand, the USA and the UK (Australian Institute of Family Studies 1999; Geballe 2000; Parliamentary Monitoring Group 2001; Paediatrics and Child Health 2004).

As the young may not be able to verbalize their feelings, signs of distress such as soiling, eating disorders, behaviour and social difficulties may be misinterpreted. The negative emotions of older children may be manifest by their challenging and risk-taking actions such as self-harm, social withdrawal, alcohol and drug abuse or even prostitution. If the future looks intolerable, some may feel unwilling to make the effort to battle against seemingly insurmountable odds, or prolong their misery by taking self-protective action.

Instead, they may turn to attractive, accessible and immediate means for amelioration of their suffering that act adversely in the long term. Sadly, these behaviours often alienate those adults who could care for those most in need of their help.

Difficult to prove

Part of the power of the modes of indirect bullying preferred by girls is that it is established before anyone recognizes it for what it is. These modes of attack take place under the eyes of adults who may fail to identify their potency to harm. In addition, as a group of girls is often involved, it is a more powerful process than the one-to-one fight more usually occurring between boys.

Difficult to challenge

Culprits rarely admit to using indirect aggression (Lagerspetz *et al.* 1988; Bjorkqvist *et al.* 1992b; Eslea and Smith 1994). This may be because they fear sanctions or because they do not recognize their actions as bullying. Young people may know that it is unfair to exclude a girl from their group, yet dismiss such actions as trivial. Adults supporting the girl may find it difficult to challenge culprits who proffer excuses and seek escape routes. Only the recipient can know how terrifying it can be to get 'the look' from her attacker, or how stigmatizing it is to have no one speak to her for the whole school day. If challenged, female bullies often state that it is their right to choose their own friends.

No physical clues

There is a less obvious distinction between the powerful and the vulnerable among girls than is present between boys. I have often found it possible to identify boys who are bullies, and those at risk, by observing their behaviour and demeanour. The most powerful girls may not be those most visibly dominant in the peer group as the smallest, or most demure girl may be manipulating the rest.

Victims may not understand it is bullying

Only recently have we begun to understand the structure and powerful negative effects of behaviours such as social exclusion (Munthe 1989; Hawker and Boulton 1996). Victims are quickly demoralized by verbal abuse and may only make sense of what has happened to them by believing their attackers and accepting that they are unworthy of their friendship. They assume their unhappy situation is due to their having no value as friends. Sadly, if they blame anyone, they blame themselves.

Peers misunderstand

Peer witnesses may miss, or misinterpret, the covert attacks of girls, making it more difficult for the peacemakers to challenge the culprits. There is a clearer line of demarcation drawn by young people between overtly negative behaviours, more frequently used by boys, and acceptable social mores and practice, making it easier for willing peers to take appropriate action.

Why is girls' bullying so destructive?

Enmeshed relationships

It would seem that we have allowed girls to think of their negative behaviour as the norm. This results in those observing the bullying seeming to play no active part in, and taking no responsibility for, the distress of the target. The structure of girls' friendship groups, involving the emotional enmeshment of the members, adds to the potency of the bullying attacks. If there is a tight, cohesive bond within a group, there may be no need to use the more overt forms of aggression to cause distress: the hidden mechanisms of insult, gossip, rumour and ostracism may be powerful and damaging enough (Bjorkqvist *et al.* 1992b; Ahmad and Smith 1994; Crick and Grotpeter 1995). If the majority of those in a close friendship group behave in an unfortunate manner to one of the members, this gives tacit permission to the rest to join in the attacks. Importantly, any wishing to challenge the powerful may feel daunted, helpless and in fear of reprisals or scorn, and so fail to protect the vulnerable girl.

Emotional support

Girls choose friends who are similar to themselves, who share their values and interests, and with whom they can discuss the intimate details of their lives. Girls enjoy sharing emotions, secrets and confidences (Lever 1976; Gottman and Parker 1986). This adds potency to the loss of a close friend as they would lose not only a playmate but also a counsellor who would listen to their concerns and anxieties. The girls in the activity club named this as a highly valued quality in a friend.

Some girls disclosed intimate feelings and information about family quarrels and break-ups to each other and gained solace at a surprisingly sophisticated level. Adults may underestimate the skills that even young children display in offering emotional support to their friends. As some discussed serious issues concerning family matters with their friends, it was imperative that their confidences were respected. Being trustworthy was a quality highly valued by these girls. Betraying a confidence, or spreading gossip, was enough to break a relationship acrimoniously and all would hear that the culprit was not to be trusted.

Supportive peer relationships may be more important nowadays than in the past owing to the fragmentation of family structures (Asher and Coie 1990). To gauge the power of the loss of a close friend, we may consider that many lifelong relationships begin at school. Adults may consider children to have less powerful emotions than those older, but the young are unseasoned in ways of coping with loss. An ostracized girl is in a vulnerable position as she may find it difficult to cope emotionally on her own and be eager to gain acceptance back into the group. This gives permission, and opportunity, for the bullies to continue their attacks. Many girls pay a high cost for the intimacy of their friendships. As the close friendship bonds forged between girls are so highly valued, they offer a power base open to manipulation.

Emotional awareness

Adolescence has been termed a 'time of storm and stress' for many (Hall 1904), and 'a time of fusion of emotion and reason' (Gottman and Mettatal 1986). At this age, there is a growing awareness, along with confusion, regarding opposing emotions such as trust and wariness, dependency and independence. It is during adolescence that these conflicting emotions fuse within an individual schema so that we eventually come to terms with everyone having positive and negative attributes. This may lead to girls, being more emotionally involved with their peers than are boys, changing their allegiances to each other frequently in their attempt to come to terms with the opposing facets in the personalities of their friends.

Unpredictability

As it is most often the friends or acquaintances of targeted girls who attack them, they feel unprepared, betrayed and confused. The attacks of girls, due to jealousy, pique, irritation or other emotive reasons, often occur unexpectedly, making it difficult for girls to prepare for, and cope with, the emotional repercussions. Bullying between boys is more predictable as it is more common for those physically strong to attack the weak. As the rough-housing play of boys starts from an early age, they soon gain an indication of where they stand on the dominance hierarchy (Omark *et al.* 1973; Petit *et al.* 1990; Smith and Boulton 1990). This allows for those aware of their physical vulnerability to put in place, and practise, strategies such as avoidance and deflection thus enabling them to adjust or amend their social position.

Moving the goalposts

Girls evaluate and compare themselves to others on their own terms using subjective evaluations. If they do not wish to have a girl as a friend, they simply change their demands. Girls making critical comments can move their goalposts as their judgements are subjective. They may claim justification for the attacks because their target comes from an affluent family or one socially disadvantaged; they may say a girl is too talkative or too quiet, too fat or too thin. If they wish to attack, they will find a rationale. In this way, the victim feels powerless; she can never attain the standards demanded. Dominant girls may tell a vulnerable girl that she is 'a fat loser' but, if she loses weight, they will call her 'stick pin'. Only when the target realizes that, in trying to meet their demands she is on a fool's errand, is there any hope of her coming to terms with the situation.

Boys are more likely to use tangible measures to judge each other. They judge a boy a worthy companion by an informal audit of his strength and physical skills, and the ability to defend himself and others rather than assessing his personal qualities. This objective evaluation of visible, measurable skills could make rejection easier to bear. It would seem easier to be excluded from games because of inadequate skill than because you are deemed worthless as a person.

No escape route for girls

Targeted girls rarely find avoidance tactics successful. As the attacks relate to their social relationships and unstable friendships, it is most often girls with whom the targets are familiar that perpetrate the bullying (Lagerspetz *et al.* 1988; Munthe 1989; Roland, cited in Besag 1989; Olweus 1993; Rivers and Smith 1994). The bullies may have been friends of their target, even recent 'best friends', thus making it difficult for girls under attack to use the avoidance tactics accessible to boys. Male bullies pick on the vulnerable even if he is a stranger met on the way home from school. Their target may be able to use avoidance strategies such as changing his route to school or altering his time of entering and leaving. Avoiding the bullies can be an effective means of escape for boys as it is often a case of 'out of sight, out of mind'; this is not so with girls who may have been friends in the recent past.

The hostage situation

The psychological, emotional and social facets integral to the covert modes of bullying make them more difficult to cope with than physical attacks as they primarily involve the manipulation of the emotions of the target. The strategies employed to exclude, ostracize, ridicule or demoralize another girl may be more sophisticated than has been acknowledged. This is because these behaviours thrive on the victim being in a situation equivalent to a hostage situation where one party is obviously the more powerful. The uncertainty of what will happen increases the power of the attacker while decreasing the power of the hostage. One minute the attackers are friendly, the next they are abusive; the bullies may entice a girl into their group but the next minute they reject or attack her. The uncertainty of not knowing how the bullies will behave increases the victim's tension and distress. A combination of hope and despair confuses the cognitive processes, making the strategy one of the most powerful psychological mechanisms for holding the victim passive in the abusive situation.

Behaviours common to a bullying and hostage situation

- *Repetitive threat.* The accumulation of threats increases their potency while diminishing the victim's resistance.
- *Brainwashing.* Repeated abusive comments lower the self-esteem of the victim, leading to further feelings of helplessness and vulnerability. Victims come to believe they are to blame for not defending themselves and that rationales given by the perpetrators for the attacks are valid.
- *Degradation.* A girl constantly called an abusive name, possibly by the whole class or year group, may come to believe the bullies. It is difficult to retain self-belief when faced with repeated insult. In addition, her shame may prevent her from seeking help.
- *Physical or emotional isolation.* The process of systematic separation of the target from relevant others can be identified in most forms of bullying. A girl enticed into a group may find herself in a socially precarious situation. Should she lose her status in the new group, it is unlikely that her old friends will welcome her back.
- *Name calling.* Name calling is a traditional way of denigrating a victim as the names used are demeaning and often dehumanizing such as 'bitch' or 'cow' (Besag 1989).
- *Rhymes and rhythm.* Bullies often sustain their bullying by incorporating rhymes and rhythmic cadences in their attacks. Chanting and singing, accompanied by humorous content and gestures, encourage the participation of bystanders.
- *Intermittent attacks.* The unpredictability of the attacks makes the emotional repercussions particularly potent. We can prepare for danger – a surge of adrenaline helps us prepare for a fight-or-flight response – but we cannot prepare for a surprise attack.

The synchronized spirals

Over time, the increase in the power, competence and confidence of the attacker is matched by a corresponding decrease in the confidence and self-esteem of the victim (Figure 16.1).

Cycle of abuse

There appears to be a cyclical pattern present in many forms of abuse (Figure 16.2).

Emotional effects of the abuse

- Powerlessness – the victim feels unable to fight or flee and so flounders.
- Hopelessness – no help seems available.
- Uncertainty – the attacks are unpredictable
- Trapped – the victim feels emotionally or physically trapped.
- Guilt – the victim has no access to effective defence strategies.
- Shame – the victim feels ashamed and denigrated by the nature of the abusive attack and by feeling unable to take effective defensive action.
- Fear – of attack and possible reprisals should they seek help.
- Anxiety – may lead to depression.
- Loss of identity – due to denigrating name calling.

In summary, modes used by females to establish dominance, such as demeaning another girl by ignoring her, dismissing her comments, by use of sarcasm or ostracizing her from the group, may be more powerful than the 'sword' of overt dominance used by boys (Underwood *et al.* 2001)

Confidence and self-esteem of the victim

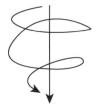

Power, competence and confidence of the attacker

Figure 16.1   The synchronized spirals.

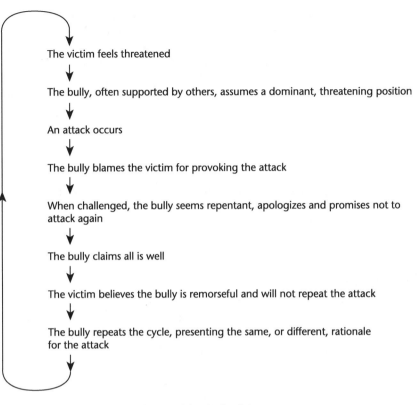

The victim feels threatened

The bully, often supported by others, assumes a dominant, threatening position

An attack occurs

The bully blames the victim for provoking the attack

When challenged, the bully seems repentant, apologizes and promises not to attack again

The bully claims all is well

The victim believes the bully is remorseful and will not repeat the attack

The bully repeats the cycle, presenting the same, or different, rationale for the attack

Figure 16.2   Cycle of abuse.

Can't break away

Adults are often mystified when a girl refuses to leave an abusive friend or group. Encouraging her to stay away may be futile; she may only want to resume the close relationship she once enjoyed with the girls now bullying her. One study found that 78 per cent of older adolescent girls kept links with those involved in accusations and aggressive attacks targeting them once a conflict was over (Campbell and Muncer 1987). As discussed earlier, there would seem to be a need among most girls for affiliation and emotional connectedness. A combination of reluctance to make an emotional break from the group, alongside an eagerness for resumption of the friendship, contributes to the fractious nature and instability in girls' groups.

The reluctance of the victim to leave the group may be due to her feeling that she will be under a harsh spotlight where all will be aware of the shame of her rejection. However, to understand this more fully, it may be helpful to consider the psychology of abuse. Why do so many abused adults stay in an abusive relationship? Why do the emotional ties remain long after a physical separation? The downward spiral of abuse results in the victim feeling confused, unworthy, demoralized and, above all, helplessly trapped in the situation as there is little emotional and psychological energy to spare to think clearly and logically. Victims come to believe that if only it were possible to meet the expectations of the attackers, they would gain their acceptance, if not their respect. This often leads the victim on a futile path striving to comply with the demands of the abuser.

Friends difficult to replace

Once rejected, ridiculed and shunned for personal reasons, it may be hard for a young girl to believe that she is worthy of acceptance. Her loss of self-esteem, and fear of rejection, may make it hard for her to integrate into alternative groups.

A social death

A characteristic of girls' bullying is that the aggressors ensure their victim is isolated for as long as they take an interest, even when their provocative attacks have ceased. The target is in an emotionally vulnerable position having no access to emotional or physical support. The bullies may not be satisfied with excluding her from their friendship circle but ensure that no others befriend her by the use of malicious gossip and threats, or by enticing her previous friends into their group. They find effective ways of influencing others, even those in a distant locality, so that the exclusion can feel like social death for a girl. The target will not know whether the exclusion is to be short or long term, thus adding to the trauma. The stigmatization and isolation could continue for the rest of the girl's school career, or the bullies may resume the friendship prior to attacking another girl.

Why me?

There appears little overt rationale in the choice of a girl selected for rejection, or ridicule, so she is often left confused and bewildered (Munthe 1989). She may never know why she was a victim or later allowed back into the group. As targets often find no reason for the attacks, they have no idea how to remedy the situation.

Lack of reparative work

Once all self-esteem and confidence are lost, the victim is defenceless and in a precarious situation. Adults freed from a hostage situation often have recourse to reparative work with a psychologist or therapist. It is by no means certain that young victims, similarly emotionally or psychologically damaged by bullying, will have any such support.

Suggested approaches

1   There needs to be some recognition and acceptance of depression in the young and develop relevant preventative strategies. See Section 7 for suggestions.
2   Sensitive, informed and factual discussion about emotions such as sadness and depression should be tackled at home and at school. Young people need to recognize and understand the difference between sadness and depression. Sadness usually has a focus so we often know the reason for our sadness. It is transitory and we can cheer ourselves up. It does not affect other areas of our functioning so we can get on with our life and continue our normal pattern of behaviour.
3   Young people need to recognize and have access to a range of resilience techniques. These need to be practised in advance of difficulties occurring.
4   Simple techniques have been proven to be effective as part of a therapeutic approach. Physical movement and exercise results in chemical changes in the body that bring about an enhanced emotional state. A mantra could be 'Lift your body, lift your spirits' or 'Up, out and about'.
5   Encourage the girl to take up a hobby or interest and to get passionate about something. This will take her mind off the problem in addition to offering a way of meeting new friends.
6   Encourage her to do something for someone else – to start a club or games group for younger people, to offer to do some gardening or walk a dog for someone who needs help.
7   Depression is pervasive and invades all thoughts. A diary can show that the bullying is less frequent and severe than was thought.
8   Girls need to know that they are not to blame for the attacks, as they tend to blame themselves.
9   Girls need to understand that the attacks are deliberately used to cause distress and pain and are intentionally personal and destructive.

17 The green-eyed god

Why do girls compete?

Emotional and practical rationales for gender differences in preferred modes of aggression have been given in previous chapters, but they do not address the puzzle as to why girls are so disputatious within their friendship groups. Boys jostle for status, dominance and to display their physical prowess but this does not appear to be the source of the disputes between girls. Much of the trouble erupting between girls, resulting in the fractured nature of their friendship bonds, appears sourced in feelings of jealousy. However, there has been little explanation given for why this should lie at the root of their unstable friendships. What clouds the issue is that there is often no obvious, factual reason for others to be jealous of a targeted girl so, as it remains unclear what the aggressors gain from their attacks, the source of their rejection remains a mystery (Munthe 1989; Pipher 1994; Simmons 2002; Wiseman 2002).

Boys need an audience

The primary rationale for bullying that emerges in the case of boys is the need of some to demonstrate, or confirm, their physical power over others (Bowers 1973; Wachtel 1973; Olweus 1978, 1993). Just as the cockerel stands on the dung heap to crow, many boys seem to have the need to prove, to themselves and others, that they hold a dominant position in the group. It is rare for bullying episodes between boys to occur without the involvement of bystanders, albeit in the passive role of 'silent observers' (Besag 1989; Bjorkqvist *et al.* 1992b; Sharp and Cowie 1998). Boys like to have an audience to appreciate their dominance. They use the presence of the 'gallery' to boost their confidence, display their power and ward off challenge (Bowers 1973; Wachtel 1973). A gathering crowd will incite male bullies to escalate a physical attack, whether it is a fight between young lads on the school field or men in a pub brawl. Boys who attack others often have members of their group in the roles of assistants to help them, and reinforcers to encourage and support them in their attacks (Bjorkqvist *et al.* 1992b). It is less common to see females fighting in front of a crowd as their modes of aggression, being covert, lend themselves less effectively to a large audience. Some modes used by girls, such as gossip, are most potent if spread rapidly among a large number, but these are not carried out in front of a crowd. In summary, although both boys and girls appear to use aggression in the context of power, they seem to employ it in different ways.

The rough and tumble play of young boys, such as wrestling, kick boxing and fighting, is considered an acceptable manner of testing out strength and confidence. This results in there being an established hierarchy of dominance in a boys' group from an early age (Pellegrini and Smith 1998), whereas girls' friendship groups seem to be more egalitarian than hierarchical (Charlesworth and Dzur 1987; Campbell 1995). There was a hierarchical structure in some of the groups of girls in the class studied but these were difficult even for the girls to identify. The most dominant girls may be less clearly identifiable than in male groupings as all decisions among girls appear to go to arbitration, resulting in long negotiations that usually end in compromise (Cross and Madson 1997). All may need to be comfortable with the final decision. However, as happened in the groups of girls studied, it is likely that one person more usually has her own way, or point of view accepted, or at least the last word signalling the end of the conversation. Other members, sometimes silently and grudgingly, may defer to her seemingly superior knowledge, negotiating skills, verbal or physical dominance. Those who ignore the convention of egalitarian female group dynamics do so at their peril as they may be labelled 'bossy' and are either 'cut down to size' or ostracized.

Fight for your man

Perhaps we can look to the adult world for rationales to explain the fractious nature of girls' friendship groups. In comparison with adult males, Campbell (1995) suggests that adult females have a different mode, source and reason for their aggression. Women fight over the selection and acquisition of a mate (Campbell 2004). They would seem to fight over ownership of a man, whether the relationship is in existence, in anticipation, or merely in hope. A woman may attack another dressed provocatively, or thought to be flirtatious, if she believes her man is the target. This predatory behaviour may exist only in her imagination but can result in a violent attack. Campbell suggests that female aggression is triggered by three principal areas of challenge: attacks on sexual reputation; competition over accession to desirable partners; and jealousy with regard to propriety and ownership of partner and resources. In other words, females fight not only over who gets the best mate but also in relation to keeping him faithful. Advances in science may have some influence on those who see their primary role as motherhood. There are new ways of child bearing, such as *in vitro* fertilization and surrogate parenting, that do not require the male–female attraction bond for the production of offspring. Eventually, this may lessen the angst of women to secure a desirable mate.

Females also fight to protect their sexual reputation. Campbell found that many of the most fiercely fought battles among the young women she studied concerned refuting accusations of sexual infidelity. A study of sexual bullying among girls in one secondary school offers similar findings (Duncan 1999). Much of the abusive language used among girls concerns accusation of sexual infidelity and promiscuity. Duncan found accusations of sexual licence the most provoking of all attacks, and the violent repercussions triggered by such verbal attacks considered to be justified by all. Even the much younger girls attending the activity club used sexual name calling and accusations in their attacks on other girls.

The local Lothario

The fight is on among girls surprisingly early for the male considered the best in the bunch. The three rationales given by Campbell (1995) for aggression among young women – attacks on sexual reputation; competition for desirable partners; jealousy with regard to ownership of partner and resources – were already in evidence in the class studied by the time the girls were only 11 years old. The more physically mature and precocious of these girls were already arguing and fighting over whom they considered the most attractive male in the class. This was in terms of his strength, his ability to defend himself and others, and his level of maturity and physical attractiveness, all factors given as rationales for selection. The young lad favoured by the girls was not interested in the role of local Lothario allocated to him. Boys attracting this attention can be oblivious to the intense interest in them despite the quarrels, arguments and fights among the girls for ownership.

I have found jealousy concerning boys considered as future, present and past partners is often at the source of conflicts between adolescent girls. The manifestation of this jealousy may obscure an underlying rationale. Girls may only compare each other in terms of dress or attractiveness, without direct reference to any boy, but jealousy regarding competition for male partners most often underlies their disputes and fractured friendships. Girls in their early teens, and perhaps younger, need to assimilate norms of behaviour and to negotiate procedures in their attempts to secure boyfriends that are new to them. Novices to the procedures encounter much heartache as they struggle to learn the game play. In their eagerness to acquire a particular boy, some consider it necessary to employ devious means.

Many subtle facets are in evidence within the conflicts of girls. Even if a girl is not in a relationship with a particular boy, her proprietorial attitude may continue to cause mayhem. Established members of a class, or community, view a newcomer with a suspicion that may be justified as males are thought to be attracted to novelty when seeking a partner (Marsh and Paton 1984; Campbell *et al.* 1993). Characteristically, an aggrieved, jealous or possessive girl will blame another girl for a boy's infidelity or lack of interest. Girls rarely blame the boy for any transgression, even if he is at fault (Keise 1992; Campbell 1995; Duncan 1999).

A further cause for the jealousy, and subsequent aggression, occurring among girls relates to competition for those considered optimum male partners. This is a multifaceted process where several dynamics intertwine. As girls link their relationships with boys to status, how they are to secure a desired partner is a major concern to many young girls and women (Schofield 1981; Goodwin 1990). Many consider they need a male partner to give them an identity and status. The higher the status of the male, the higher is their reflected status as an attractive female. The more precocious girls in the class studied ranked themselves according to how they considered they fared in attracting prized boys. Those flaunting their ability to attract the desirable boys came under attack from other girls.

The above rationale does not explain why girls too young to be interested in securing a male partner quarrel acrimoniously. As noted in Chapter 9, girls appear from a very early age to enmesh themselves in their female friendships in the manner of lovers. Information collated from research findings, supported by many conversations with adolescent girls, indicates that, as they move into the teenage years, they form small friendship groups, leaving behind the intense dyad relationships. Perhaps, at this time, they transfer their jealousies and angst from their lover-like dyad female friendships to their emotional connections with boys.

The beauty industry

It could be argued that western culture encourages aggressive female competition, albeit tacitly. Many of the most profitable industries in the world relate to the search of women to seek, possess and hold on to desirable partners. The beauty industry is one of the most flourishing, encompassing counter sales of make-up products, fashion items, jewellery, publications and the promotion of female icons. In addition, the vast bank of literature focused towards female sales often relates, directly or indirectly, to the search and securing of a desirable male. As stated earlier, most females must attract males if they are to engage in the reproductive process. This results in many spending fortunes to retain a youthful appearance in order to present themselves as still being of childbearing years, as this indicator of youthfulness is a potent draw for males.

This is so even though a child may not be the desired outcome of either partner. In recent years, there has been an unprecedented boom in the plastic surgery industry as a youthful appearance is still attractive to many men. An informal perusal of dating advertisements shows males seek desirable physical features in a female partner, but also emphasize an ideal age that clearly lies within the relatively narrow band of childbearing years.

Optimum providers

Having attracted her male, the female must ensure she has access to the means to provide for any future offspring (Campbell 1995). Traditionally, males have been the main provider, or had chief access to essential resources. Whereas males appear to seek attractive women of childbearing years, men advertising for partners tend to state that they are homeowners to advertise their financial status. This tacitly proclaims they can provide for a female partner and her offspring.

When desirable males are in short supply, as in areas and times of financial and social disadvantage, female competition for them is relatively high (Draper and Harpending 1988). There is evidence that intra-female aggression takes more direct and physical forms in conditions of resource scarcity; girls living in areas of social and economic disadvantage appear to use physical aggression more readily than others (Campbell *et al.* 1985; Campbell and Muncer 1987; Ness 2004). However, there may be other reasons why female aggression is an accepted modus operandi in localities of economic disadvantage, such as the need for effective survival skills. Nonetheless, a positive correlation appears to exist between rates of female unemployment and welfare dependency and females' use of aggression over desirable male partners (Campbell *et al.* 1985; Campbell and Muncer 1987). It may be that hard times produce 'hard' women. Ness (2004) describes how structural and cultural factors promote violence between females of African-American and Hispanic origin in the impoverished inner-city areas in west and north-east Philadelphia. In her comparison of female aggression in pre-colonial and colonial Zambia, Glazer (1992) found that physical aggression became more pervasive between women when they had little control over access to or the distribution of resources.

Most females have a higher threshold in the use of physical aggression than males and seem able to delay a violent response to provocation more easily (Campbell 1995). This being so, they require correspondingly more powerful provocation to trigger them into action. However, studies indicate that, when necessary, females will fight in any way possible for access to essential resources such as the best male provider. Arguments over partners erupting between young females can be verbally and physically violent. Women can and do fight, but usually in less obvious, and perhaps more imaginative, ways than their male counterparts. It is still rare to see women fight physically in public unless excessive intake of alcohol has lessened their inhibitions.

Sex and pecs

If females compete for the best mate, what are the characteristics that they find attractive? How do they identify the optimum provider? Females tend to look for sexual potency in the form of a strong male presenting as sexually mature, athletic and with clear gender differentiation (Weisfeld 1987). These characteristics overtly signal an attractive male and covertly identify a sound provider. Some consider symmetrical facial features to be the most attractive as this links to sound genetic inheritance, consequently health and strength. The label of athleticism relates to the high status of males who are household names in sport and icons of both men and women. Evolutionary psychology would frame this attraction as the male showing physical strength and therefore capability of being an effective provider. However, not all agree that physical characteristics provide reliable information about male reproductive potency (Symons 1979; Buss and Schmitt 1993).

As females compete for husbands and relationships, not just for copulation and healthy offspring, they are attracted to other factors in addition to physical attributes. Females may be drawn initially towards physically attractive males, but seek those who offer resources and protection for themselves and their young in the long term (Gangestad and Thornhill 1997). Young girls may be attracted to a partner by looks alone but, as they grow older, take into consideration his ability to protect and care for them and their children.

The oldest swinger in town

Looks alone can offer no guarantee of producing offspring but it seems that a presentation of physical strength gives out signals of the ability to provide. These signals are attractive to women but do not emanate only from the young male with a strong physique, as financial security attracts females looking for a good provider. Signals such as an expensive car, high salary and corresponding lifestyle are highly desirable in a male. As a man gets older, these become more important, replacing the physical strength and attractive appearance of earlier years. The 'oldest swinger in town' combines fading youth with compensatory signals of wealth. His long locks, bare chest and energy on the dance floor (traditionally linked to youth and virility), plus expensive suit, watch and car (later monetary acquisitions), are bids to attract desirable females of childbearing age. The profile of the optimum young male may be changing as physical strength no longer predicts the male ability to provide in the way that it did when work involved hard physical labour. Interestingly, there are now fewer male icons and box office stars displaying a powerful physique. Perhaps both males and females are beginning to respond to changes in lifestyles, thus altering their preferred characteristics in a mate.

Evolutionary change does not happen overnight and echoes of our past are evident. Males continue to show off the attributes of strength, fitness and sound gene heritage in order to attract females (Buss 1989). Although physical strength is no longer necessary for employment, males are still photographed in 'sex and pecs' poses. Female 'glamour' poses, highlighting the hips and breasts, primary features of a sound childbearing body, are still prevalent in magazines aimed at the male market.

Relevant to the arguments above is the finding that young people at the age of puberty, approximately 11 years old, appear to reach a peak in display of aggression (Eron *et al.* 1983; Bjorkqvist *et al.* 1992b; Olweus 1993) that may relate to preparation for the process of mate selection. Girls begin sexual development typically three years before they can conceive, so this is a time to experiment emotionally and compete for high-status males before the possibility of gestation. As stated earlier, the girls in the study, aged from 10 to 11 years, were already competing for whom they considered the most desirable male in the class. Research would show that the peak in aggression is particularly marked in the case of males at this time. This could be because they are preparing to fight for first choice of female partner, and because they wish to display their ability to defend themselves and others (Campbell 1995). As stated earlier, there is a measurable decrease in aggression among older boys presumably because, once they have established a dominance hierarchy, there is less need for confrontation (de Waal 1982; Olweus 1993; Ellis 1995). The process of challenge and testing out may continue longer in the case of girls, albeit in a lower key, as their dominance is not as structured, or as visible, as that of boys (Miller *et al.* 1986; Crick and Ladd 1990; Goodwin 1990). However, there may be less gender difference when a fuller picture of aggression is considered, as female aggression is usually less visible and has only recently been under scrutiny (Hawker and Boulton 1996).

Sexual reputation

The majority of quarrels and insults issued between young adolescent girls involve accusations about a girl's sexual reputation, provocative clothing and appearance (Duncan 1999). These can give rise to violent reactions, as happened in the group of girls studied. In an evolutionary context, the power of these attacks would stem from a reputation for fidelity being essential if the female is to be chosen by a male as a long-term partner (Draper and Harpending 1988). The male needs to know that the mother of his child will prioritize her child's welfare over other considerations. Sexual accusations are distressing as they are not easy to defeat, so that gossip focusing on sexual reputation is especially destructive (Marsh and Paton 1984). It is impossible for a girl to deny that she is no longer a virgin as she can give no evidence to her accusers. The best course of action is to fend off such accusations before they develop (Sanford and Eder 1984; Campbell 1995).

A further factor contributing to the instability of girls' friendships may be the pressure of conflicting messages about appearance and behaviour aimed at young girls and which must be assimilated and processed at speed. The general values and concerns of pre-adolescent and adolescent girls are identified as social status, appearance and interpersonal relationships with both boys and other girls (Schofield 1981, 1982; Goodwin 1980; Schofield 1982; Eder 1985; Maccoby 1999). Eder considers that there is an ongoing renegotiation process among girls concerning appearance, such as the use of more make-up or a more daring dress code, because girls develop rapidly and so change their norms and values at speed. They must assimilate a myriad of messages arriving from the adult world as well as sift out the most relevant coming from their peers.

Girls need to straddle an imaginary boundary where they must appear sexually attractive to appeal to males, yet keep up a front of non-provocative decorum to maintain their friendships with other girls. This is not an easy road to travel and a girl must tread carefully if she is to remain a non-threatening member of the friendship group yet secure a desirable male partner. If a quarrel develops over a boy then, regardless of who is at fault, it is likely to focus on the provocative dress and behaviour of the accused girl in leading the 'innocent' boy astray (Eder 1985; Campbell 1995)

It is at the age when competitiveness is at a peak, and girls are particularly conscious of their own physical appearance, that they are at the lowest ebb in self-confidence and self-esteem (Coleman 1966; Simmons *et al.* 1973; Schofeld 1981, 1982). Currently, the media promote an anorexic look, yet many males prefer a shapely girl. Physical maturity is considered to increase status among girls (Savin-Williams 1979; Weisfeld and Billings 1988; Harris 1995), but those less physically mature may view the early curvaceousness of another girl as a threat (Tobin-Richards *et al.* 1983). Young girls appear to rank themselves and others on a shifting scale of indeterminate structure that contributes to their intense monitoring of each other and an adherence to a supposedly egalitarian ethos in the group.

In summary, the fractured nature of the friendship bonds between girls appears to be based in powerful feelings of jealousy. If this jealousy is based on competition for an optimum provider, whether for emotional commitment or material provision, why do girls too young to be interested in securing a male partner quarrel acrimoniously? As noted in Chapter 9, from a very early age, girls appear to enmesh themselves in their female friendships in the manner of lovers. Information collated from research findings, supported by many conversations with adolescent girls, indicates that, as they move into the teenage years, they form small friendship groups, leaving behind intense dyad relationships. Perhaps, at this time, they transfer their jealousies and angst from their lover-like dyad female friendships to their emotional connections with boys. This could explain why the lives of girls are enriched by powerful emotional bonds to other girls that later include males, but hidden below these enhancing emotions are the petty suspicions and jealousies that characterize their relationships.

Suggested approaches

1   Help girls to recognize that jealousy is a very powerful emotion. Evolutionary psychology would suggest that it is a survival strategy to help females protect their partnerships with males. Girls may be interested in discussing how male–female relationships may be changing as females are no longer necessarily dependent on males for economic support. Discuss what other changes are taking place that could affect these relationships.

2   Discuss the negative effects of jealousy. Who benefits and who loses? Girls need to understand, discuss and accept difficult emotions such as jealousy, rage, depression and revenge when experienced by themselves and others. They need support and education in how to handle these emotions in regard to their own safety and that of others.

3   Ask what triggers jealousy in girls of their age and why they think this is. Help girls to understand that, instead of being upset, they could view jealousy as a compliment. The target has some quality, possession or physical feature that others envy.

4   It would appear that males and females require different things from their relationships but rarely express this candidly. This leads to misunderstandings and disputes that can eventually destroy a partnership. This could be explored, highlighting the gender differences in behaviour and attitudes noted in this work and how these could affect male–female relations.

5   Explore with girls how gender differences in expectations, behaviour and attitudes could help complement a relationship rather than destroy it. What would need to be in place to bring this about?

SECTION 6
Case Studies

18 Case studies

Juggling for position

Many of the covert, subtle strategies used by girls, as they jostle for position or dominance in their friendship groups, fall into the category of bullying behaviour as defined in Besag (1989), depending on the intent of the perpetrator and the effect on the recipient. Even when used among friends, as is most often the case with girls, the aim is to acquire power at the expense of others. Male and female adults signal and establish dominance by exercising power strategies, whether in the boardroom, criminal gang, a seemingly benign social setting such as a book club, or even among family members. However, there would appear to be gender differences in the modes used. Research carried out among university staff in Finland found a gender difference in how staff members treated their students (Bjorkqvist *et al.* 1994). A process of collusion and rejection operated far more covertly and intentionally among female staff towards female students than among male staff towards male students. The case studies given here illustrate some of the strategies used by girls in their attempts to acquire or maintain power.

These case studies are drawn from the interactions of the girls attending the activity club as well as those witnessed during many years of working with girls in a wide variety of schools and other settings. Although girls draw on the modes of attack described in the case studies, many boys too will include such approaches in their repertoire. The case studies illustrate that most girls use several strategies in conjunction to form a complex, powerful assault on their target. The complexity of these attacks confuses the victim as well as those trying to identify the strands in an attack with the aim of providing remedial support. The case studies also illustrate that most of the strategies commonly employed by girls draw primarily on their linguistic skills.

The suggested approaches given at the end of each case study are presented in brief as many that are relevant have been given more fully at the end of previous chapters.

The dispenser of wisdom

One way commonly used by those wishing to establish or maintain dominance over an individual or group is by publicly distributing advice and support while dismissing as worthless that offered by others. Distributing advice or information is a traditional way of gaining, displaying and maintaining dominance for both males and females (Savin-Williams 1980). The cowboy hero in the traditional scenario always had a feasible strategy to offer in time of peril, thus becoming the indispensable leader, until another usurped his position by force of strength or by offering superior strategies. Autocratic or defensive managers know that knowledge is power and so retain all information in an attempt to hold on to this power and to demonstrate that they are indispensable.

Both boys and girls aim to gain power and status by offering the group effective advice or information. Group members may vie to display that they are the most accomplished, hold most knowledge, or have most experience at whatever is under discussion. Unless the power lies with a covert provocateur, the leader must be seen to make the decisions regarding the group and to take responsibility for them. To do this she may take on the role of 'wise woman', to be consulted at every turn. Successful challenges from other girls could result in her displacement. Unlike most boys, girls mop up every titbit of information about those they admire or idolize, as is seen from the proliferation of magazines aimed at a young female readership. Boys may pin up photographs of their female fantasies but rarely search out details of their personal lives. A girl offering exciting, tantalizing gossip has a chance of increasing her status in the group. She may not achieve the role of leader in this way, but her ability to source important or engaging information may help a leader to ward off challenges.

Put downs

The leader must seize every opportunity to discredit moves made to encroach upon her role, otherwise her influence over the group could fade. In parallel to displaying information themselves, those who aim for dominance often quash the contributions of others quickly and effectively. The ubiquitous put down is a successful mode of destroying challenge. This may be an abusive personal or evaluative remark, or it may be of a passive nature whereby the leader ignores the contributions of a targeted girl while listening attentively to the opinions or advice of others. Cursory dismissal of the contributions of the target makes it clear that she is unworthy of attention. By ignoring, scorning or ridiculing her suggestions, the leader can speedily cause even a robust girl to become demoralized. These powerful, destructive tools are most effective if used in a conspicuous manner before peers. The public arena is essential to advertise the victim's so-called ineptitude, foolishness or worthlessness. This is equivalent to the audience that boys seek for their bullying behaviour in order to display their physical power and prowess (Wachtel 1973).

The cold shoulder

Dominant members of the group can display their rejection of a girl in several ways. The colloquial phrase 'cold shoulder' describes physical, social or psychological rejection. It is a form of put down and encompasses a number of manoeuvres. It could be turning the back towards someone, talking past a previously close friend to another nearby, or issuing invitations while deliberately ignoring the presence of the target girl. Although the recipient will recognize such manoeuvres as being shunned and rejected, these subtle signals are difficult to identify, intercede or challenge. As it is difficult for anyone outside the group to implement any effective intervention, these strategies remain high in the repertoire of those wishing to denigrate or demote others.

Divide and conquer

Some girls become friendly with others solely as a revenge strategy to cause distress to former friends (Bjorkqvist *et al*. 1992b). This may be because the friend has been disloyal by becoming friendly with another girl, or perhaps she is threatening the leader's role. A dominant girl will recognize immediately anyone trying to upstage her. Should she identify anyone making a bid for her enviable position, her reaction must be swift and effective if she is to retain her magisterial position. This queen knows the rule of divide and conquer. The fastest mode of demolishing the power of a usurper is to appoint another girl second-in-command thus cutting out the aspirant to the throne. Alternatively, she may instigate quarrels solely to realign allegiance.

CASE STUDY
Geraldine

Geraldine and Marcia are 16 years old and close friends. Geraldine has considerable influence over the other girls as she is clever, attractive, chatty and good fun. Her flamboyant personality allows her to direct others to do what she wants or thinks best. She has good organizational skills so things go well when she suggests a place to go or something to do. She finds her schoolwork well within her capability and helps those struggling to complete their assignments. The group often meets up in the evenings and at weekends and they support each other if anyone is worried or in trouble.

Marcia is not as clever as Geraldine but manages her schoolwork without any problem. She does not take things as seriously as Geraldine does. She wants to go to the local college to study hairdressing, whereas Geraldine wants to enter the sixth form and try for a university place as she has hopes of becoming a vet.

Geraldine can be harsh in her use of language. She often ignores good suggestions made by others, later presenting them as her own, and counters opposition with dismissive or demeaning comments in such a forceful manner that others fail to challenge her. This is an effective way of preventing others from attempting to defend her target. Geraldine has a range of inventive and powerful put downs that she uses to quell opposition. Her dominance remains unopposed and the other girls accept this and do not think of her use of directive language and effective put downs as bullying them into compliance and submission.

Geraldine realized that the other girls were spending a great deal of time with Marcia while she was studying. They chatted about where they had been and what they had done, and they started to pay more attention to Marcia than to her. They listened more to Marcia when she was speaking, and acted on her suggestions without waiting to hear what Geraldine had to say. They laughed more at Marcia's jokes than at Geraldine's, and Marcia had begun to cut across what Geraldine said without apologizing. Geraldine began to feel she was invisible to the other girls and left out of the group.

When a pop group gave a concert in the area, the girls chose to go on the night the tickets were cheapest although they knew that Marcia could go but Geraldine could not. Geraldine was furious. She felt it was unfair to treat her in this way after she had been such a loyal friend and she was determined to regain her influence. She complimented everyone as much as possible, she cleverly challenged every idea that Marcia put forward and carefully courted one of the more powerful girls to be her closest friend. Marcia soon realized that she had lost her powerful position. Marcia felt confused, realizing that she had been deposed, but she could not understand what had happened.

Suggested approaches

1   The case illustrates the complexity of many cases. Geraldine was a popular and generous girl although she was a dominant leader who could not tolerate opposition easily. She was a benign dictator.

2   Discussion could be a more effective mode than instruction to make girls aware of the complexities of such cases.
    •   Could the situation have been avoided?

- Who was responsible for this situation – only Geraldine?
- What was the role of the bystanders? What could they have done?
- Awareness of the distress such behaviours cause may have alerted the bystanders to behave more sensitively.

3   Prior awareness of the distress that negative language and other non-physical bullying causes could have been beneficial. However, some girls refuse to change their behaviour and may even add the strategies discussed to their repertoire of negative behaviours.

4   Discussions of what is expected from friends before problems arise can be useful. Expectations may include loyalty, trust, consideration, negotiation and a 'better for both' solution to problems.

Malicious gossip

A common mode used to attack a girl is to remove her support network by setting up negative gossip or lying about her. This is particularly powerful if the gossip or lies appear to prove her untrustworthy. The malicious gossip occurring in the class studied came primarily from two girls outside specific friendship groups who wished to be included. These girls also used other forms of negative language, such as insults and grassing, in bids to devalue the qualities of others in stable relationships in order to replace them or to gain entry into various cliques. These bids were misjudged as neither girl realized that these disruptive behaviours only strengthened the determination of others to reject them.

It is difficult to identify the author of abusive names written in a toilet, or to find the source of malicious gossip. Although it only needs a few written or spoken words to destroy a girl's sexual reputation, it is impossible to challenge a statement saying that she has had sexual relations as there is no easy way to prove she is still a virgin.

CASE STUDY
Diane

Diane is a lively girl of 12 years who is a prodigious gossip. She is inventive, humorous and she relates her embellished tales with gusto, complete with actions and amusing voices. Sadly, these often target those not in her favour. Fortunately, few girls take any notice of what she says although all enjoy the tales.

Diane recently quarrelled with Sally, the most powerful girl in the group, and spread gossip about her. She has told the other girls that Sally has told lies to the teachers about them to get them into trouble. Most of the girls ignored the gossip but Sally feels that she is not as popular as before. Diane has also threatened the other girls by saying she will 'get them' if they support Sally.

Before a disco held in school, the girls decided they would wear their prettiest clothes even though it was to be a casual affair. On the evening of the party, Diane made the most vulnerable girl telephone Sally, saying that the girls had changed their minds and had decided to wear jeans instead of party clothes. Sally arrived at the party to find she was the only girl in jeans. As she lived some distance from the school, she had to face the sniggers and rude comments of the other girls while waiting for her parents to collect her.

Abusive, sexualized graffiti about Diane appeared in the girls' toilets in school. Most of the girls thought Sally wrote it to take her revenge. Diane and Sally accused each other of starting the trouble. As both could be argumentative and querulous, it was difficult for the teachers to sort out what was really happening and what to do about it.

Suggested approaches

1   Discussions about means of repairing relationships could be helpful.
2   These girls had been friends and perhaps regretted their behaviour. Mediation could have been a possible solution.
3   Once in dispute, it may be difficult to apologize or make amends without support from an impartial source such as a teacher or student mediator.
4   Awareness that malicious gossip is slander, and graffiti libel, in the adult world, and that both carry sanctions, may have been an effective preventative measure.

Gossip via technology

Girls often use a range of modern technology as modes of aggressive communication. The power and effectiveness of these modern techniques make it possible to destroy the reputation of a girl within minutes. Gossip can be posted around the school population at surprising speed, wrongly claiming a girl to be promiscuous or a boy gay. Many young people are more *au fait* with these modes of communication than are the adults trying to police them.

Only recently have adults come to realize what a fast and fruitful mode new technology is for those wishing to abuse others. As with other forms of abuse, it is difficult for adults to be aware of what is going on. Shut away in a bedroom, a young person could be sending or receiving abusive messages without an adult's knowledge. There are many reasons why young people find it difficult to tell adults that they are being bullied (Besag 1989). A vulnerable child may not turn to classmates or adults for protection or support owing to the frightening and secretive nature of bullying.

Exchanging secrets

The quality of the emotional investment girls give to their friendships leads to disclosures and subsequent issues of loyalty. Girls enjoy friendships where they can discuss intimate issues and they prize those who can keep secrets. This exchange of secrets plays an important part in their friendships and they spend a great deal of time sitting in their bedrooms sharing confidences. This is aptly termed their 'bedroom culture' by Lees (1993).

It would seem that the severe feelings of rejection experienced by targeted girls are often exacerbated by the dual process embedded within girls' friendships: the closeness of the best-friend relationship juxtaposed with the fear of rejection. Once the relationship breaks down, feelings of rejection fuse with those of betrayal and anxiety. Those who were close now have the additional power of intimate knowledge of the rejected girl, and disclosure of her secrets can be a powerful mode of attack. The trading of secrets and disclosures adds to the tension, and fear of betrayal, that infiltrates many relationships. A common tactic is for one girl to ask another to exchange secrets. A gullible girl will disclose a true secret but the dominant girl invents one. This puts the latter in a powerful position from which to make a future attack disclosing the true secret of her victim to others. As hers is false, she has no fear of any disclosure.

Unlike boys who may avoid or hide from their attackers, girls often remain caught up in the situation as most conflict between girls occurs between friends or acquaintances. It is more difficult for a girl to avoid or escape her attackers as they will be familiar with her habits and routines. It is common for boys to be ignorant of the name of their victim whereas girls frequently gather detailed information about their target. Unlike most male bullies, females make it their business to know the personal details of their victim in order to make their attacks personal and destructive. A determined girl may elicit personal details about her target's family, even inveigling her way into the parental bedroom, so she has potent ammunition with which to launch her attacks. The attacker may have accrued this bank of information incidentally when the girls were close friends; however, once the friendship links are broken, this personal information rapidly becomes ammunition. Subsequently, the nature of the attacks and repercussions are often more destructive for girl victims than for boys.

CASE STUDY
Andrea

Andrea and Liz were close friends in their final year of school. Both were academically able and hoped to gain a university place. Andrea had an offer from the university of her choice, but Liz only received an offer from her third choice. Andrea played the violin in the school orchestra and was in the local tennis team. Liz did not play tennis but started to attend the club to seek out Andrea's boyfriend while he watched her play. Andrea admitted to her boyfriend that she was jealous. He had not realized that Liz was trying to steal him from Andrea and promised to ignore her overtures. Liz was resentful when she realized the boy no longer paid her attention.

Liz and Andrea used to exchange confidences and often slept at each other's house at weekends. Liz told the other girls all she knew about Andrea's private affairs and started to spread gossip about Andrea's parents. Liz had unintentionally collected a great deal of personal information about the family over the years, and she began to use it with malicious intent.

In one of her whispering campaigns, Liz wrongly claimed that Andrea copied her assignments from websites. In fact, Andrea's sudden improved standard of work was because she had decided to study law and needed to work extremely hard to achieve her goal. The situation escalated quickly. Andrea heard the girls whispering about her, and heard them chanting rude comments, but they stopped and giggled when they were certain she had heard them. She found notes stuck on her property calling her a slag and a cheat. She did not know to what they referred.

Liz left anonymous threatening, obscene messages on Andrea's answerphone. She even threatened to give Andrea's name to a paedophile ring. Things came to a head when Andrea was accused of stealing money. Liz had manipulated a conversation with a teacher so that it appeared that only Andrea had been in the room when the money was stolen. Luckily, Andrea was able to show she had a dentist appointment at that time. It was clear that Liz had been responsible for the gossip. Liz realized that the situation had got out of hand as she had not intended things to go so far. As both girls were about to leave school, no action was taken, but Liz felt too embarrassed to attend the leaving festivities and none of her previous friends made contact with her once they had left school.

Suggested approaches

1   Girls need to be aware of the danger of disclosing private information. They should be aware of trading secrets as any personal information may be used against them later.

2   Discussion of the role of the other girls in the group, and what they could have done differently, could be a useful starting point for other work as outlined in Section 7.

3   It is essential that girls realize how serious some bullying behaviours can be. Threats concerning paedophiles or implying theft could warrant contacting the police. Discuss the concepts of libel and slander.

4   Posters for helplines dedicated to young people are displayed in most schools, yet some young people find it difficult to make a necessary call. It may be useful to familiarize the girls with what to expect should a call be necessary.

5   Mediation may have been a successful approach in the early stages of this dispute.

6   Discuss the short-term and long-term repercussions of negative behaviours. Also refer to the final case study (Marie).

Little Miss Joker

A potent form of bullying is that of the game or joke. Physical attacks common among boys include Chinese burns on the arm, arm locks, wrestling and other modes of painful, so-called play fighting. A physically powerful boy can routinely jump on another, causing irritation if not pain. Tugging hair, a mode preferred by girls, can be painful but passed off as a playful greeting. Verbal forms of such attacks include name calling, sarcastic, barbed or critical comments, and cruel jokes. Bullies carry out such behaviours in public to display their physical dominance and to humiliate the vulnerable. Whatever the nature of the attack, the culprit negates responsibility by claiming that 'it was just a bit of fun'. This technique forms a multifaceted attack.

*   The target receives the painful attack or abusive comment intended to hurt and humiliate.
*   The target is denounced as having no sense of humour.
*   If the witnesses are laughing and the victim is left feeling unsure of whether or not there are grounds for complaint.

The parrot provocateur

It is not always clear who holds the power in a group, even to the members, as the instigator of quarrels may not be in evidence when disputes occur. A covert provocateur keeps a low profile so that others find themselves identified as the troublemakers. *Tertius gaudens* is a phrase used to describe this process whereby one gains advantage from the quarrels of others (Simmel 1964). Many girls are unaware of the subtle manipulation of them by the more powerful members of the group. One girl in the class studied used her linguistic skills in a subtle and sophisticated manner to control and manipulate the attitudes and decisions of others although no one realized her influence over them.

CASE STUDY

Lynette

Lynette is 11 years old and has plenty of material possessions as she comes from an affluent family. She wears fashionable clothing, owns an expensive mobile phone and has holidays abroad. She has two older brothers and a younger sister who is 2 years old. Lynette appears to love her little sister but there have been times when she has been spiteful and aggressive towards her. Her mother says that Lynette is jealous of her sister but that she must learn to get used to the situation.

Lynette has a group of friends who appear to appreciate her sense of humour but not everyone enjoys her jokes. She makes sarcastic and cruel comments to girls she does not like to make them feel foolish or inadequate. She couches the comments in humour so they are genuinely funny to all but the victim. If challenged, Lynette says, 'It was just a joke', in a babyish voice to make the other girls laugh. These comments make those targeted feel even worse as she is publicly announcing they have no sense of humour. As the others laugh and fail to challenge Lynette, her targets think that what she has said about them must be true and so they rarely complain. Lynette is always present whenever there are quarrels although she appears to take no part. As she keeps a low profile, her teachers do not consider her a troublemaker. The other girls include her in the group but she does not have a close friend.

One teacher has become aware of how Lynette is manipulating the other girls. When the girls are chatting, Lynette picks up words or phrases from their conversation and repeats them. She is selective and repeats only the negative comments. In this way, she emphasizes and exaggerates any critical and adverse remarks made by the girls about others. She is giving a carefully edited re-run of the conversation.

The language Lynette uses cements the attitudes she wishes to promote, thus encouraging the girls to adopt her opinions. In this way, Lynette is manipulating and directing the girls in their attitude towards others. Her motivation is to demote some girls while promoting those with whom she is friendly.

Suggested approaches

1   All need to be reminded that a joke or game is only so by the definition that all are enjoying it and it is the responsibility of all participants to ensure this is so. Anyone unsure should leave immediately.

2   A put down is a demeaning comment and not a joke. All should recognize such behaviours as negative and respond appropriately.

3   Witnesses to these attacks have a significant role to play in defending the target. They should make it clear that they are not participating in the 'game' and do not find it amusing. They should challenge the bully without being unpleasant if they feel confident enough to do so. If not, they should leave the scene immediately.

4   Anyone listening to malicious gossip, or adding comments to support the gossip, is as much at fault as the instigator. They are giving 'permission' for the behaviour.

5   Listeners must make challenges as soon as they recognize malicious gossip. The more powerful girls have an influential role to play as they can more easily break the negative gossip sequence.

The vicarious attack

It lies within the power of some girls to persuade others to bully their targets on their behalf. In this way, the bully is bullying one girl to bully another. Alternatively, the bully may tell a girl that the target girl has maligned her, stolen her boyfriend, or some other lie that she knows will incite the girl to anger, hoping the unsuspecting girl will attack her target. Meanwhile, the bully stands by quietly waiting for the drama to unfold. Although the bully has orchestrated the attack, she has a good chance of remaining undetected and escaping sanction.

CASE STUDY

Carrie

Carrie is a well-built, attractive girl of 11 years with a lively personality and a good sense of humour. She has friends but not the close dyad relationship she desires. Carrie considers herself a leader but she does not have leadership skills. She dominates conversations, wanting to take the final decision and be in charge of the social life of the other girls. When thwarted in any way, she becomes aggressive and threatens those she considers to have opposed her. Her family, and extended family, have a reputation for aggression. It is a close family, with most members living in the same locality, and Carrie mirrors the dominant role her family holds in the community.

Carrie is often at loggerheads with someone and uses many strategies to make life difficult for those she does not like, one of the more obvious being her physical aggression. The others girls are extremely wary of upsetting her as she is known to be an effective fighter and Carrie uses her size and reputation to threaten them. She does not need to risk getting into trouble for being physically aggressive as her threat is enough to ward off those who know her. If she looks at a girl in a certain way, known among the girls as 'getting the look', it is enough to frighten her target.

Recently, Carrie has quarrelled with Janice. It is difficult for them to avoid each other as both girls live in the same street. They are both in the local Irish dance team and this fuels their competitive attitude and incites their jealousy. One way in which Carrie enforces her power is to ask members of her family to threaten other girls. Her older cousin, Paul, attends a nearby school so Carrie asked him to pass the message to Janice that Carrie was 'going to get her'. Janice knew that this was no vain threat and that Paul would bring his friends to help if the quarrel escalated. This is rarely required as the threat of attack is enough to frighten most of the other girls into submission. This makes it difficult to challenge Carrie as there is never any evidence to prove she has issued a threat.

A few days ago, Janice heard a street phone ring as she passed. When she picked up the receiver, as was the custom in the neighbourhood, an unknown adult male voice stated, falsely, that everyone knew that she had slept with all the boys on the estate. No one could imagine who had spoken on the phone as no one knew Janice would be walking along the road at that time and there had been no one in sight.

Janice discovered that the boyfriend of Carrie's older sister had a flat overlooking the phone box. She suspected it was his voice and that Carrie was in the flat and saw Janice walking by, or had primed the boy in advance to make such a verbal attack should he see Janice pass his flat.

Carrie would use the threat of her family members in other ways in a bid to get what she wanted. She would ask Paul to approach a boy she liked and ask him to be her boyfriend while, in parallel, she would declare to the other girls that this boy had asked her to be his girlfriend. The emotional involvement of the parties in these alliances was skewed, the target boy remaining passive, so they never developed past the verbal stage of Carrie claiming her target as her boyfriend in front of the other girls. However, this prevented the boy from making friendships with other girls until Carrie lost interest in him and it was safe to do so.

Suggested approaches

1   This type of bullying needs to be considered in the context of other types of aggression. There was an obvious intent to cause distress to the target although no physical violence was employed. It must be

made clear that covert behaviours such as 'the look' and verbal and physical threats are as harmful as direct attacks.

2   Girls need to know that even if bullies have only made threats indirectly, through an assistant, they are as culpable as if they had made the threats in person.
3   All should be aware that anyone colluding with the bully is equally as culpable and should not escape sanctions.
4   Witnesses to such behaviour have a responsibility to support the target by challenging the bully and assistant. If they are not confident enough to do this, they should alert an adult to what is happening. This can be done anonymously if necessary.
5   Discussion about leadership skills, and the difference between democratic and autocratic leadership, may encourage a change of attitude in the bully.
6   Explore the issues of jealousy and friendship skills.
7   Girls need to be aware that it is common to attack a girl's sexual reputation, or that of family members, and understand that such accusations are rarely based on fact. They should try to challenge the bully or alert adults to these serious insults.
8   It would be useful to have a meeting with a member of the family if appropriate.
9   The bully could be given a legitimate leadership role under covert, close supervision.

The absent bully

It is possible for a girl in another class, year group, or even a different school to instigate a hate campaign or destructive gossip about her target.

CASE STUDY
Shelley

Carol-Anne and Clare are in the same class in school. They live near to each other, their parents are on good terms and they have been friends since birth. Shelley recently moved into the area and was admitted to the same school.

Shelley soon started to cause trouble by inviting either Carol-Anne or Clare to her house without inviting the other friend. This caused jealousy between Carol-Anne and Clare that soon escalated into distressing quarrels. Their parents said that the best line of action would be for them to accept Shelley's invitations only if they could go to her house together. This settled things for a while, but Shelley began to lie to the girls, telling one that she had invited the other when this was not the case.

When challenged, Shelley would say that she had forgotten to invite the other girl. As the arguments and quarrels quickly escalated, their teacher suggested that the girls told each other whenever they were going to Shelley's house so they could go together. If one could not go, neither should go. Both girls agreed to this but Shelly became aggressive towards them, complaining that no one would be her friend. She asked her parents to arrange for her to move to another school and they agreed to do so.

Shelley deliberately made friends with other girls in the school she had left. She has started sending them text messages about Carol-Anne and Clare. These were malicious lies and Carol-Anne and Clare became afraid of her. They are now isolated as the other girls in the class are also afraid of Shelley who threatens them with aggression if they are friendly with Carol-Anne or Clare.

Suggested approaches

1   Shelley may have problems not yet identified. It could be advantageous for the appropriate personnel in the two schools to discuss the matter as she may need extra academic, emotional or behavioural support from staff in school.
2   Shelley has already been to at least three schools. A discussion with her parents could identify underlying issues.
3   The teacher's suggestion that both girls only go to Shelley's house if they could go together was a good one.
4   The issue of the girls in the class who are threatened needs to be addressed.
5   A sensitive investigation is required to ensure Shelley is not bullying girls in her new school.
6   Such cases can be discussed among staff to elicit further ideas so that a bank of knowledge about bullying, and how best to address the issues, gradually develops. Compilation of brief notes, over time, could form a handbook to which all staff can have immediate access. It would be best to change the names of the girls for staff discussion.

Intermittent reinforcement

A dominant girl may use one of the most powerful psychological techniques to maintain control, that of intermittent reinforcement. The powerful girl builds tension and a sense of uncertainty to keep all on their toes. Will the favour they enjoy today be there tomorrow? These periodic cycles of inclusion and exclusion serve to unnerve the group members thus manipulating them into submission and dependency.

The girls in the study regularly issued invitations to each other for after-school activities. These invitations could cause as much upset as the more formal invitations to birthday parties as this was when changes in allegiance were signalled, and when those on the periphery of the friendship circles became aware of where they stood.

CASE STUDY

Kerry

Kerry is a girl of 9 years. She comes from a more financially advantaged home than the other girls in her class and subsequently has more possessions. Her parents have a caravan and she is able to invite her friends to join the family for weekends away. Kerry has many relatively expensive clothes she lets other girls try on when they are at her home, and make-up with which they can experiment.

The other girls eagerly await invitations to Kerry's house, especially for sleepovers at the weekend. All hope for an invitation to go away in the caravan; even to play in the caravan at the front of Kerry's house is exciting. Each Friday, the girls wait to see if Kerry will invite them that weekend.

The strong desire of the other girls to go to Kerry's home gives Kerry a great deal of power over them. Kerry gets them to do her bidding throughout the week by promising to invite them, or threatening that she will not invite them if they do not comply. She is like a princess ruling her subjects as she gets the other girls to do her homework, carry her books and belongings, and run the errands that her mother asks her to do. Kerry is never short of a partner, or someone to sit next to for lunch, and she is invited to all parties.

The other girls know that Kerry is manipulating them, but the attraction of her possessions and the caravan is too strong to resist. Kerry has become increasingly more demanding, manipulative and aggressive. One by one, the others have started to ignore her as they realize she does not keep her promises and she just invites them home on a whim.

The girls have started to challenge Kerry, telling her she is boastful, and they no longer want to be her friend. They find her untrustworthy and now exclude her from the group. Kerry cannot see why this is happening and she has become more antagonistic and aggressive. The other girls have retaliated and the situation has escalated. The school was not aware of the seriousness of the situation; the teachers know the girls are quarrelsome but they had not recognized the dynamics of the situation as it primarily concerned what the girls did in the evenings and weekends. The level of aggression has escalated so quickly that it has become a matter for the parents and the community police.

Suggested approaches

1 Kerry appears not to understand the concept of friendship. She expects to be the recipient but not the provider of friendship. Discussions about loyalty, trustworthiness and reliability could be beneficial.
2 The school, community and families could have communication links in place that would alert all to issues such as this.
3 The retaliatory behaviour of the girls in the group needs to be addressed.
4 The role of observers and assistants to aggression occurring out of school needs to be discussed with students and adults in the community.
5 Discussions with the police should be held to identify any legal implications.

The jealous friend

Disputes between girls may come from one girl trying to make her friendship with another exclusive, the more dominant girl refusing to allow others to encroach upon the relationship. This may be because she is jealous, possessive and fears losing her friend to another. As stated previously, the girls in the study valued their friendships highly. As the fear of losing a close friend was realistic, it was always in the forefront of their minds.

A possessive friend is not only controlling the dyad friendship, she is also controlling the group in a passive manner. She is preventing a friendship group forming around her friend, fearing that she would lose her influence over her. Once alienated from her supportive network, the less dominant girl, manipulated into such a situation, could find herself in a vulnerable position. If there is a dispute within the dyad, her previous friends may not welcome her back and she may find herself excluded from their friendship circle. Separated from her friends, she is in a position where her jealous, powerful friend can bully or manipulate her. The bully may not have intended this at the start, but the pattern of abuse begins with the gradual separation of the vulnerable from any means of support, thus allowing the abusive relationship to continue unchallenged. The abuse may escalate in frequency and intensity as the victim continues to suffer a loss of self-esteem and confidence.

CASE STUDY

Vivienne

Vivienne and Juliet are 8 years old and close friends. They live in the same area so they spend a lot of time together in school and at home. Juliet is a happy, popular girl, with several friends in school and the neighbourhood. She has a good sense of fun and an excellent singing voice and often breaks into song while playing. As the other girls love to join in, this has become an integral part of their play.

Vivienne is jealous of Juliet's popularity and becomes upset when Juliet wants to play with other girls. She cajoles Juliet into playing exclusively with her and sulks if she does not comply. Vivienne becomes unpleasant if other girls approach when she and Juliet are playing together and she argues, makes spiteful comments, pinches them or pushes them away. Vivienne keeps a close watch on the other girls in the class and tries to get them into trouble with the teachers if they threaten her friendship with Juliet.

Vivienne lies to Juliet, telling her that the other girls have been criticizing her and gossiping about her. On hearing this, Juliet challenged her other friends. Vivienne denied she had lied and said the other girls were lying to Juliet because they were jealous of their friendship. This has caused a great deal of trouble between Juliet and her other friends. Vivienne is so spiteful to the other girls that no one plays with Juliet when Vivienne is around. This is a successful strategy in keeping her rivals at a distance. There were other girls on the periphery of this duo but the aggressive attitude of Vivienne does not allow any friendship group to form. Juliet has a good friend in the class that she sees out of school who will not approach her when Vivienne is present. Vivienne has attained her goal and has Juliet to herself.

Suggested approaches

1   Friendship issues, such as what makes a good friend need to be discussed.
2   The dangers of having just one dominant friend need to be discussed.
3   Training in assertiveness could be appropriate for Juliet.
4   Vivienne may need help to understand how to make and develop friendships. Juliet may be the only girl she has managed to keep as a friend.
5   There may be other issues connected to Vivienne's need to dominate her friend. Academic, social and home factors may need to be considered as she may be lacking self-esteem and confidence.
6   Strategies such as Circle of Friends (Newton *et al.* 1996) may be considered.

Girls from minority cultures

As previously stated, it is easy to miss, or misunderstand, the difficulties facing girls who come from ethnic minority cultures as they sometimes face specific problems. Several teachers mentioned that they were aware of a particular form of truancy occurring among some girls. This appears to stem from a desire to experience a sense of autonomy and freedom, and a taste of Western culture, that can be difficult to achieve within their communities.

Observations showed parents escorting even older girls to school and collecting them at the end of the school day, and several girls stated that they usually remained within their extended family network and communities when away from school. Teachers reported that some girls arrive at school but, once their parents are out of sight, change into the Western style of clothing and go off for a day of freedom. If forbidden the mobile phones, so beloved of the young, the ingenuity of some girls leads them to find ways of buying the phones themselves, such as saving their dinner money to purchase one. The girls may use them to view their film and pop idols or to contact boys. Some girls claim boys have contacted them as this signifies popularity with boys and so status over other girls. These claims are similar to those made by girls from other cultures for the same reasons.

These behaviours, clearly forbidden by their parents, leaves these girls open to gossip, blackmail and threats from other girls. It is not always their parents who are most feared by them as they may not speak fluent English and may be unfamiliar with the school system. Older brothers of the girls, or other males in the extended family, are those frequently delegated to keep a watchful eye on young girls. These older boys know of all the temptations and dangers that face girls as they have fewer restrictions and have usually been through the same school system as the girls. Just the knowledge that other girls know about their behaviour can cause these girls a great deal of stress. As mentioned earlier, the label 'shameful' has a powerful resonance as this means a girl is shaming her family and the whole community.

From my limited experience, I would suggest most girls from minority cultures appear to mix happily with those from other cultures in school but, when they have free time, they join others from their ethnic group whenever possible. This would appear to be so for any minority community in any area of the world, especially if the language used in the home is not one in general use in their locality. This can be the case with many of these girls.

It may be that some girls more easily integrate into school life in Britain for a variety of reasons. The history of immigration into Britain means that some ethnic minority groups will have had a longer period of assimilation than other groups. These families are likely to be better established into the cultural mores of British life and are probably better versed in the English language, including the local dialect and accent, than more recent immigrants. In addition, they will have had more time and opportunity to have succeeded in training and found appropriate employment. These factors would suggest we need to consider a range of issues specific to the differing ethnic minority groupings before we apply knowledge gained from research carried out with one to any other.

CASE STUDY

Jasmina

Jasmina is a girl of fifteen years whose parents came to Britain some years ago. The family lives in the traditional manner in their community and, although both her parents speak some English, they prefer to speak their Pakistani dialect so this remains the dominant language in the home. Jasmina attends the local comprehensive school where her older sister and brother went but they have now left.

Jasmina is having some difficulties in school as she is finding the work hard. She finds it impossible to keep up with the speed the teachers speak while concentrating on the lessons. These have recently become more challenging as she is preparing for external exams. Jasmina has always found the work difficult but her sister helped her in the evening. However, her sister married a few weeks after leaving school and now lives some distance away. There are learning mentors in the class but none are designated to support Jasmina as they help those students with identified special educational needs. There has been no detailed assessment of Jasmina's difficulties as she is a quiet, well-behaved girl who always presented her homework and managed in class. An additional problem is that Jasmina has a slight hearing difficulty that has been over-looked. She finds it difficult to hear and concentrate when the learning mentors are speaking aloud while helping the other students.

Some girls from Jasmina's class invited her to truant with them. She went with them once but was very afraid in case her brother found out and has refused to go again. These girls think she may tell the teachers or other girls who will then inform their families. They have threatened Jasmina and said she must go with them so that she too will get into trouble if they are discovered. Jasmina lies awake at night and does not know what to do. They have taken money from her and they laugh at her timidity. They have threatened that if she does not go with them they will tell her family that she has a boyfriend and is shaming the community.

One of the boys in the class has started to tease and torment her and sometimes tries to pull her hajib from her head. The other girls laugh at her distress. She feels as though he has ripped her clothing off when he does this but she does not want to tell her family as they may take her from the school. Jasmina is afraid to tell a teacher and she is fearful her brother will make things worse if he knew. She is too frightened to go to school but does not know what to do.

Suggested Approaches/Bhd

1   Jasmina's educational needs require assessment by the Special Educational Needs specialists in the school or by external services.

Language difficulties and cultural confusions can mask educational problems.

2   Jasmina had acquired a functional level in the English language but found difficulty in accessing the more complex language needed for the curriculum required for external examinations. Extra tuition and guidance would be helpful with regard to additional reading matter for her curriculum requirements and for informal social and instructional language.

3   Jasmina's medical needs require assessment. There had been an unidentified deterioration in her hearing. As she was reticent to seek help, the school staff had not realised her difficulties.

4   Shy girls such as Jasmina need to be directed to an adult, such as a learning mentor or personal tutor, in advance of problems occurring. They will then feel more confident and comfortable in approaching these people should difficulties arise.

5   Strong communication links with the families and communities of these students can provide school staff with a bank of information regarding the more subtle cultural mores. This can be drawn upon to identify possible areas of difficulty specific to the student.

6   Meetings and workshops for families and members of the community can be organised by the school in conjunction with relevant professionals to form networking links so that problems can be foreseen.

7   Relevant continuing professional development is essential for all adults working with these students.

As with other ethnic minority groups, girls of Afro-Caribbean origin may have specific problems regarding bullying. It would seem that many of these girls and boys like to give an impressive presence, a 'buona figura', to the world. Some teachers interviewed wryly suggested that sometimes they felt that some of these students regarded coming to school to chat and show off their sense of style to their friends an essential element of school life. For some girls, their presentation is of such importance that any personal criticism or ridicule can lead to an aggressive attack on others that can quickly escalate. However, several teachers considered that under the humour and gleeful chat of many girls of Afro-Caribbean origin there was, sometimes, a sense of unhappiness and insecurity.

Some of the girls studied came from matriarchal families without a male authority figure. In such cases, as in some Asian families, an older male relative may take on the role of monitoring the girls' social behaviour. Although there is often pride in securing a boyfriend, to become pregnant is considered shameful so that malicious gossip regarding a girl's reputation could be as destructive as for many girls elsewhere. Bullying among these girls was often in the form of insults directed forcefully to the target or her mother, giving the 'evil eye' or 'the look', or crowding around their target.

CASE STUDY
Rose

Rose's family is well-established in Britain. Her great-grandparents came here from Africa after the war. Her father left home soon after she was born. Her mother works in the local laundrette so she has as many material possessions as the other girls she knows. Rose was a happy girl until a few months ago. She was doing well at school and she hoped to go to the local college to study beauty care and hairdressing. Her teachers were pleased with her progress, and her mother, grandmother and older sister, who lives with her partner and baby nearby, were proud of her.

Rose is a quiet girl who looks much older than her 14 years. She is a Christian and sings in the choir at church. Recently the choir sang on a local television programme and Rose sang a solo. Her friends in the choir go to a different school but she had friends in school. Some girls in her school saw the programme and have started to pick fights with her on their way home from school. Several other girls saw what was happening and became her friends and protectors. These girls are older than Rose and go to the local clubs and pubs at weekend. They encourage Rose to go with them as she looks old enough to be admitted. Rose does not want to do so as she would feel out of her depth. She is not interested in that kind of social activity and would rather be with her friends in the choir.

These girls have now turned on her and say she is a baby. They mock her clothes, her more studious attitude and her singing. They have threatened to take her money and her mobile phone. She now leaves her phone at home but is worried as her mother often phones her after school to arrange to meet her in town. The attackers push and jostle her in the corridor and they call Rose and her mother abusive names. They have spread gossip around saying she is pregnant.

Rose does not know what to do. She feels too ashamed of what they say to tell a teacher, especially as her head of year is male. She does not want to worry her mother and she feels awkward about talking to her sister over the phone about such sensitive matters. Rose is afraid of any teachers finding out, as the bullies will think she has complained and she fears reprisals. Rose now fears these girls and the others who bullied her previously.

Suggested approaches

1 Rose should know she is able to approach any teacher if she wishes to discuss a problem.

2 Rose could send an anonymous letter to a teacher in school whom she would feel comfortable talking to, explaining her situation.

3 Schools should have links with families and members of the community as shown in the previous case study.

4 Many adults are unaware of some of the common triggers for bullying. These include media attention given to the target and even a bereavement in the family of the victim.

5 Rose could try to talk to an adult in her church about the problem.

6 If Rose discussed the problem with her friends in the choir it may make her feel better. They may be able to give her some ideas to try and they would give her emotional support.

7 Rose could contact Childline, Kidscape or a dedicated website such as www.bullying.co.uk.

8 If the school has a peer support system, this would be a good line of approach.

False friends

One of the more distressing means of attack is for a group of girls to persuade another to hold a party and invite a crowd of friends. Often they choose someone who will be flattered to think that, at last, they are inviting her into the high-ranking group of social stars, but they fail to turn up and they make sure no one else attends.

CASE STUDY

Hannah

Hannah is an 8-year-old girl who has recently moved into the area. She has not managed to make any real friends in her new school even though she has tried hard to be accepted. She has taken her books and toys to school to show the other girls and offered to let them borrow them. One or two girls have done so but have not brought them back, saying they have been lost. Some have been returned dirty and spoilt.

Hannah has always found it difficult to make new friends. She is a quiet girl, and feels awkward in groups, but she longs to have a friend to talk to and to do things with in the evenings and at weekends. She had a good friend at her last school and she is missing her badly. Hannah told her parents she had made some friends, knowing they want her to be happy at school. She is aware that neither of her parents wanted to move house but it had been necessary because of her father's job. She suspects that her parents are unhappy in the new home so she has not told them how lonely she feels as she does not want to worry them.

Dionne sits next to Hannah in class and has started to play with her in the playground. Hannah was delighted as Dionne is very popular. Hannah thought that if Dionne became friendly with her, she would soon be included in the games of the other girls. Dionne found out it was soon to be Hannah's birthday and told the other girls, who all made a fuss of Hannah. They persuaded Hannah to ask her parents to give her a birthday party at a local fast-food restaurant. Hannah was reluctant to do so as she knew her parents had spent a lot of money on the house move. In addition, she suspected the girls were being friendly with her only so she would invite them to her party. Eventually, they persuaded her to ask for the party. Her parents were delighted that she had made so many friends.

On the day of the party, Hannah and her parents waited in anticipation for the guests to arrive. No one came. Hannah was extremely upset and her parents were distressed on her behalf. Worst of all, on her return to school the next day, she had to face the giggles, sneers and taunts of the girls who had duped her.

Suggested approaches

1   Girls need to be wary of unexpected invitations or of agreeing to do something with those not previously friends.
2   Hannah may need help to make friends in her new school. If this is not possible, she could be given help to make friends out of school.
3   The bullies should be identified and made aware that their behaviour was an aggressive act and could carry sanctions.
4   Those who colluded with the bullies should be made aware of how influential they had been. Discussion could help them understand that they could have behaved differently without fearing reprisals from the bullies.
5   Hannah may benefit from assertiveness training.

CASE STUDY

Marie: a retrospective case

In recent years, adults have more readily admitted to bullying others when younger. Marie is a woman in a prominent position in her community. When at school, she and her friends were jealous of the academic achievements of Jane, a girl in the same class. Just prior to the university entrance exams, they hid Jane's essays, books and notes as a joke, even though they knew that it was cruel and could destroy Jane's chance of academic success. Failing her exams would mean that she could not follow her chosen career. Luckily, Jane achieved the required exam results.

Ever since the episode, 40 years ago, Marie has felt a strong sense of remorse. After training to teach, she married a local farmer and had to return to live in the next village to Jane. Marie saw Jane regularly in her professional role and continues to see her in the neighbourhood. She is faced with her past most days and urges that bullies need to be aware that acts considered a joke at the time may haunt them in future years.

SECTION 7
Remediation, Reparation and Resolution

19 Strategies for supporting individual girls

Why is bullying still with us?

Over the past twenty years, there has been a steady input of funded initiatives addressing bullying (DfES 2002). Awareness raising, specific programmes, curriculum input and extra personnel have been introduced into our schools. Why do distressing cases still emerge and young people continue to witness bullying on a regular basis? Bullying remains difficult to resolve and is recognized as being, in the words of Mona O'Moore, a 'tough nut to crack' (Smith *et al.* 2004: 285).

- *We may have been too simplistic in our approach.* Bullying is a complex behaviour only relatively recently investigated (Olweus 1978; Besag 1989). As with all behavioural issues, there will not be one, simple answer to the problem. If there were an easy solution, young people would have discovered it for themselves.
- *We have only recently considered the significance of gender differences.* Although gender differences were noted in earlier work (Besag 1989), there was little rigorous research available to guide and inform gender-specific remedial approaches.
- *Bullying is a difficult area to research.* The subtle interactions that pass between young people require research methodologies that depend on sophisticated equipment and a generous time allocation. This makes it an expensive area to investigate in appropriate detail. We may have covered the more obvious and simplistic interactions but have yet to make headway into the equally influential covert areas of bullying.
- *It is a false premise to suppose that we are able to eradicate bullying.* Bullying is a behaviour that lies on the spectrum of aggression and, as is the case with other types of aggressive behaviours, it will be with us for some time to come.

- *We may have taken a generalized approach without matching remedial approaches to specific problems.* We may need to match the resolution more closely to the problem. One size does not fit all. Strategies that are effective with 10-year-old boys using physical aggression may not work with a group of adolescent girls attacking the sexual reputation of another.
- *We may not have considered the child as an individual and what lies in his or her power to address the problem.* We need to consider factors such as personality, experience and level of confidence for each child before deciding on a remedial approach.
- *We may not have been cognisant of the specific bullying action and situation.* We need to have appropriate information before we are able to support the victim in choosing a feasible approach.
- *We may need to support victims more closely by discussing exactly how they are going to put their own resolutions into practice.* They need to think through exactly what they are going to do, how they are going to do it, and consider all possible consequences of their actions.

Outlined below is a range of strategies found to be effective in addressing bullying. Further information is given in the following publications by this author among others:

Bullies and Victims in Schools (Besag 1989)
We Don't Have Bullies Here! (Besag 1992)
Coping with Bullying (Besag 1999), CD-ROM available from Rotary Clubs or the author (see p. 216 for contact details)
Preventing and Responding to Bullying in Schools (Besag 2005), available from PBM, 7 Quinton Close, Merseyside PRB 2TD

Strategies for adults supporting girls

The first line of approach in any remedial work with girls must be to ensure that everyone, students and relevant adults, fully understand the problem and the possible ramifications of bullying behaviours. We need to make all girls aware of the sophisticated modes of bullying used under the guise of quarrels and friendship. They need to recognize and understand the nuances of the situations they may encounter. The multifarious modes of indirect aggression used by girls are potent and destructive. If girls do not understand, or accept, that gossiping, social exclusion and other such modes of indirect aggression are bullying behaviours, they will not fully appreciate the distress or danger the victim is experiencing. If this is genuinely the case, we cannot blame them for using these harmful tactics. It is beholden on us to protect the emotional as well as the physical well-being of our young. We must remember that it is every child's right to go to school in safety. All adults need to be aware of the signs of stress, even though bullying may not be at the root of the problem. A list of warning signs is given in Besag (1989, 1992).

Listening and talking to girls

General principles

- Come to terms with your own emotional responses to the problem. Try not to overemphasize the effects. Separate your own priorities, fears and anxieties.
- It is important to give some thought to the level of distress experienced by the victim. The girl may be in a state of shock or distress.
- Understand that the victim may not be ready to talk about the bullying.
- If you are a parent, the victim's priority may be to protect you. We socialize girls to care, so she may be wary of disclosing what has happened.
- She may feel too embarrassed to talk. Some bullying acts are extremely demeaning.
- Consider her telling you as a disclosure and treat it sensitively.
- She may consider herself a social failure and no one can help her.
- Let *her* do the talking. She may only want you to listen.
- Let her know that you want to help and are willing to listen at any time and *nothing* will shock you.
- Be prepared for her emotions being a mixed bag of fear, shame, helplessness, anger and revenge. Help her to accept these as normal responses.
- Use active listening by giving your full attention.
- Avoid closed questions she can respond to with single words such as yes or no.
- Aim to keep questions in the third person – 'Tell me about the bullying in school', 'Tell me what kinds of things happen'.
- Avoid giving advice. Help victims to develop their own problem-solving approach that they can use in other situations in the future.

Essential requirements

- Avoid interruptions.
- Avoid sitting higher than her.
- Sit slightly askew rather than face-to-face as that can be threatening.
- Sit with an open posture rather than with arms folded and leaning forward.

- Appear relaxed, calm and speak slowly.
- Offer genuine praise, for example for courage, action, temper control, clear thinking.
- Acknowledge the courage it may have taken for her to seek help.
- Find out what she wants and seek her permission before taking any action.

Stages of disclosure

It is often difficult for a victim to admit to the bullying. The following stages may be in evidence:

1 Denial – the victim denies the bullying.
2 Partial disclosure – the victim admits there is bullying but says she is not the target.
3 Disclosure but dismissal – the victim admits she is bullied but dismisses it.
4 Disclosure and acceptance – the victim is ready to talk.
5 Problem solving.

Problem solving

It is important that the girl shares in a problem-solving approach. This empowers her and is an effective way of raising self-esteem. In addition, she will feel more confident if required to face problems in the future. Solution-focused practice is a well-proven problem-solving technique. The following procedure is an abbreviated form. Further information and training are available from the author (see page 216 for contact details). The publication by De Shazer (1985) is a good starting point.

Start with general conversation using topics that are of interest to the girl and find something about which you can offer genuine praise. When you think she is ready to talk about the bullying, ask the following:

1 What is the problem?
2 How does it make you feel?
3 Feed back in an abbreviated form what the girl has said. This shows you have listened and understood and it helps to clarify her thoughts.
4 What have you tried that was successful, even partially?
5 What else could you try?
6 What are your options?
7 What could be the outcome of each option? It is important to take the girl down the path of each action she suggests so that she is clear

about possible outcomes. This helps to clarify which would be the best option and forms a brief rehearsal for future action.

8 What is your best choice?
9 How are you going to go about doing this?
10 Recognize this process may have been difficult for her and praise her for working with you.

It is important to check that all is well. The victim may say everything has improved even though the situation remains the same.

Suggested strategies

It is possible to teach girls a range of coping strategies. Several have already been included in the body of this work. They can be divided into the following categories.

- Confront
- Avoid
- Deflect
- Cope

and

- Immediate
- Medium term
- Long term

Immediate strategies

1 It is important to encourage the girl to do something active. Action triggers mood-enhancing endorphins, especially if the activity involves being in the fresh air. Encourage her to get outside. Suggest she thinks about taking an older person's dog for a walk. Doing something for someone else often helps to raise a depressed mood. She may like to do their gardening or shopping occasionally. This will help her focus on something other than the bullying.
2 Help her to find other friends and to meet new people.
3 Encourage her to try a new activity. A sense of achievement is a morale booster. Genuine praise increases self-worth. A passion can deflect stress and anxiety. Following a passion always raises the mood.
4 Encourage the victim not to seek reprisals as this could continue the negative interactions.

5 Encourage her to try to ignore the hurtful things said by the attackers. We all have faults. The bullies are simply picking on the faults of others rather than acknowledging their own.

6 Help her to think of the bullying impersonally as a bad habit that must be broken.

7 Recognize the power and destructive nature of some attacks. Suggest she gives herself time to heal.

8 Help her to recognize whether she is sad, unhappy or depressed.

9 Discuss her usual resilience techniques. Is she a shopaholic or a chocaholic? Does she prefer to talk to friends, visit someone or somewhere, or listen to music? What else could she do? She could make a list and circle those strategies that have worked in the past. It may be time to consider new strategies.

10 Encourage her to be creative. She may like to write a poem about how she feels, draw a picture or create a collage, write a song, bake a cake, design a dress or make jewellery.

11 Encourage her to reinvent herself for fun. She could update her clothes with a new belt, scarf or a flower, put new combinations and colours together, shorten trousers to make crop jeans, try a new hairstyle or make-up.

12 Encourage her to concentrate on her schoolwork, hobby or talent. Suggests that she does her best and puts her energies there. She may not have the most friends but she may achieve at a level higher than she thought possible.

13 There is life after school. Encourage her to set her goals for high marks, being awarded a certificate, winning a scholarship or a gaining a good CV.

14 Arrange for her to visit where she would like to work even if it will be a few years yet before she goes out to work. Ask if she could spend a morning in a hairdresser's salon, a garage, a veterinary surgery or animal sanctuary. Ask if she could help in a shop or library. Help her set a goal for the future.

15 Suggest she organizes her work, tidies her desk or bedroom. She may be resistant, but having a clear-out can help her feel better. Clutter clutters the mind. Help her to redecorate her room.

16 Encourage her to keep smiling. Remind her that the endorphins released when she smiles will help to raise her mood.

17 She may wish to do voluntary work for a charitable organization, with younger or older people or animals. She could help with a youth club. Suggest she looks in the phone book for ideas and information or asks in school, the local library, neighbours or relatives.

18 She could ask family members or other adults what they did when they had problems.

19 Girls who enjoy being in a group could think about group activities such as playing music, learning a foreign language or joining a dance class. She could join a fitness or swimming club. Playing a sport may help her to make new friends. Help her to seek out a club where she can share a hobby or skill.

20 Enquire about evening classes.

21 Designated holidays are a way of making friends. Someone may know a family abroad for an exchange visit.

22 Many successful entrepreneurs have started something because there was nothing to meet their own needs. Suggest she starts a club.

23 Ask her to write down all the distressing things that have been said then burn the paper for her.

24 Encourage her to keep a diary and to write down only the good things that happen each day. This can help highlight that the bullying is not happening all the time.

25 Sometimes it helps to keep a diary writing down the bullying attacks. This is a useful record for those supporting the girl and it serves the same purpose for the girl as the diary above.

Confronting the attacker

If the girl wishes to resolve the situation by confronting the bully or bullies, an indirect mode may be best in the first instance. An adult could facilitate the writing of a letter, the making of a tape recording or production of some other mode of communication whereby the attackers understand the distress they have caused. A sensitive judgement must be made by the adult supporting the girl regarding how to present this to the bullies as they may already be fully aware of the effects of their behaviour. If this is so, the best approach may be for the adult in charge to let the bullies know that their behaviour, their understanding and responses, are known and that sanctions will be imposed if the bullying continues. If they do not wish to include the target girl in their group, they must leave her alone and let her make other friends.

A meeting with the bully should be arranged only if the victim feels confident. It may be preferable for an adult to be there to act as mediator if necessary.

Avoiding, deflecting or de-escalating an attack

The appearance of confidence is a sound protective factor and goes a long way in warding off attack. Young people need to learn how to stay calm when under attack, but *ignoring* is a skill that needs to be taught and practised. Parents, teachers and older students can help. The following techniques can be used to get out of a bullying situation without losing face. It is necessary to have a few well-chosen sentences prepared. All these responses need rehearsal and practice.

Fogging
The victim deflects insults by using phrases such as 'You may think I am fat, but I am happy with my weight', 'That may be your opinion but I don't think so', 'The trouble is my mum's such a marvellous cook'.

Broken record
When under pressure to comply, it is best to give a response such as 'No. I don't want a drink, thank you.' This is repeated without giving any explanation or digressing from the refusal. If an explanation or excuse for the refusal is given, the persuaders then have leverage to argue, thus wearing down their target's resistance.

Humour
The use of humour is a powerful defence strategy. Encourage the victim to see the funny side of the taunts. It is better to laugh at yourself than be laughed at by others. It is important to ensure the victim does not think you are dismissing her claims as unimportant.

Concentration techniques
It is helpful to use concentration techniques to deflect the mind, and subsequently the emotions, on something other than the bullies. The following are examples of using cognitive techniques to take the mind off what is happening so that the victim gives the outward appearance of ignoring the bullies.

1. Prepare a mantra
A mantra could be the victim's name and address recited repeatedly in as much detail as possible. Alternatively, if confronted by the attackers, the victim concentrates on a mental exercise such as reciting a multiplication table or counting backwards.

2. Imagination techniques
Encourage the victim to imagine:

- she is inside a clear plastic tube where no harm can come to her;
- she is a turtle and can pull her head into her shell for protection;
- she is in a safe place or with a special person;
- she imagines she is protected by the armour of her choice. This could be that of Darth Vader, a medieval knight, a magic cloak, James Bond's bulletproof vest and equipment. She may prefer a magic wand, a book of spells or magic dust.

3. A secret place
The victim can imagine:

- she has a special, secret place;
- she has won a special holiday or a competition;
- she has been invited to compete in an international contest of some kind;
- she has won a date with her favourite star;
- a preferred, powerful adult or older student is by her side to protect her. This could be someone from a novel, film or a music icon.

All such techniques need to be practised, perhaps with a parent or older student, so that they become automatic when faced with a tormentor. The power of these strategies is in imagining the fine details as this focuses the mind. It is useful to think of all the senses. This could be the feel, sound and smell of the armour as the wearer moves, or the sound of the sea lapping against the shore of an island, or feel of the snow when imagining a skiing holiday.

Long-term strategies

Desensitization
This process has been described in the suggested approaches at the end of Chapter 12.

Forget these friends
Encourage the girl to meet new friends. Friends do not need to be same sex or age as her and she may feel more comfortable with older or younger welcoming people. She could spend time with a relative, neighbour or older friend until she feels confident. They may have useful advice to offer. She may find it easier to talk to them about the bullying if she feels ashamed or is afraid of worrying her parents, or is anxious about reprisals if her parents go to the school and her attackers find out.

Talk about the bullying
Encourage her to talk openly with family and friends and discuss the issues with those she can trust in advance of an attack so that she is prepared.

Self-talk
Problem-solving self-talk is a positive way forward. These techniques need tuition and practice.

A brief form of solution-focused practice can be used based on that given above. A pencil and paper may be useful to jot down ideas.

1   What is the problem?
2   How does it make me feel?
3   What have I tried to do about it that was successful – even partially?
4   What else could I try?
5   What are my options?
6   What could be the outcome of each option?
7   What is my best option?
8   How shall I go about doing it?

Cognitive interventions – turning negative thoughts to positives
Refer to publications such as Trower *et al.* (1988) and Squires (2002).

Sadness and depression encourage us to think in a negative way. *There is always another side to the cloud.* For example, a girl walking across the playground, fearing the bullies, thinks: 'They are ignoring me. They think I am not worth speaking to.' It may be that this is an erroneous assumption. Change this thought around to: 'They haven't seen me. I'll smile and say hello as I walk past. They may acknowledge me. I won't have lost anything. I'll just give it a try.' Or change it around to: 'They may not have heard me yesterday. They were not expecting me to speak. I'll speak clearly and smile and see if they speak or smile.'

Remember, it takes time to build up friendships. Even if you have known the girls a long time, now may be the right time to aim to move things forward and make a connection.

Give the girl time for reflection so she can make a considered choice. Never encourage immediate action that she may regret.

Specific strategies for parents and carers

See the section above for relevant suggestions.

The emotions of parents are likely to be powerful if their child is under attack (see Figure 19.1). Parents have a strong, ethological response to protect their offspring by attacking those they think have harmed them in some way. Be rational. Sleep on any plan. Avoid the daily inquisition at the door, 'What did they do to you today?'

Lighten the load
*   Enjoy fun things together such as art or music, or try something different such as scuba diving. The local swimming baths will have information.

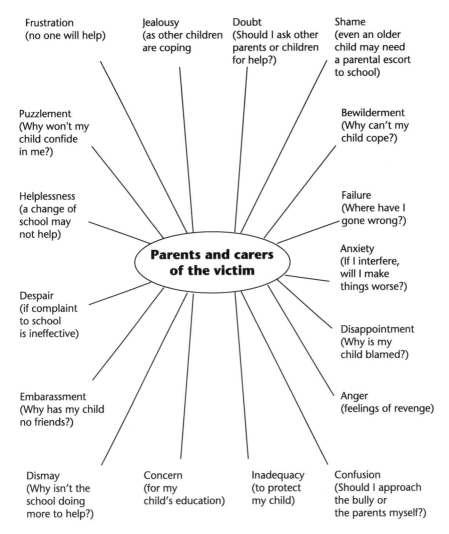

Figure 19.1 Reactions of parents and carers of the victim.

- Go to the cinema, to a restaurant or go out for the day. Try to go away for a few days.
- Make home a place of safety and comfort, a sanctuary and a refuge.
- Comfort your daughter, hug her and try to meet any special requests. Show you respect her. Encourage friends and siblings to help.
- Cook a special meal or bake a surprise cake.
- Join an appropriate group, such as tennis, golf, cookery or Pilates, and take her along.

Talk to the school

- Ask if your daughter can move seat, group or class. In extreme cases, a new school may offer a new start.
- Ask the school for help to find ways forward. It is rarely your sole responsibility.
- Ask about parent workshops.
- Get advice from Kidscape or ChildLine.
- Ask about other services such as the Bullying Alliance, Connexions, the local Educational Psychology Service, community services, the Mental Health Service. Ask the school or local library for addresses and information.
- Look on the web.
- If necessary, contact the police.

Restoring self-esteem and confidence

Your daughter will need your support and help owing to her low confidence and self-esteem.

- Smile at her whenever appropriate. This will make you both feel better.
- Talk in positive terms and look forward to the future. Avoid dwelling on the past.

Programme to develop confidence

The aim is to integrate the young person as soon as she is comfortable, into the peer group. To push an isolated young person into a club or disco will only display their friendless state and social rejection to all. The programme is only an outline and needs to be adapted according to individual needs and progress.

1. Young people and adult groups

It is advisable to start with groups that include both young people and adults. Adults are often welcoming, tolerant and forgiving. Introductory groups at which parents accompany their children could be computers, music, weight training, chess, self-defence, craft, woodwork, dance classes, dog training, flower arranging, computer animation, photography.

The advantages of this process are that such activities offer a degree of social interaction, but from a position of safety as participants may choose how and why they become involved with others. Strong structures and adult support are needed at this stage. The opportunities to be gained include:

- Experimenting with safe social settings.
- The chance to practise and increase skills and techniques to enhance self-image, self-confidence and self-esteem.

- Companionship and friendship.
- An exchange of ideas and information.
- A newly acquired skill increases confidence.
- A new skill can increase kudos.
- As the emphasis is on learning techniques there should be less emphasis on social interactions than in a casual peer group setting.
- The adult is able to observe the social behaviour of the child, which can be enlightening.
- A shared interest between parent and child is the basis of a supportive relationship.
- The young person can try out approach behaviours towards others in the supportive presence of their parents.
- Young people often respond better to adults other than their parents in a learning situation.
- This could lead to a special interest or hobby that could be pursued in a group where they can work in parallel with others rather than in full interaction.
- A skill-based group is less threatening than a social group.

2. The peer group
Social confidence and ease can be gained by children initially working alone but in communication with others: fan clubs, correspondence (e.g. chess, pen pal), voluntary work (e.g. hospital radio, library work), or working with animals or plants.

3. Interacting peer group
These are groups where peer social interaction can take place under supportive adult supervision. This could be a computer, drama or music club or badminton. There should be the opportunity for the young person to make as much, or as little, social communication as they like.

4. Regular groups
As soon as possible the young person should be eased into regular groups supported by adults: school, church, community, disco, quiz nights. An older child may be willing to accompany them initially if appropriate. Any skill the child can display, unobtrusively, can be used to gain validity of purpose within the group, such as offering:

- a service: sell tickets, make coffee, keep scores, buy supplies;
- a talent: accounts, posters, music, costumes, photography;
- enthusiasm: organize trips, guest speakers, draw up rotas;
- hard work: tidy, fetch and carry, make refreshments.

5. Public groups
The final stage will be to attempt entry to fully independent groups such as a public disco, party or sports club.

Coping

Prepare
You cannot change the world, so strengthen the young person's coping skills as in the strategies outlined above. These skills can be honed through rehearsal, preparation, desensitization and role play.

Things to avoid saying
- Why are they doing this – what have you done?
  Change to: Let's think what can be done.
- I'm going to school to complain.
  Change to: What would you like me to do? Do you want me to talk to someone in school?
  Victims often do not want any action taken. They are happy that someone knows and will support them if necessary.
- All girls behave like this.
  Change to: Some girls behave like this when they are angry or jealous.
- What happened? You were close friends.
  Change to: Tell me about when it started. What did you notice? When does it happen? Is there anything we can do?
- You are too sensitive. They don't mean it.
  Change to: How can you tell they're not joking?

Working with girl bullies

Why is the girl bullying? The rationale should give indications for remedial approaches.

- Is she jealous? Why is this?
- The girl may be targeting those displaying similar faults or failings to hers.
- She may lack confidence or feel a failure.
- The bullying may be for attention
- She may think of the bullying as fun.
- She may be taking friends from other girls as she is afraid she will have none.
- The group may be encouraging the bullying.
- Encourage her to use her strengths positively.

20 What can the school do?

Sanctions or attitude change?

In tackling bullying it is rarely effective to start by simply challenging the culprit. Reprimands, sanctions and punishments alone will not necessarily eradicate undesired behaviour. To rely solely on this approach is costly in terms of both time and money, and often an ineffective use of both resources. Punishment means someone has to supervise the offender as opportunities may remain for repetition of the attack. It is obvious that even severe sanctions do not eradicate all undesired behaviours; the recidivist rate remains high although our prisons have been full for centuries. We need to use these approaches only as a last resort. A spectrum of approaches for addressing bullying, as given below, is available so that it is beholden on us to start with low-key strategies, moving towards sanctions and punishment only if, and when, these are necessary.

An important role for all

There is a role and appropriate action for the victims, bullies and observers, schools, families and communities in addressing this problem. Standing around doing nothing could encourage the bullying. The media and retail trades must be accountable for promoting unacceptable attitudes in the impressionable young and shaping the culture within which bullying thrives. Even the most counter-suggestive among our young are covertly seeking guidance and forming their attitudes and social mores, so leaving them open to exploitation. Witnesses of bullying often feel angry, distressed, confused and helpless. We need to give them clear guidelines on how to respond if they are not to experience the bullying in a vicarious manner.

Whole-school approaches

Research has shown that intervention by schools in an effort to tackle bullying can be effective. Below is a summary of research findings collated from individual research papers and books. A summary can be found in Smith *et al.* (2004).

1   For various reasons, interventions have been more effective in primary schools than in secondary schools. However, all schools that implemented preventative and protective strategies did better than the control group.
2   Success depends on the quantity and quality of adult involvement.
3   The whole-school approach and school policy are important but these can be vague terms. Their effectiveness depends on the detail of the implementation.
4   Class management was an important factor. Significant elements were the classroom climate, class rules against bullying, class meetings, classroom activities and curriculum work.
5   Student participation and peer interventions were noted as effective factors.
6   The involvement of staff included: discussion groups; the perceived importance of tackling bullying to all the staff and senior management; staff consensus on what needed changing; the coordination of responses; availability of information for staff and continuing professional development, including contributions from experts.
7   Supervision included: break-time supervision; staff vigilance; intervention in playground bullying; the redesign of the schoolyard.
8   Meetings with parents of victims, bullies and all other children were effective, as was adult awareness and involvement in the programme.
9   Talks and individual intervention plans for bullies and victims, including a discipline plan for bullies, were effective.

The above shows that emphasis must be placed on preventing bullying rather than simply responding to events. The aim should be to create an appropriate ethos and an emotionally literate school.

Given below is a range of procedures and measures of good practice which parents and schools need to have in place in order to address bullying. These form the bedrock upon which to start in considering gender differences in interventions. However, most of these programmes and strategies are applicable to working with boys as well as girls.

Immediate approaches

1   It is essential that the victim feels safe. Ensure she knows that there is to be a determined effort to stop the bullying. If necessary, call a multidisciplinary meeting.
2   All students should have access to a member of staff with whom they can discuss personal matters comfortably. Each student should feel free to choose whom to approach when worried.
3   Strategies given earlier are appropriate for schools to use when preparing an immediate response for a victim.

Medium-term approaches

A survey
An anonymous survey could reveal that many students come across bullying in some form in their school career. Questionnaires for primary and secondary school are given in Besag (1992).

Support for younger students
It could be useful for older students to make a booklet of advice, or a brief film, for younger students, drawing on what they found helpful. Older students can talk to younger students about issues such as bullying.

Art
Girls enjoy working together but adults need to keep a close eye on their social interactions. Following a discussion group, give the girls pieces of paper cut to the size and shape of leaves. Ask them to paint one side of the paper to resemble a leaf. The girls write with coloured pens some of the bullying acts, words and phrases they have received, used or witnessed in the past on the reverse of their leaf. Without anyone else seeing what has been written, each girl pastes her leaf on to a wall collage of a bonfire to signify the destroying of these bullying behaviours.

Ask victims to draw or write on a flipchart all the good things they feel about themselves. It is a powerful exercise if others volunteer to do this for them. They can draw round the student lying on the floor and fill in the outline with compliments. These comments could be put on a T-shirt.

Drama
Many girls enjoy drama and dance. They could prepare a drama to present to younger students. Some may prefer to do the music or costumes for a production.

Older students as models

Older students from the school or local college of further education can work with small groups of girls on a project. For example, this could be an art project for the school or community. It is most effective if done on a weekly basis over several weeks. The older students model behaviours such as negotiation, mediation, empathy and compliments while working with the students. They are able to give recognition and respect to the more vulnerable students. The girls think the end product is the reason for the working groups. Only the older students know that the underlying rationale is to improve the girls' social behaviour.

Conflict resolution

Many girls only want someone to hear their side of a quarrel, making it impossible for them to discuss the problem rationally. A mediator ensures that both sides of the story are given an equal and impartial hearing. This may be enough for the girls to resume their friendship. Mediation is not a technique to use if a vulnerable victim has to face a powerful bully. Both disputants must feel comfortable about trying the mediation. Primary schools, as well as secondary schools have effective student mediators.

Long-term approaches

An effective approach is for the school to have a training day on bullying which incorporates a variety of workshops for staff. Teachers could choose an area of interest outside their usual role at school and prepare a day for a group of students around their choice e.g., a maths teacher could help students compose a rap song or drama. Further information is given in Besag (1992).

Building up friendship skills

A strong supportive friendship network is the most powerful protective factor. Those without friends often feel rejected and lonely and quickly lose confidence and self-esteem. The peer group may fail to include a child from thoughtlessness rather than active rejection. Programmes such as Circle of Friends (Newton *et al.* 1996) can develop group awareness of those children who feel isolated and rejected. Staff may be able to help in building up friendship networks, internal or external to school, by identifying other students with similar interests.

Building confidence, self-esteem and assertiveness

Once lost, it is difficult to restore confidence and self-esteem. The best response is to ignore any defensive behaviour and embark upon a *practical* plan of action, discussing the bullying as little as possible. It is possible for young people to learn by teaching others. For example, the girls could help in a toddler group alongside professionals and parents. Many peer supporters began their training because they were bullied and wanted to help others. It would be essential to check that the peer supporters are comfortable with their role. If the focus is on the task rather than social behaviour, these students often gain in confidence.

A vulnerable student may progress best in an adult-based group, gradually working towards inclusion in adult-controlled peer groups and finally to groups and events both peer run and peer based without adult supervision (see 'Programme to develop confidence' in the previous chapter).

Working with bullies in schools

Aim to match the bullying actions to a spectrum of responses, starting with a low-key response. We need to 'give every child a chance to change' (Besag 1992).

Stage 1: Awareness raising

- Awareness of the effect of their actions can be effective in changing the behaviour of many bullying children as young people can confuse leadership and dominance. Use low-key discussions to highlight the difference.
- Many bullies have excellent communication and leadership skills (Sutton *et al.* 1999). Encourage them to use these skills in a positive manner. Offer the opportunity to run coaching sessions for the academic programme or games skills. They could set up groups based on hobbies or activities or lunchtime clubs. They need to work with older students who model appropriate behaviour.
- Girls asked why they bullied others blamed boredom (Owens, Shute and Slee 2000). Teasing and taunting others was an enjoyable way to pass the time. Organizing games, clubs and other activities may help. However, this may have been an excuse and not an accurate response.
- Some young people do not have a full repertoire of social behaviours. They have not learnt the skills of bartering, empathy, negotiation and reciprocity. In anger or frustration, they turn to demanding, domineering and forceful responses. In summary, they have an egocentric attitude and see only their point of view and needs. A relevant intervention programme is given at the end of this chapter.

The role of the peer group

As bullying is hidden from adult eyes, the most powerful avenue for change is that of working with the peer group. Young people themselves are the eyes, ears and knowledge of the school. They know what is happening in the social sub-curriculum organized by young people themselves that is more important to the individual child than any academic programme (Besag 1989). There are many ways the peer group can address bullying:

- Send a letter to school from home alerting staff to bullying they have witnessed.
- Set up a bully box in school. Students post notes to alert staff.
- They could call a girl away from a group on a pretext if it looks as though she is in trouble.
- As with boys who like an audience, those who stand by, even the silent observers, are fuelling the fire. By standing by, they are giving silent permission for the bullying to continue. They must move away and seek help.

The ripple effect of bullying
A most effective strategy is for the whole peer group to make it known to bullies that others consider their behaviour unacceptable. Some who bully may be popular among the group owing to their sense of humour, but this may be at the expense of another child. If safe to do so, the witnesses should challenge the bullies. If this is not possible, they should walk away. To stay and watch, even though they are uncomfortable or angry about the bullying, is giving the bullies an audience that they will read as permission.

Peer support systems
Schools are increasingly using peer support systems as central to their anti-bullying policies. It is possible for a school to have more than one system in place at any one time as each can be used to address the issue of bullying in a different way. Any peer support system needs to be implemented with caution. Such schemes are one of the most valuable and effective ways of addressing bullying, yet it can be dangerous to introduce a scheme without careful preparation and follow-up. The peer supporters must be properly trained. Once trained, they must then be supported with regular high-quality adult supervision from teachers trained in the methods of peer support. Poorly trained and supported peer support systems can leave the vulnerable at risk.

Stage 2: Avoid the blame game

- If discussions with the bullies fail to bring about change, low key, more structured approaches could be considered such as the No Blame Approach (Maines and Robinson 1992) or The Method of Common Concern (Pikas 1989).

- Some children use bullying as a way of getting friends. The strategy of Circle of Friends (Newton *et al.* 1996) could be useful if the bully is acting in this way due to feelings of rejection or isolation.

Stage 3: Emotional literacy

Some children are unable to respond appropriately to questions such as 'How do you think Sarah feels being left out of things?' They will not have an understanding of empathy and reciprocity if they have not been trained to consider how others feel or react to their actions. The use of games is an effective way to experience turn taking, negotiating and understanding the emotions of others. Many who would dismiss 'lecturing' from an adult will learn these skills during the course of playing board games or similar activities (Besag 1989).

Stage 4: Specialist services and sanctions

The research of Olweus (1978) and Sutton *et al.* (1999) found that some who bully have little remorse and may enjoy watching the distress of their target. If we do not identify and challenge this attitude, we are giving these bullies permission to dominate the more vulnerable for their own need or gratification. They will see no reason to change and so continue to hold this belief into adult life. Those who have serious behaviour or personality disorders will need support from the local Educational Psychology Service, Behaviour Support Team or Community and Adolescent Mental Health Service.

Challenging girls

Some girls enjoy giving a public display of their aggression towards others. This means that public sanctions could be counterproductive. Many highly aggressive girls suffer from mental health problems such as feelings of alienation, loss, helplessness and depression, and turn to challenging and deviant behaviours owing to these powerful negative emotions. Research now points to many having the ability to meet challenges and achieve; they simply do not want to meet the goals most adults set down for them (Houghton and Carroll 2002). It is essential that we support these girls, either in schools or in specialist care, as the long-term prognosis for them is pessimistic with regard to their physical and mental health, their place in the community and future parenting (Collishaw *et al.* 2004).

Suggested approaches for girls in gangs

- Avoid tackling the ringleader first.
- Approach those on the periphery.
- Aim to cut off the support and supply of whatever they are getting from the gang, such as drugs, money or excitement.

- Go with their choices and decisions as far as possible, amending them if necessary.
- Support near approximations to appropriate behaviour.
- Identify the rewards gained from being in the gang and match with more appropriate goals and rewards if feasible.
- Where possible, break up their territory.
- Consider alerting the police to adults housing the girls.
- Identify the group dynamics – the leader, assistants, reinforcers and followers.
- Encourage resilience skills such as dealing with peer and adult pressure, aggression control, recognizing manipulation techniques and dominance.
- Develop tangible and sought-after skills such as driving, computer skills, presentation skills.
- The curriculum content and style could be amended where possible to encompass a flexible, innovative approach, a supportive and tolerant delivery, and be dedicated to genuine needs.
- Parental responsibility should be addressed with support from external services if necessary.

If the girl is truanting this must be addressed as she will be putting herself at risk. The benefits of being out of school need to be matched by those gained by being present. It may be possible to reward all the class if the truant attends. This rewards others for encouraging her and offering her friendship and support. It avoids their feeling resentful seeing someone rewarded for attending school. Girls who truant are often troubled and at great risk, and so warrant as much support as possible.

Student–parent programme

One way of helping girls to develop appropriate social behaviour is to encourage them to attend a programme of weekly sessions with their parents, although it is usually the mother who attends.

A feasible programme would run for six sessions of one hour per week for six weeks. As these girls are often truants, and difficult to manage in class, it is usually possible to run the sessions during school time. Professionals external to school who are involved with the girls may help run the sessions.

A programme to develop emotional literacy could be drawn up to include relevant elements from the three skills modules (see below). The programme could include drama, role play, discussions and mediation techniques. This type of work has brought about change in girls excluded from school and in those involved with the juvenile justice system.

A programme to develop emotional literacy

Emotional skills
- Identifying and labelling emotions.
- Expressing feelings.
- Assessing the intensity of feelings.
- Managing feelings.
- Delaying gratification.
- Controlling impulses.
- Reducing stress.
- Differentiating between feelings and actions.

Cognitive skills
- Self-talk – an inner dialogue.
- Self-awareness.
- Reading and interpreting social cues.
- Understanding behavioural norms.
- Understanding the perspective of others.
- Problem solving and decision making.

Behavioural skills
- Non-verbal communication.
- Verbal communication.

Sanctions

We discontinue those behaviours that are not rewarding. We need to ensure that the bullies are not gaining in any way from their behaviour. In some cases, the local police or community officers may wish to speak to the aggressors. A specialist unit, internal or external to the school, may need to be considered if others are at risk.

Restorative justice

A system of restorative justice is used very effectively in many parts of the world and is now used widely within the judicial system in the UK. The process allows the perpetrator to meet the victim in a safe environment, to hear of the effect of their attacks and to make reparation. This system is an effective way of addressing bullying in the community.

If there are serious concerns regarding the victim or bully or others who are affected, advice may be sought from the local police service, the local education authority or publications such as Fiddy and Hamilton (2004).

Supportive Friends

Is a specific training that gives older students the skills to approach, befriend and support those students who are depressed or even suicidal. The present author holds the only UK licence for this training. Training sessions are available for those wishing to train students in this work. Contact Val Besag for further details:

valbesag (Training and Publications)
tel. 0191 281 7298
email: valbesag@valbesag.co.uk
website: www.valbesag.co.uk

References

Adams, B.N. and Bristow, M. (1979) Ugandan Asian expulsion: rumour and reality. *Journal of Asian and African Studies*, 14: 191–203.

Ahlgren, A. (1983) Sex differences in the correlates of cooperative and competitive school attitudes. *Developmental Psychology*, 19: 881–888.

Ahmad, Y. and Smith, P.K. (1994) Bullying in schools and the issue of sex differences. In J. Archer (ed.) *Male Violence*. London: Routledge.

Alder, P.A. and Alder P. (1984) The carpool: a socializing adjunct to the educational experience. *Sociology of Education*, 57(4): 200–209.

Alder, P.A. and Alder, P. (1995) Dynamics of inclusion and exclusion in pre-adolescent cliques. *Social Psychology Quarterly*, 58(3): 145–162.

Allan, G. (1996) *Kinship and Friendship in Modern Britain*. Oxford: Oxford University Press.

Allport, G.W. (1954) *The Nature of Prejudice*. New York: Addison-Wesley.

Almirol, E.B. (1981) Chasing the elusive butterfly: gossip and the pursuit of reputation. *Ethnicity*, 8: 293–304.

Answers.com (2005) Stanford Prison Experiment: Information from Answers.com. http://www.answers.com/topic/stanford-prison-experiment

Apter, T.E. (2001) *The Myth of Maturity: What Teenagers Need from Parents to Become Adults*. New York: Norton.

Archer, J. (2001) Evolving theories of behaviour. *The Psychologist*, 14(8): 414–430.

Archer, J. and Coyne, S. M. (2005) An integrated review of indirect, relational, and social aggression. *Personality and Social Psychology Review*, 9(3): 212–230.

Arnold, D.H., Homrok, S., Ortiz, C. and Stowe, R.M. (1999) Direct observation of peer rejection acts and their temporal relationship with aggressive acts. *Early Childhood Research Quarterly*, 2: 183–196.

Artz, S. (2005) To die for: violent adolescent girls' search for male attention. In D. Pepler, K. Madsen, C. Webster and K. Levene (eds) *The Development and Treatment of Girlhood Aggression*. Mahwah, NJ: Lawrence Erlbaum.

Asher, S.R. and Coie, J.D. (eds) (1990) *Peer Rejection in Childhood*. New York: Cambridge University Press.

Asher, S.R., Parker, J. and Walker, D.L. (1996) Distinguishing friendship from acceptance: implications for intervention and assessment. In W. M. Bukowski, A. Newcomb and W.W. Hartup (eds) *The Company They Keep*. Cambridge: Cambridge University Press.

Australian Institute of Family Studies (1999) *Creating a 'Child-friendly' Social*

Environment: A Strategy to Reclaim Our Children from Risk? http://www.aifs.gov. au/institute/pubs/wise.html

Bailey, F.G. (ed.) (1971) *Gifts and Poisons: The Politics of Reputation.* New York: Schocken.

Baron-Cohen, S. (2003) *The Essential Difference.* London: Penguin.

Baron-Cohen, S. and Hammer, J. (1997) Is autism an extreme form of the male brain? *Advances in Infancy Research,* 11: 193–217.

Basow, S.A. and Rubin, L.R. (1999) Gender influences on adolescent development. In N.G. Johnson, M.C. Roberts and J. Worell (eds) *Beyond Appearance: A New Look at Adolescent Girls.* Washington, DC: APA.

Bavelas, J.B., Rogers, L.E. and Millar, F.E. (1995) Interpersonal conflict. In C. West and D.H. Zimmerman (eds) *Handbook of Discourse Analysis,* Vol. 4. London: Academic Press.

BBC News (2001) *Children as young as six 'suicidal'.* http://news.bbc.co.uk/1/hi/ health/1432317.stm (accessed 11 July).

Belle, D. (1989) Gender differences in children's social networks and supports. In D. Belle (ed.) *Children's Social Networks and Social Supports.* New York: Wiley.

Bem, S.L. (1993) *The Lenses of Gender: Transforming the Debate on Sexual Inequality.* New Haven, CT: Yale University Press.

Benenson, J.F. (1993) Greater preference among females than males for dyadic interaction in early childhood. *Child Development,* 64: 544–555.

Benenson, J.F., Apostoleris, N.H. and Parnass, J. (1997) Age and sex differences in dyadic and group interaction. *Developmental Psychology,* 33: 538–543.

Bergmann, J. (1987) *Discreet Indiscretions* (translation). New York: Aldine de Gruyter.

Bergsmann, I. (1994) Establishing a foundation: just the facts. *National Juvenile Female Offenders Conference: A Time for Change.* Laurel, MD: American Correctional Association.

Berndt, T. (1979) Developmental changes in conformity to peers and parents. *Developmental Psychology,* 15: 608–616.

Besag, V.E. (1989) *Bullies and Victims in Schools: A Guide to Understanding and Management.* Milton Keynes: Open University Press.

Besag, V.E. (1992) *We Don't Have Bullies Here!* Newcastle upon Tyne: Val Besag.

Besag, V.E. (1999) *Coping with Bullying.* Ashington: Coping with Life (CD-ROM).

Besag, V.E. (2005) *Preventing and Responding to Bullying in Schools.* Ainsdale: Positive Behaviour Management.

Besnier, N. (1989) Information witholding as a manipulative and collusive strategy in Nukulaelae gossip. *Language in Society,* 18: 315–341.

Bjorkqvist, K. (1994). Sex differences in physical, verbal, and indirect aggression: a review of recent research. *Sex Roles,* 30(3/4): 177–188.

Bjorkqvist, K., Osterman, K. and Kaukianinen, A. (1992a) The development of direct and indirect aggressive strategies in males and females. In P. Niemela and K. Bjorkqvist (eds) *Of Mice and Women: Aspects of Female Aggressiveness.* New York: Academic Press.

Bjorkqvist, K., Lagerspetz, K. and Kaukiainen, A. (1992b) Do girls manipulate and boys fight? Developmental trends regarding direct and indirect aggression. *Aggressive Behaviour*, 18: 117–127.

Bjorkqvist, K., Osterman, K. and Lagerspetz, K. (1994) Sex differences in covert aggression among adults. *Aggressive Behaviour*, 20: 27–34.

Boden, D. and Zimmerman, D.H. (1991) *Talk and Social Structure: Studies in Ethnomethodology and Conversation Analysis*. Oxford: Basil Blackwell.

Borja-Alvarez, T., Zarbatany, L. and Pepper, S. (1991) Contributions of male and female guests and hosts to peer group entry. *Child Development*, 62: 1079–1090.

Boulton, M.J. and Hawker, D.S. (1997) Non-physical forms of bullying among school pupils: a cause for concern. *Health Education*, 2: 61–64.

Boulton, M.J. and Smith, P.K. (1994) Bully/victim problems in middle-school children: self perceived competence, peer perceptions and peer acceptance. *British Journal of Educational Psychology*, 62: 73–82.

Bowers, K.S. (1973) Situationalism in psychology: an analysis and a critique. *Psychological Review*, 80: 307–336.

Brenneis, D. and Lein, L. (1977) You fruithead: a socio-linguistic approach to children's dispute settlement. In S. Ervin-Tripp and C. Mitchell-Kernen (eds) *Child Discourse*. New York: Academic Press.

Buhrmester, D. (1996) The need to belong: desire for interpersonal attachments as a fundamental human motivation. *Psychological Bulletin*, 117: 497–529.

Buhrmester, D. and Furman, W. (1987) The development of companionship and intimacy. *Child Development*, 58: 1101–1113.

Bullying Online (2005) *Helping Children and Their Parents with Bullying*. http://www.bullying.co.uk/

Buss, D.M. (1981) Sex Differences in the evaluation and performance of dominant acts. *Journal of Personality and Social Psychology*, 40: 147–154.

Buss, D.M. (1989) Sex differences in human mate preferences: evolutionary hypotheses tested in 37 cultures. *Behavioural and Brain Sciences*, 12: 1–49.

Buss, D.M. and Schmitt, D.P. (1993) Sexual strategies theory: an evolutionary perspective on human mating. *Psychological Review*, 100: 204–242.

Cairns, R.B., Cairns, B.D., Neckerman, H.J., Ferguson, L.L. and Gariepy, J.L. (1989) Growth and aggression: childhood to early adolescence. *Developmental Psychology*, 25: 320–330.

Campbell, A. (1991) *The Girls in the Gang*. Oxford: Blackwell.

Campbell, A. (1993) *Men, Women and Aggression*. New York: Basic Books.

Campbell, A. (1995) A few good men: evolutionary psychology and female adolescent aggression. *Ethology and Sociobiology*, 16: 99–123.

Campbell, A. (2004) *Woman's Hour*, BBC Radio 4, 10 October.

Campbell A. and Muncer, S. (1987) Models of anger and aggression in the social talk of women and men. *Journal for the Theory of Social Behaviour*, 17: 489–512.

Campbell, A., Bibel, D. and Muncer, S.J. (1985) Predicting our own aggression: person, subculture or situation? *British Journal of Social Psychology*, 24: 169–180.

Campbell A., Muncer S. and Gorman B. (1993) Sex and social representations of aggression: a communal-agentic analysis. *Aggressive Behaviour*, 19: 125–135.

Charlesworth, W.R. (1996) Cooperation and competition: contributions to an evolutionary and developmental model. *International Journal of Behavioural Development*, 19: 25–38.

Charlesworth, W.R. and Dzur, C. (1987) Gender comparisons of preschoolers' behaviour and resource utilization in group problem solving. *Child Development*, 58: 191–200.

Chesney-Lind, M. (2001) Girls, violence and delinquency: popular myths and persistent problems. In S. White (ed.) *Youth and Justice* (Handbooks of Law and Social Science). New York: Plenum.

Chesney-Lind, M. and Sheldon R. (1998) *Girls, Delinquency, and Juvenile Justice*. Pacific Grove, CA: Brooks/Cole.

Chung, T.Y. and Asher, S.R. (1996) Children's goals and strategies in peer conflict situations. *Merrill Palmer Quarterly*, 42(1): 125–147.

Coffield, F. (1983) Entrée and exit. *The Sociological Review*, 31(3): 520–545.

Coie, J.D. (1990) Towards a theory of peer rejection. In S.R. Asher and J.D. Coie (eds) *Peer Rejection in Childhood*. Cambridge: Cambridge University Press.

Coie, J.D. and Dodge, K.A. (1998) Aggression and antisocial behavior. In W. Damon and N. Eisenberg (eds) *Handbook of Child Psychology*, 5th edn. *Vol. 3: Social, Emotional, and Personality Development*. New York: Wiley.

Coleman, J.S. (1966) *Equality of Educational Opportunity* (The Coleman Report). Washington, DC: US Government Printing Office.

Collins, W.A. and Laursen, B. (1992) Conflict and relationships during adolescence. In C.U. Shantz and W.W. Hartup (eds) *Conflict in Child and Adolescent Development*. New York: Cambridge University Press.

Collishaw, S., Maughan, B., Goodman, R. and Pickles, A. (2004) Time trends in adolescent mental health. *Journal of Child Psychology and Psychiatry*, 45: 1350–1362.

Cook, K. (1992) Matrifocality and female aggression in Margariteño society. In P. Niemela and K. Bjorkqvist (eds) *Of Mice and Women: Aspects of Female Aggressiveness*. New York: Academic Press.

Cowen, E.L., Pederson, A., Babigian, H., Izzo, L.D. and Trost, M.A. (1973) Long-term follow-up of early detected vulnerable children. *Journal of Consulting and Clinical Psychology*, 41: 438–436.

Crick, N.R. and Grotpeter, J.K. (1995) Relational aggression, gender and social psychological adjustment. *Child Development*, 66: 710–722.

Crick, N.R. and Ladd, G.W. (1990) Children's perceptions of the outcomes of social strategies: do the ends justify being mean? *Developmental Psychology*, 26: 612–626.

Crick, N.R., Casas, J.F. and Mosher, M. (1997) Relational and overt aggression in preschool. *Developmental Psychology*, 33(4): 579–588.

Crick, N.R., Werner, N.E., Casas, J.F., O'Brien, K.M., Nelson, D.A. *et al.* (1999)

Childhood aggression and gender: a new look at an old problem. In D. Bernstein (ed.) *Nebraska Symposium on Motivation*. Lincoln: University of Nebraska Press.

Crombie, G. and Desjardins, M.J. (1993) Predictors of gender: the relative importance of children's play, games and personality characteristics? Paper presented at the biennial meeting of the Society for research in Child Development, New Orleans, March 1998.

Cross, S.E. and Madson, L. (1997) Models of self: self construals and gender. *Psychological Bulletin*, 122: 5–37.

Crozier, W.R. and Dimmock, P.S. (1999) Name-calling and nicknames in a sample of primary school children. *British Journal of Educational Psychology*, 69: 517–531.

Cummins, J. (1984) *Bilingualism and Special Education: Issues in Assessment and Pedagogy*. Avon: Multilingual Matters.

Daly, M. and Wilson, M. (1994) Evolutionary psychology of male violence. In J. Archer (ed.) *Male Violence*. London: Routledge.

Daniels-Beirness, T. (1989). Measuring peer status in boys and girls: a problem of apples and oranges. In B.H. Schneider, G. Attili, J. Nadel and R. P. Weissberg (eds) *Social Competence in Developmental Perspective*. Amersdam: Kluwer Academic.

Davies, B. (1984) Friends and fights. In M. Hammersley and P. Woods (eds) *Life in School: The Sociology of Pupil Culture*. Milton Keynes: Open University Press.

Denham, S.A. (1998) *Emotional Development in Young Children*. New York: Guilford Press.

Dent, S. (2004) *Larpers and Shroomers: The Language Report*. Oxford: Oxford University Press.

De Shazer, S. (1985) *Keys to Solutions in Brief Therapy*. New York: Norton.

de Waal, F.B.M. (1982) *Chimpanzee Politics*. London: Jonathan Cape.

DfES (Department for Education and Skills) (2002) *Bullying: Don't Suffer in Silence. An Anti-bullying Pack for Schools*, 2nd edn. London: DfES.

Diagnostic and Statistical Manual of Mental Disorders IV (1994) Washington, DC: American Psychiatric Association.

Douvan, E. and Adelson, J. (1966) *The Adolescent Experience*. New York: Wiley.

Draper, P. and Harpending, H. (1988) A sociobiological perspective on the development of human reproductive strategies. In K. MacDonald (ed.) *Sociobiological Perspectives on Human Development*. New York: Springer Verlag.

Dunbar, R. (1996) *Grooming, Gossip and the Evolution of Language*. London: Faber & Faber.

Duncan, N. (1999) *Sexual Bullying*. London: Routledge.

Eagly, A.H. and Karau, S.J. (1991) Gender and the emergence of leaders: a meta-analysis. *Journal of Personality and Social Psychology*, 60: 685–710.

Eckerman, C.O., Davis, C.C. and Didow, S.M. (1988) Toddlers' emerging ways of achieving social coordination with a peer. *Child Development*, 60: 440–453.

Eckert, P. (1990) Cooperative competition in adolescent 'girl talk'. *Discourse Processes*, 13: 91–122.

Eder, D. (1985) The cycle of popularity: interpersonal relations among female adolescents. *Sociology of Education*, 58: 976–985.

Eder, D. (1990) Serious and playful disputes: variations in conflict talk among adolescent females. In A. Grimshaw (ed.) *Conflict Talk: Sociolinguistic Investigations of Arguments in Conversations*. Cambridge: Cambridge University Press.

Eder, D. (1991) The role of teasing in adolescent peer culture. *Sociological Studies of Child Development*, 4: 181–197.

Eder, D. and Enke, J.L. (1991) The structure of gossip: opportunities and constraints on collective expression among adolescents. *American Sociological Review*, 56: 494–508.

Eder, D. and Kinney, D. (1995) The effect of middle-school extracurricular activities on adolescents' popularity and peer status. *Youth and Society*, 26: 298–324.

Eder, D. and Sanford, S. (1986) The development and maintenance of interactional norms among early adolescents. In P. Adler and P. Adler (eds) *Sociological Studies of Child Development*, Vol. 1, pp. 283–300. Greenwich, CT: JAI Press.

Eder, D., Evans, C. and Parker, S. (1996) *School Talk: Gender and Adolescent Culture*. New Brunswick, NJ: Rutgers University Press.

Ellis, L. (1995) Dominance and reproductive success among nonhuman animals: a cross-species comparison. *Ethology and Sociobiology*, 16: 257–333.

Ensminger, M.E. and Slusarcick, A.L. (1992) Paths to high school graduation or dropout: a longitudinal study of a first-grade cohort. *Sociology of Education*, 65(2): 95–113.

Erikson, K.T. (1968) Notes on the sociology of deviance. In T.J. Scheff (ed.) *Mental Illness and Social Processes*. New York: Harper and Row.

Eron, L., Huesmann, L.R., Brice, P., Fischer, P. and Mermelstein, R. (1983) Age trends in the development of aggression, sex typing and related television habits. *Developmental Psychology*, 19: 71–77.

Ervin-Tripp, S. (1979) Children's verbal turn-taking. In E. Ochs and B. Schieffel (eds) *Developmental Pragmatics*. New York: Academic Press.

Erwin, P. (1985) Similarity of attitudes and constructs in children's friendships. *Journal of Experimental Child Psychology*, 40: 470–485.

Eslea, M. and Mukhtar, K. (2000) Bullying and racism among Asian schoolchildren in Britain. *Educational Research*, 42: 207–217.

Eslea, M. and Smith, P. K. (1994) Anti-bullying work in primary schools. Poster presented at the Annual Conference of the Development Section of the British Psychological Society, University of Portsmouth, September 1998.

Farrington, D.P. (1991) Childhood aggression and adult violence: early precursors and life outcomes. In D. Pepler and K.H. Rubin (eds) *Development and Treatment of Childhood Aggression*. Hillsdale, NJ: Lawrence Erlbaum.

Farrington, D.P., Loeber, R. and Stouthamer-Loeber, M. (2003) How can the relationship between race and violence be explained? In D.F. Hawkins (ed.) *Violent Crime: Assessing Race and Ethnic Differences*. New York: Cambridge University Press.

Feingold, A. (1994) Gender differences in personality: a meta-analysis. *Psychological Bulletin*, 116: 429–456.

Ferguson, T.J. and Rule, B.G. (1988) Children's attributions of retaliatory aggression. *Child Development*, 59: 961–968.

Feshbach, N.D. (1969) Sex differences in children's modes of aggressive responses toward outsiders. *Merrill-Palmer Quarterly*, 15: 249–258.

Feshbach, N.D. and Sones, G. (1971) Sex differences in adolescent reactions toward newcomers. *Developmental Psychology*, 4: 381–386.

Festinger, L. (1954) A theory of social comparison processes. *Human Relations*, 7: 117–140.

Fiddy, A. and Hamilton, C. (2004) *Bullying: A Guide to the Law*. Colchester: Children's Legal Centre.

Fillion, K. (1997) *Lip Service The Myth of Female Virtue in Love, Sex and Friendship*: London: HarperCollins.

Fisher, R. and Ury, W. (1983) *Getting to Yes: Negotiating Agreement Without Giving In*. New York: Penguin.

Flannery, K.A. and Watson, M.W. (1993) Are individual differences in fantasy play related to peer acceptance levels? *Journal of Genetic Psychology*, 154: 407–416.

Frazer, J. G. (1923) *The Golden Bough*, 3rd edn. London: Macmillan.

Galen, B.R. and Underwood, M.K. (1997) A developmental investigation of social aggression among children. *Developmental Psychology*, 33: 589–600.

Gangestad, S.W. and Thornhill, R. (1997) The evolutionary psychology of extra pair copulation: the role of fluctuating asymmetry. *Ethology and Sociobiology*, 18: 65–88.

Gaskell, E.C. (1985) *Cranford*. Wantage: Black Swan; first published 1853.

Ge, X., Conger, R.D. and Elder, G.H., Jr (1996) Coming of age too early: pubertal influences on girls' vulnerability to psychological distress. *Child Development*, 67: 3386–3400.

Geary, D.C. (1998) Male, female: the evolution of human sex differences. Washington DC: American Psychological Association.

Geballe, S. (2000) *The State of Children's Mental Health in Connecticut: A Brief Overview*. http://www.ctkidslink.org/publications/h00ChldMH06.pdf

Geertz, C. (1983) *Local Knowledge: Further Essays in Interpretive Anthropology*. New York: Basic Books.

Gilbert, P. (1992) *Depression: The Evolution of Powerlessness*. Hove: Lawrence Erlbaum.

Gilmore, D. (1978) Varieties of gossip in a Spanish rural community. *Ethnology*, 17: 89–99.

Glaser, B. and Strauss, A. (1967) *The Discovery of Grounded Theory: Strategies for Qualitative Research*. Chicago: Aldine.

Glazer, I.M. (1992) Interfemale aggression and resource scarcity in a cross-cultural perspective. In: P. Niemela and K. Bjorkqvist (eds) *Of Mice and Women: Aspects of Female Aggressiveness*. New York: Academic Press.

Gluckman, M. (1963) Gossip and scandal. *Current Anthropology*, 4: 307–316.

Goffman, E. (1963) *Behaviour in Public Places*. London: Collier Macmillan.

Goffman, E. (1968) *Stigma: Notes on the Management of Spoiled Identity*. Harmondsworth: Pelican.

Goodman, R.F. and Ben-Ze'ev, A. (eds) (1994) *Good Gossip*. Lawrence, KS: University of Kansas Press.

Goodwin, M.H. (1980) 'He-said-she-said': formal cultural procedures for the construction of a gossip dispute activity. *American Ethnologist*: 7: 674–695.

Goodwin, M.H. (1990) *He-said-she-said: talk as social organization among black children*. Bloomington, IN: Indiana University Press.

Gottman, J. and Mettatal, G. (1986) Speculations about social and affective development: friendship and acquaintanceship through adolescence. In J.M. Gottman and J.G. Parker (eds) *Conversations of Friends: Speculations on Affective Development*. Cambridge: Cambridge University Press.

Gottman, J.M. and Parker, J.G. (eds) (1986) *Conversations of Friends: Speculations on Affective Development*. Cambridge: Cambridge University Press.

Gray, J. (1998) *Men Are from Mars, Women Are from Venus*. London: HarperCollins.

Greer, S. (1995) *Supergrass*. Oxford: Clarendon Press.

Grice, H.P. (1975) Logic and conversation. In P. Cole and J. Morgan (eds) *Syntax and Semantics. Vol. 3: Speech Acts*. New York: Academic Press.

Grotpeter, J.K. and Crick, N.R. (1996) Relational aggression, overt aggression and friendship. *Child Development*, 67(5): 2328–2338.

Hall, G.S. (1904) *Adolescence: Its Psychology and Its Relation to Physiology, Anthropology, Sociology, Sex, Crime, Religion, and Education*. New York: Appleton.

Hargreaves, D.H. (1967) *Social Relations in a Secondary School*. London: Routledge & Kegan Paul.

Harris, J.R. (1995) Where is the child's environment? A group theory of socialisation. *Psychological Review*, 97: 114–121.

Hartup, W.W. (1983) Peer relations. In P. Mussen (ed.) *Handbook of Child Psychology*, 4th edn. New York: Wiley.

Hartup, W.W. (1992) Friendships and their developmental significance. In H. McGurk (ed.) *Childhood Social Development*. Hove: Lawrence Erlbaum.

Haviland, J.B. (1977) *Gossip, Reputation and Knowledge in Zinacanton*. Chicago: University of Chicago Press.

Hawker, D. and Boulton, M.J. (1996) Sticks and stones may break my bones: the effect of bullying on victims. Paper given at the British Psychological Society Annual Conference, Brighton, 1998.

Hawley, P. H. (1999) The ontogenesis of social dominance: a strategy-based evolutionary perspective. *Developmental Review*, 19: 97–132.

Hedstrom, K.E. (1984) A study of repairs in speech. *Stockholm Papers in English Language and Literature*, 4: 69–101.

Heidigger, M. (1962) *Being and Time*. New York: Harper & Row.

Hey, V (1997) *The Company She Keeps: An Ethnography of Girls' Friendship*. Buckingham: Open University Press.

Hines N.J. and Fry D.P (1994) Indirect modes of aggression among women of Buenos Aires, Argentina. *Sex Roles*, 30: 213–236.

Houghton, S., and Carroll, A. (2002). Longitudinal rates of self-reported delinquency of at-risk and not at-risk high school students. *Australian and New Zealand Journal of Criminology*, 35(1): 99–113.

Hoyenga, K.B. and Hoyenga, K.T. (1993) *Gender-related Differences: Origins and Outcomes*. Boston: Allyn & Bacon.

Hughes, L.A. (1988) 'But that's not really mean': competing in a cooperative mode. *Sex Roles*, 19: 669–687.

Hutchins, E. (1991) The social organisation of distributed cognition. In L. Resnick, J.M. Levine and S.D. Teasley (eds) *Perspectives on Socially Shared Cognition*. Washington, DC: American Psychological Association.

Hyde, J.S. (1990) Meta-analysis and the psychology of gender differences. *Signs: Journal of Women in Culture and Society*, 16: 55–73.

Joe, K.A. and Chesney-Lind, M. (1995) Just every mother's angel: an analysis of gender and ethnic variations in youth gang membership. *Gender and Society*, 9: 408–431.

Jones, D.C., Costin, S.E. and Ricard, R.J. (1994) Ethnic and sex differences in best friendship characteristics among African American, Mexican-American, and American adolescents. Poster session presented at Society for Research on Adolescence, San Diego, CA.

Katz, A., Buchanan, A. and Bream, V. (2001) *Bullying in Britain: Testimonies from Teenagers*. East Molesey: Young Voice.

Kaukiainen, A., Bjorkqvist, K., Lagerspetz, K., Osterman, K., Salmivalli, C. *et al.* (1999) The relationships between social intelligence, empathy, and three types of aggression. *Aggressive Behavior*, 25: 81–89

Keenan, K. and Shaw, D. (1997) Development and social influences on young girls' early problem behaviour. *Psychological Bulletin*, 121(1): 95–113.

Keise, C. (1992) *Sugar and Spice? Bullying in Single-sex Schools*. Stoke-on-Trent: Trentham Books.

Kennedy, J.H. (1990) Determinants of peer social status: contributions of physical appearance, reputation, and behavior. *Journal of Youth and Adolescence*, 19: 233–244.

Klein, M. (1946) *Writings. Vol 3: Notes on Some Schizoid Mechanisms*. London: Hogarth Press.

Kochman, T. (1983) The boundary between play and non-play in black verbal duelling. *Language in Society*, 12: 329–337.

Kupersmidt, J.B. and Patterson, C.J. (1991) Childhood peer rejection, aggression, withdrawal, and perceived competence as predictors of self-reported behavior problems in preadolescence. *Journal of Abnormal Child Psychology*, 19: 427–449.

LaFontana, K.M and Cillessen, A.H.N. (2002) Children's perceptions of popular and unpopular peers: a multi-method assessment. *Developmental Psychology*, 38: 635–647.

Labov, W. (1972) *Language in the Inner City: Studies in Black English Vernacular*. Philadelphia, PA: University of Philadelphia Press.

Ladd, G.W. and Kochendorfer, B.J. (1996) Linkages between friendship and adjustment during early school transitions. In W.M. Bukowski, A. Newcomb and W.W. Hartup (eds) *The Company They Keep*. Cambridge: Cambridge University Press.

Lagerspetz, K.M.J., Bjorkqvist, K. and Peltonen, T. (1988) Is indirect aggression typical of females? Gender differences in aggressiveness in 11–12-year-old children. *Aggressive Behaviour*, 14: 403–414.

Larson, R. and Asmussen, L. (1991) Anger, worry, and hurt in early adolescence: an enlarging world of negative emotions. In M.E. Colten and S. Gore (eds) *Adolescent Stress: Causes and Consequences*. New York: Aldine de Gruyter.

Lees, S. (1993) *Sugar and Spice: Sexuality and Adolescent Girls*. London: Penguin.

Lemert, E. (1972) *Human Deviance: Social Problems and Social Control*, 2nd edn. Englewood Cliffs, NJ: Prentice Hall.

Lever, J. (1976) Sex differences in the games children play. *Social Problems*, 23: 478–487.

Loeber, R. and Hay, D. (1997) Key issues in the development of aggression and violence from childhood to early adulthood. *Annual Review of Psychology*, 48: 371–410.

McCabe, A. and Lipscomb, T.J. (1988) Sex differences in children's verbal aggression. *Merrill-Palmer Quarterly*, 34: 389–401.

McLloyd, V.C. (1983) The effects of the structure of play objects on the pretend play of low-income preschool children. *Child Development*, 54(3): 626–635.

Maccoby, E.E. (1990) Gender and relationships: a developmental account. *American Psychologist*, 45: 513–520.

Maccoby, E.E. (1999) *The Two Sexes: Growing up Apart, Coming Together*. Cambridge, MA: Harvard University Press.

Maccoby, E.E. (2002) Gender and group process: a developmental perspective. *Current Directions in Psychological Science*, 11(22): 54–58.

Maccoby, E.E. and Jacklin, C.N. (1974) *The Psychology of Sex Differences*. Stanford, CA: Stanford University Press.

Maccoby, E.E. and Jacklin, C.N. (1987) Gender segregation in childhood. In H. Reese (ed.) *Advances in Child Development and Behavior*, Vol. 20, pp. 239–288. New York: Academic Press.

Magnusson, D., Stattin, H. and Allen, V. (1986) Differential maturation among girls and its relation to social adjustment in a longitudinal perspective. In P. Baltes, D. Featherman and R. Learner (eds) *Life Span Development and Behaviour*, Vol 7. Hillsdale, NJ: Lawrence Erlbaum.

Maines, B. and Robinson, G. (1992) *The No Blame Approach*. Bristol: Lame Duck.

Malone, M.J. (1997) *Worlds of Talk: The Presentation of Self in Everyday Conversation*. Oxford: Polity Press and Blackwell.

Maltz, D. and Borker, R. (1982) A cultural approach to male–female miscommunication. In J. Gumperz (ed.) *Language and Social Identity*. New York: Cambridge University Press.

Manning, M. and Sucklin, A.M. (1984) The function of aggression in the pre-school and primary years. In N. Frude and H. Gault (eds) *Disruptive Behaviour in Schools*. Chichester: Wiley.

Marsh, P. and Paton, R. (1984) Unpublished manuscript cited in Campbell (1995).

Maynard, D. (1985) On the functions of social conflict among children. *American Sociological Review*, 50: 207–223.

Menesini, E. (1997) Behavioural correlates of friendship status among Italian schoolchildren. *Journal of Social and Personal Relationships*, 14(1): 109–121.

Menesini, E. (1998) Bullying among Italian school children. Paper given at the E.C. Conference, Gateshead, Tyne and Wear.

Merten, D. (1997) The meaning of meanness: popularity, competition, and conflict among junior high school girls. *Sociology of Education*, 70: 175–191.

Meyer Spack, P.M. (1985) *Gossip*. New York: Knopf.

Miller, P.M., Danaher, D.L. and Forbes, D. (1986) Sex-related strategies for coping with interpersonal conflict in children aged five and seven. *Developmental Psychology*, 22(4): 543–548.

Miller-Johnson, S., Moore, B.L., Underwood, M.K. and Coie, J.D. (2005) African American girls and physical aggression: does stability of childhood aggression predict later negative outcomes? In D. Pepler, K. Madsen, C. Webster and K. Levene (eds) *The Development and Treatment of Girlhood Aggression*. Mahwah, NJ: Lawrence Erlbaum.

Muncer, S., Campbell, A., Jervis, V. and Lewis, R. (2001) Ladettes, social representations and aggression. *Sex Roles*, 44: 33–44.

Munthe, E. (1989) Bullying in Scandinavia. In E. Roland and E. Munthe (eds) *Bullying: An International Perspective*. London: David Fulton.

Ness, C.D. (2004) Why girls fight: female youth violence in the inner city. *Annals of the American Academy*, 595: 32–48

Newcomb, A.F. and Bagwell, C.L. (1996) The developmental significance of children's friendship relations. In W.M. Bukowski, A.F. Newcomb and W.W. Hartup (eds) *The Company They Keep: Friendship in Childhood and Adolescence*. New York: Cambridge University Press.

Newton, C., Taylor, G. and Wilson, D. (1996) Circle of Friends: an inclusive approach to meeting emotional and behavioural needs. *Educational Psychology in Practice*, 11(4): 41–48.

Nicolopoulau, A. (1997) Worldmaking and identity formation in children's narrative play-acting. In B. Cox and C. Lightfoot (eds) *Sociogenic Perspectives in Internalization*. Hillsdale, NJ: Lawrence Erlbaum.

Nilan, P. (1991) Exclusion, inclusion and moral ordering in two girls' friendship groups. *Gender and Education*, 3(1): 163–182

Nilan, P. (1992) Kazzies, DBT's and tryhards: categorisations of style in adolescent girls' talk. *British Journal of Sociology of Education*, 1(2): 201–213.

Nolen-Hoeksema, S. (2001) *Abnormal Psychology*, 2nd edn. Boston: McGraw-Hill.

Obeidallah, D. and Earls, F. (1999) *Adolescent Girls: The Role of Depression in the Development of Delinquency*, FS000244. National Institute of Justice, Washington, DC: US Government Printing Office.

Olweus, D. (1978) *Aggression in Schools: Bullies and Whipping Boys*. Washington, DC: Hemisphere.

Olweus, D. (1991) Bully/victim problems among schoolchildren: basic facts and effects of a school based intervention program. In D. Pepler and K. Rubin (eds) *The Development and Treatment of Childhood Aggression*. Hillsdale, NJ: Lawrence Erlbaum.

Olweus, D. (1993) *Bullying at School: What We Know and What We Can Do*. Oxford: Blackwell.

Omark, D.R., Omark, M. and Endelman, M. (1973) Formation of dominance hierarchies in young children. In T.R. Williams, (ed.) *Psychological Anthropology*. The Hague: Mouton.

Opie, I. and Opie, P. (1959) *The Lore and Language of School Children*. Oxford: Clarendon Press.

Osterman, K., Bjorkqvist, K., Lagerspetz, K., Kaukiainen, A., Huesmann, L.R. and Fraczek, A. (1994) Peer and self-estimated aggression and victimization in 8-year-old children from five ethnic groups. *Aggressive Behavior*, 20: 411–428.

Owens, L.D. (1996) Sticks and stones and sugar and spice: girls' and boys' aggression in schools. *Australian Journal of Guidance and Counselling*, 6 (May): 45–55.

Owens, L.D. (1999) Physical, verbal and indirect aggression amongst South Australian school students. Unpublished PhD thesis.

Owens, L.D., Shute, R. and Slee, P. (2000) Guess what I just heard! Indirect aggression among teenage girls in Australia. *Aggressive Behaviour*, 6: 67–83.

Paediatrics and Child Health (2004) *Commentary*. http://www.pulsus.com/Paeds/09_04/gand_ed.htm

Parker, J.G. and Gottman, J.M. (1989) Social and emotional development in a relational context: friendship interaction from early childhood to adolescence. In T.J. Berndt and G. Ladd (eds) *Peer Relationships in Child Development*, pp. 95–132. New York: Wiley.

Parkhurst, J.T. and Hopmeyer, A. (1998) Sociometric popularity and peer-perceived popularity: two distinct dimensions of peer status. *Journal of Early Adolescence*, 18: 125–144.

Parliamentary Monitoring Group (2001) *Report of the Portfolio Committee on Social Development on Study Tour to Britain*. http://www.pmg.org.za/docs/2002/com-reports/020227pcsocialreport.htm

Pearson, P. (1999) *When She Was Bad: How Women Get Away with Murder*. London: Virago.

Pellegrini, A.D. (1988) Elementary-school children's rough and tumble play and social competence. *Developmental Psychology*, 24: 802–806.

Pellegrini, A.D. and Smith, P.K. (1998) Physical activity play: the nature and func-tion of a neglected aspect of play. *Child Development*, 69(3): 577–598.

Pepler, D. (1996) A peek behind the fence: what we have learned about bullying. Paper presented at the conference 'Putting the Brakes on Violence', York University, Toronto, August.

Pepler, D., Connolly, J. and Craig, W. (2004) Bullying and Harassment: Experiences of Minority and Immigrant Youth.

Petit, G.S., Bakshi, A., Dodge, K.A. and Coie, J.D. (1990) The emergence of social dominance in young boy's play groups: developmental differences and behavioural correlates. *Developmental Psychology*, 26:1017–1025.

Pikas, A. (1989) The common concern method: for the treatment of mobbing. In E. Roland and E. Munthe (eds) *Bullying: An International Perspective*. London: David Fulton.

Pipher, M. (1994) *Reviving Ophelia: Saving the Selves of Adolescent Girls*. London: Random House.

Rauste-von Wright, M. (1989) Physical and verbal aggression in peer groups among Finnish boys and girls. *International Journal of Behavioral Development*, 12(4): 473–484.

Reicher, S. and Potter, J. (1985) Psychological theory as intergroup perspective: a comparative analysis of 'scientific' and 'lay' accounts of crowd events. *Human Relations*, 38: 167–189.

Richardson, D.R. and Green, L.R. (1999) Social sanction and threat explanations of gender effects on direct and indirect aggression. *Aggressive Behavior*, 25: 425–434.

Rivers, I. and Smith, P.K. (1994) Types of bullying behaviour and their correlates. *Aggressive Behavior*, 20: 359–368.

Rodkin, P.C., Farmer, T.W., Pearl, R. and Van Acker, R. (2000) Heterogeneity of popular boys: antisocial and prosocial configurations. *Developmental Psych-ology*, 36(1): 14–24.

Roland, E. (1988) personal communication.

Roland, E. and Idse, T. (2001) Aggression and bullying. *Aggressive Behavior*, 27: 446–462.

Rose, A.J. and Asher, S.R. (1999) Children's goals and strategies in response to conflicts within a friendship. *Developmental Psychology*, 35: 69–79.

Rosenberg, F.R. and Simmons, R.G. (1975) Sex differences in the self concept of adolescence. *Sex Roles*, 1: 147–159.

Rosnow, R.L. and Fine, G.A. (1976) Inside rumours. *Human Behaviour*, 3(8): 64–68.

Rosnow, R.L. and Fine, G.A. (1996) *Rumour and Gossip: The Social Psychology of Hearsay*. New York: Elsevier.

Rowe, D.C. (1994) *The Limits of Family Influence: Genes, Experience, and Behaviour*. New York: Guilford Press.

Sacks, H., Schegloff, E.A. and Jefferson, G. (1974) A simplest systematics for the organization of turn-taking in conversation. In J.N. Schenkein (ed.) *Studies in the Organization of Conversational Interaction*. New York: Academic Press.

Salmivalli, C. and Kaukiainen, A. (2004) Female aggression revisted: variable- and person-centred approaches to studying gender differences in different types of aggression. *Aggressive Behavior*, 30: 158–163.

Salmivalli, C., Lagerspetz, K.M.J., Bjorkqvist, K., Osterman, K. and Kaukiainen, A. (1996) Bullying as a group process: participant roles and their relations to social status within the group. *Aggressive Behaviour*, 22: 1–15.

Sanford, S. and Eder, D. (1984) Adolescent humour during peer interaction. *Social Psychology Quarterly*, 47: 235–243.

Savin-Williams, R.C. (1979) Dominance hierarchies in groups of early adolescents. *Child Development*, 50: 923–935.

Savin-Williams, R.C. (1980) Social interactions of adolescent females in natural groups. In H.C. Foot, A.J. Chapman and J.R. Smith (eds) *Friendship and Social Relations in Children*. Chicester: Wiley.

Schoeman, F. (1994) Gossip and privacy. In R.F. Goodman and A. Ben-Ze'ev (eds) *Good Gossip*. Lawrence, KS: University of Kansas Press.

Schofield, J. (1982) *Black and White in School: Trust, Tension or Tolerance?* New York: Praeger.

Schofield, V.W. (1981) Complementary and conflicting identities: images of interaction in an interracial school. In S.A. Asher and J.M. Gottman (eds) *The Development of Children's Friendships*. New York: Cambridge University Press.

Seligman, M.E.P. and Peterson, C. (1986) A learned helplessness perspective on childhood depression: theory and research. In M. Rutter, C.E. Izard and P.B. Read (eds) *Depression in Young People*. New York: Guilford Press.

Sharp, S. (1995) How much does bullying hurt? The effects of bullying on the personal well-being and educational progress of secondary aged students. *Educational and Child Psychology*, 12(2): 81–88.

Sharp, S. and Cowie, H. (1998) *Counselling and Supporting Children in Distress*. London: Sage.

Simmel, G. (1964) *Conflict and the Web of Group Affiliation*. London: Collier-Macmillan.

Simmons, R.G. (2002) *Odd Girl Out: The Hidden Culture of Aggression in Girls*. San Diego, CA: Harcourt.

Simmons, R.G., Rosenberg, F.R. and Rosenberg, M. (1973) Disturbance in the self image at adolescence. *American Sociological Review*, 38: 553–568.

Smith, P.K. and Boulton, M. (1990) Rough and tumble play, aggression, and dominance: perception and behaviour in children's encounters. *Human Development*, 33: 271–282.

Smith, P.K. and Myron-Wilson, R. (1988) Parenting and school bullying. *Clinical Child Psychology and Psychiatry*, 3: 405–417.

Smith, P.K., Madsen, K. and Moody, J. (1999) What causes the age decline in reports of being bullied at school? Towards a developmental analysis of risks of being bullied. *Education and Research*, 41: 267–285.

Smith, P.K., Pepler, D. and Rigby, K. (eds) (2004) *Bullying in Schools: How Successful Can Interventions Be?* Cambridge: Cambridge University Press.

Smuts, B.B. (1987) Gender, aggression and influence. In B.B. Smuts, D.L. Cheney, R.M. Seyfarth, R.W. Wrangham and T.T. Struhsaker (eds) *Primate Societies*. Chicago: University of Chicago Press.

Snyder, H.N. and Sickmund, M. (1999) Juvenile offenders and victims 1999: A national report. Washington, DC: Office of Juvenile Justice and Delinquency Prevention.

Snyder, J., Horsch, E. and Childs, J. (1997) Peer relationships of young children: affiliative choices and the shaping of aggressive behavior. *Journal of Clinical Child Psychology*, 26: 145–156.

Squires, G. (2002) *The Theory and Practice of Changing Thinking and Feeling to Change Behaviour: Cognitive Interventions*. Ainsdale: Positive Behaviour Management.

Strauss, A.L. and Corbin, J. (1994) Grounded theory methodology: an overview. In N.K. Denzin and Y.S. Lincoln (eds) *Handbook of Qualitative Research*. London: Sage.

Sumrall, S.G., Ray, G.E. and Tidwell, P.S. (2000) Evaluations of relational aggression as a function of relationship type and conflict setting. *Aggressive Behavior*, 26: 179–191.

Sutton, J., Smith, P.K. and Swettenham, J. (1999) Bullying and theory of mind: a critique of the 'social skills deficit' view of anti-social behaviour. *Social Development*, 8: 117–127.

Symons, D. (1979) *The Evolution of Human Sexuality*. New York: Oxford University Press.

Tajfel, H. (1982) *Differentiation between Social Groups*. London: Academic Press.

Tannen, D. (1992) *You Just Don't Understand: Woman and Men in Conversation*. New York: William Morrow.

Tapper, K. and Boulton, M.J. (2004) Sex differences in levels of physical, verbal, and indirect aggression amongst primary school children and their associations with beliefs about aggression. *Aggressive Behavior*, 30: 123–145.

Thorne, B. (1993) *Gender Play: Girls and Boys in School*. Milton Keynes: Open University Press.

Thorne, B. and Luria, Z. (1986) Sexuality and gender in children's daily worlds. *Social Problems*, 33: 176–190.

Tobin-Richards, M., Boxer, A. and Peterson, A. (1983) The psychological significance of pubertal change: sex differences in perception of self during early adolescence. In J. Brooks-Gunn and A. Peterson (eds) *Girls at Puberty: Biological and Psychosocial Perspectives*. New York: Plenum Press.

Tomada, G. and Schneider, B.H. (1997) Relational aggression, gender, and peer acceptance. *Developmental Psychology*, 33: 601–609.

Toth, S.A. (1978) *Blooming: A Small-town Girlhood*. Boston: Little, Brown.

Trad, P.V. (1987) *Infant and Childhood Depression: Developmental Factors*. New York: Wiley.

Trower, P., Casey, A. and Dryden, W. (1988) *Cognitive Behavioural Counselling in Action*. London: Sage.

Tullock, J. (2000) *The Season Ticket*. London: Jonathan Cape.

Underwood, M.K. (1997) A developmental investigation of social aggression among children. *Developmental Psychology*, 33(4): 589–600.

Underwood, M.K. (2003) *Social Aggression among Girls*. New York: Guilford Press.

Underwood, M.K., Galen, B.R. and Paquette, J.A. (2001) Top ten challenges for understanding gender and aggression in children: why can't we all just get along? *Social Development*, 10(2): 248–266.

Urberg, K.A., Degirmencioglu, S.M., Tolson, J.M. and Halliday-Scher, K. (1995) The structure of adolescent peer networks. *Developmental Psychology*, 31: 540–547.

Vaillancourt, T. (2005) Indirect aggression among humans. Social construct or evolutionary adaptation? In R.E. Tremblay, W.H. Hartup and J. Archer (eds) *Developmental Origins of Aggression*. New York: Guilford Press.

Wachtel, P.L. (1973) Psychodynamics, behaviour therapy and the implacable experimenter: an inquiry into the consistency of personality. *Journal of Abnormal Psychology*, 83: 324–334.

Walkerdine, V. (1990) *Schoolgirl Fictions*. New York: Verso.

Walkerdine, V. (1992) Girlhood through the looking glass. Plenary paper presented at the Alice in Wonderland Conference, Amsterdam, June.

Warden, D., Chrisie, D. and Stevens, C. (1994) Differential perceptions of bullying and prosocial behaviour. *Proceedings of the British Psychological Society*, 3(1): 48.

Watkins, M.J. (1990) Mediationism and the obfuscation of memory. *American Psychologist*, 45: 328–335.

Weisfeld, G.E. (1987) Stability of boys' social success among peers over an eleven-year period. In J.A. Meacham (ed.) *Interpersonal Relations: Family, Peers, Friends*. Basel: Karger.

Weisfeld, G.E. and Billings, R.L. (1988) Observations on adolescence. In K.B. MacDonald (ed.) *Sociobiological Perspectives on Human Development*. New York: Springer Verlag.

White, M. (1987) *The Japanese Educational Challenge*. London: Free Press/Macmillan.

Whitesell, N.R. and Harter, S. (1996) The interpersonal context of emotion: anger with close friends and classmates. *Child Development*, 67: 1345–1359.

Whiting, B.B. and Edwards, C. (1988) *Children of Different Worlds*. Cambridge, MA: Harvard University Press.

Whitney, I. and Smith, P.K. (1993) A survey of the nature and extent of bullying in junior/middle and secondary schools. *Educational Research*, 35: 3–25.

Williams, J. and Best, D. (1990) *Sex and the Psyche: Gender Roles and Self Concepts Viewed Cross-culturally*. Beverly Hills, CA: Sage.

Wilson, M.I. and Daly, M. (1985) Competitiveness, risk taking, and violence: the young male syndrome. *Ethology and Sociobiology*, 6: 59–73, 301, 351.

Wiseman, R. (2002) *Queen Bees and Wannabes: Helping Your Daughter Survive Cliques, Gossip, Boyfriends and Other Realities of Adolescence*. London: Piatkus.

Xie, H., Swift, D.J., Cairns, B.D. and Cairns, R.B. (2002) Aggressive behaviors in social interaction and developmental adaptation: a narrative analysis of interpersonal conflicts during early adolescence. *Social Development*, 11(2): 205–223.

Xie, H., Cairns, B.D. and Cairns, R.B. (2004) The development of aggressive behaviors among girls: measurement issues, social functions, and differential trajectories. In D. Pepler, K. Madsen, C. Webster and K. Levene (eds) *Development and Treatment of Girlhood Aggression*. Mahwah, NJ: Lawrence Erlbaum.

Zarbatany, L., McDougall, P. and Hymel, S. (2000) Gender-differentiated experience in the peer culture: links to intimacy in preadolescence. *Social Development*, 9: 62–79.

Useful websites

http://www.antibullying.net/
http://www.antibullyingalliance.org/
http://www.bbc.co.uk/schools/bullying/
http://www.bullying.co.uk/
http://www.bullyonline.org/schoolbully/index.htm
http://www.ceris.metropolis.net/Virtual%20Library/education/pepler1/
    pepler1.html
http://www.childline.org.uk/
http://www.dfes.gov.uk/bullying/
http://www.kidscape.org.uk/
http://www.valbesag.co.uk/

Index

Related books from Open University Press

COUNSELLING SKILLS FOR TEACHERS
TALKING MATTERS

Gail King

Tina says she is pregnant and considering a termination. Marcus wonders whether he should tell his friends he is gay. You worry whether Gulshan has some form of eating disorder. Stephen's father is very angry with you about the school's treatment of his son.

Jane boasts to you that she and her friends were drunk and smoked cannabis at a party last night. How would counselling skills help a teacher in these situations? Gail King explores the counselling skills which teachers need in their pastoral role, and examines them using examples from teachers' typical experience.

This is a practical book written for both new entrant and experienced teachers who work with school students aged 11 to 18 in mainstream education. It describes the basic listening and responding skills, and how to conduct a helping interview. It covers issues such as professional boundaries, role conflict, self-disclosure, referring on, self-awareness, and cross-cultural awareness. It also includes teachers' legal responsibilities with respect to confidentiality, sex education and the Children Act; and an invaluable section listing relevant organizations.

Counselling Skills for Teachers tackles the pitfalls and the dilemmas faced by teachers in pastoral roles, and provides invaluable guidance as to how counselling skills can be successfully deployed.

Contents
Preface – Counselling skills in secondary education – Listening skills – Responding skills – Implications of using counselling skills – How students present issues – Teachers' legal liabilities and responsibilities – Useful organizations and addresses – Further reading – References – Index.

160pp   0 335 20000 1 (Paperback)

BEHAVIOUR IN SCHOOLS
SECOND EDITION

Louise Porter

Behaviour management in the classroom and playground is one of the most challenging aspects of teaching. The new edition of this popular book offers a comprehensive overview of the major theories of behaviour management in primary and secondary schools, illustrated with detailed case studies. The theories covered range from teacher-dominated methods to more democratic approaches. They include assertive discipline, applied behaviour analysis, the new cognitive behavioural approaches, neo-Adlerian theory, humanism, Glasser's control theory and systems theory. The emphasis is on proactive approaches to discipline which allow teachers to achieve their educational and social goals for their students and themselves. Porter also shows how to enhance students' motivation and help students become confident and independent learners.

Maintaining the balance of theory and practice, the new edition has been fully updated in light of recent research, including a strengthened discussion of inclusion and anti-bias curricula, and sections on motivation and self-esteem. References have been also been updated, making fuller use of UK research.

Behaviour in Schools is a textbook for education students and a reference for experienced teachers who want to improve their ability to cope with disruptive behaviour.

Contents
Part one: The theories – Introduction – The limit-setting approaches – Applied behaviour analysis – Cognitive-behaviourism – Neo-Adlerian theory – Choice theory – Systems theory – Critique of the theories – Part two: Motivating students – Safeguarding students – Meeting students' need for autonomy – Fostering competence – Meeting students' social needs – Part three: Beyond the classroom – Collaborating with parents – Formulating a discipline policy – Bibliography – Index.

368pp   0 335 22001 0 (Paperback)

CHALLENGING VIOLENCE IN SCHOOLS
AN ISSUE OF MASCULINITIES

Martin Mills

This is an important book in which Martin Mills provides a carefully argued analysis of gender-based violence in schools as well as a wealth of strategies for challenging its many facets. *Challenging Violence in Schools* is a grim reminder that the current narrow fixation with academic achievement needs to be broadened if schools are to act responsibly in playing their part in making the future. This book should be compulsory reading for all teachers.
Professor Pat Mahony, University of Surrey Roehampton

- Why are boys the major perpetrators of violence in schools?
- What are the significant issues which schools need to take into account when dealing with boys' violence?
- What are some practical strategies for addressing these issues?

This book explores the relationship between violence and masculinity within schools. There is a clear need to explore this relationship. A substantial amount of evidence exists which demonstrates how boys are the major perpetrators of violence in schools – from extreme acts of violence such as school shootings in the US to more common forms of schoolyard bullying – and that both girls and boys are their victims.

The book suggests that violence has been 'masculinized' in such a way that boys often perpetrate violence as a means of demonstrating their perception of what counts as a valued form of masculinity. This masculinization of violence has often meant that girls experience violence from boys who are seeking to demonstrate their superiority over girls, and it has also meant that some boys often experience violence due to their non-conformity to dominant images of masculinity. In order to support these arguments the book draws on extensive interview data collected from boys and teachers who were involved in anti-violence programs in their schools.

Contents
Introduction: challenging violence in schools as an issue – Violence and the signifiers of masculinity – The violencing of masculinity and masculinization of violence – Boyswork programs and the curriculum – Implementing change: a question of pedagogy? – Conclusion: challenging violence in schools, principles for action – Index.

160pp   0 335 20584 4 (Paperback)

LADS AND LADETTES IN SCHOOL

Carolyn Jackson

This innovative book looks at how and why girls and boys adopt 'laddish' behaviours in schools. It examines the ways in which students negotiate pressures to be popular and 'cool' in school alongside pressures to perform academically. It also deals with the fears of academic and social failure that influence pupils' school lives and experiences.

Drawing extensively on the voices of students in secondary schools, it explores key questions about laddish behaviours, such as:

- Are girls becoming more laddish – and if so, which girls?
- Do boys and girls have distinctive versions of laddishness?
- Do laddish behaviours lead to the same outcomes?
- What are the implications for teachers and schools?

The author weaves together key contemporary theories and research on masculinities and femininities with social and psychological theories and research on academic motives and goals, in order to understand the complexities of girls' and boys' behaviours.

This topical book is key reading for students, academics and researchers in education, sociology and psychology, as well as school teachers and education policy makers.

Contents
Introduction – Part 1: Theoretical frameworks: motives and behaviours – Academic motives: achievement goal theory and self-worth protection – Social motives: constructing 'appropriate' masculinities and femininities – The interplay between academic and gender identities – Part 2: From theory to practice and back again – Testing times: pressures and fears at school – School work or 'cool' work: competing goals at school – Self-defence: techniques and strategies for protecting self-worth – Balancing acts: who can balance the books and a social life? – Part 3: Implications and ways forward – Implications for teachers today – Implications for the policy makers of tomorrow – Conclusions

176pp   0 335 21770 2 (Paperback)   0 335 21771 0 (Hardback)

SEX BY NUMBERS
EXPLORING THE RELATIONSHIP BETWEEN
MATHEMATICS AND MASCULINITY

Heather Mendick

The study of mathematics, together with other 'gendered' subjects such as science and engineering, usually attracts more male than female pupils, particularly at more advanced levels. In this book Heather Mendick explores this phenomenon, addressing the important question of why more boys than girls choose to study mathematics. She combines new research with an original theoretical approach to argue that 'doing mathematics is doing masculinity'.

The book illuminates what studying mathematics means for both students and teachers and offers a broad range of insights into students' views and practices. In addition to the words of young people learning mathematics, the masculinity of mathematics is explored through historical material and cinematic representations . The author discusses the ways in which the alignment of mathematics with masculinity creates tensions for girls and women doing the subject. These tensions are sensitively explored through interviews with young women, to show how doing mathematics conflicts with their gender identities. Finally, the book explores the implications for teachers, including ways to promote gender equity in mathematics education.

This is key reading for students on courses in gender and education, mathematics education, gender and curriculum, and social justice.

Contents
Part 1: Scene setting – Engendering mathematics – Introducing the study – Part 2: Doing mathematics is doing masculinity – Being/ doing 'good at maths' – Proving something to others – Proving something to themselves – Changing directions – Part 3: Queering gender and maths – Making choices social: refusing essences in the classroom – Supporting gender transgression: being and acting different in maths – Opening up mathematics: living with uncertainty

192pp   0 335 21827 X (Paperback)   0 335 21828 8 (Hardback)

TEACHERS, PARENTS AND CLASSROOM BEHAVIOUR
A PSYCHOSOCIAL APPROACH

Andy Miller

This elegantly crafted book contains thoughtprovoking implications for all
branches of applied psychology, as well as educationists and policy makers . . .
With an increasing focus in education on evidence-based practice, this book will
be a valuable resource for practicing and trainee teachers and educational
psychologists.

The Psychologist

The most useful, insightful and coherent account of understanding and
managing behaviour in schools that I have read. It is also superbly written,
making it a pleasure to read . . . if you buy only one book this year, then it
should be this one.

Educational Psychology in Practice

This book examines the reasons why strong statements of mutual recrimination and
blame often occur in this area, before looking at policies and practices which are
co-operative, preventive and proactive in nature. But this is not solely another book of
tips and techniques. In addition to describing strategies with a proven evidence base,
it also demonstrates, within a coherent framework, how and why these approaches
achieve their aims. It provides an in-depth understanding of key psychological factors
for those in schools who are struggling in this vexed and pressing area and for that
widening group of professionals charged with working in partnership to bring about
demonstrable change.

Contents

*Introduction – Part one: The Context of Difficult Behaviour in Classrooms – Emerging
perspectives on behaviour in classrooms – Difficult behaviour in classrooms:the
psychosocial perspective – Part Two:Working with individual students, teachers and
parents – The evidence base – Strategies with individual students:the evidence base and
major challenge – Strategies with teachers and parents:an evidence base and a major
challenge – Consulting with teachers-and parents – Part three:Teacher and Pupil Cultures
– Teacher culture and difficult behaviour in classrooms – Pupil culture and difficult
behaviour in classrooms – Teacher, student and parent perspectives on behaviour:clash
and concordance – Part four:Grasping the nettle:Coherent psychosocial interventions –
Intervening within staff cultures – Across the great divide – Intervening with teachers and
parents – Conclusion – References – Index.*

216pp   0 335 21156 9 (Paperback)   0 335 21157 7 (Hardback)